War & Pieces
My Life from London to Baghdad and Back

Sandra D. Ekelund

MAPLE
PUBLISHERS

War and Pieces

Author: Sandra Ekelund

Copyright © Sandra Ekelund (2022)

The right of Sandra Ekelund to be identified as author of this work has been asserted by the author in accordance with section 77 and 78 of the Copyright, Designs and Patents Act 1988.

First Published in 2022

ISBN 978-1-915492-27-2 (Paperback)
      978-1-915492-28-9 (E-Book)

Book Cover Design and Layout by:
    White Magic Studios
    www.whitemagicstudios.co.uk

Published by:
    Maple Publishers
    1 Brunel Way,
    Slough,
    SL1 1FQ, UK
    www.maplepublishers.com

A CIP catalogue record for this title is available from the British Library.

All rights reserved. No part of this book may be reproduced or translated by any form or by any means, electronic or mechanical, including photocopying, recording or by any information storage and retrieval system without written permission from the author.

This book is a memoir. It reflects the author's recollections of experiences over time. The Publisher hereby disclaims any responsibility for them.

Author's Disclaimer

This book is subject to the vagaries of time and memory. I have done my best to make it truthful, any discrepancies or typos are unintentional.

Names have not been changed, place names may differ in spellings.

I regret any unintentional harm to any persons mentioned therein which may occur as a result of the marketing and publishing of this book.

Index

Introduction 6
Chapter 1 7
Chapter 2 15
Chapter 3 23
Chapter 4 39
Chapter 5 47
Chapter 6 50
Chapter 7 55
Chapter 8 57
Chapter 9 62
Chapter 10 65
Chapter 11 71
Chapter 12 77
Chapter 13 87
Chapter 14 89
Chapter 15 93
Chapter 16 96
Chapter 17 99
Chapter 18 103
Chapter 19 106
Chapter 20 108
Chapter 21 113
Chapter 22 117
Chapter 23 121

Chapter 24..131

Chapter 25..135

Chapter 26..142

Chapter 27..150

Chapter 28..154

Chapter 29..160

Chapter 30..165

Chapter 31..174

Chapter 32..178

Chapter 33..183

Chapter 34..191

Chapter 35..196

Chapter 36..203

Chapter 37..205

Chapter 38..212

Chapter 39..219

Chapter 40..227

Chapter 41..232

Chapter 42..236

Chapter 43..244

Chapter 44..248

Chapter 45..253

Chapter 46..260

Chapter 47..265

Chapter 48..268

Introduction

Why am I writing my life story?

"You should write a book about your life!" my children and friends have said on so many occasions when I mentioned an incident taken from my years on this earth. My life had been complicated, I had so many stories to tell, do I only write about the good times, or do I write about the sadder times and just let everything out?

I decided to take the middle road, skip over some of the awful moments, and there were many, and concentrate on just a few, even if those would make your hair stand on end.

It is also a chance for me to release my demons by writing about some events which played a part in moulding me into the person that I am today. I am a survivor rather than a victim, whatever mistakes I have made in my life I have learnt from. I have grown from an immature, shy young girl into a confident, independent woman.

What I am called?

So here I am, Sandra Dorothea Ekelund, a mother of seven children, four girls and three boys, eighteen grandchildren, and to date, one great-grandson, nice to meet you.

My name Sandra, is the female equivalent of either Alexander-Greek, meaning *protector of man,* though I have not had that inclination, or the Greek name, Cassandra, *she who entangles men,* that is not a good description of me either, though I am quite comfortable in male company, more so than the female.

I have no idea where the *Dorothea* part came in, someone on my Swedish side probably. The origin of that name is Greek, meaning *gift of God.* I doubt my mother thought I was a gift, more of a curse, she just liked that name.

I live in Bicester, Oxfordshire, UK, near my two sons Samer and Mohammed and their families. I have lived in so many areas of the UK, I have lost count.

My mother was Veronica Rose Ford, my father was Bernhard Gunner Ekelund.

Chapter 1

19th January, 1949

My father was Barney – or Scots Barney as he was known. He had been born in Ayr, Scotland in 1918.

His father was a Swedish merchant seaman named Gunnar Bernhard Ekelund, (b.1894 Johannes Fors) from Stockholm, Sweden. His mother was a local lass, Margaret Jane Cloy of Stranraer, Dumfries, Scotland (b.1898).

My grandparents had been married in 1917 in Cupar, Scotland.

I discovered only recently during my research, that my father married Kathleen Chambers in 1941 in Aylesbury. I do not know if they got divorced or if he had been widowed. Her information has been hard to find, searching through various ancestry websites.

Most of the information regarding my parents came in later years when I delved into family history research. My parents rarely spoke about their childhood and being so young I was not much interested in their lives.

I did often imagine, though, when I was young if my father was a spy, and I imagined him coming to England secretly.

He had no passport (he said), this made me think up all sorts of scenarios for him. He was not a tall man; I would say of average height with light blue eyes and sandy hair. The strangest thing is, I cannot recall his accent, which I presume to have been Scots.

My brother, Brian, once told me he thought my father had been a local minor gangster, but I took that with a pinch of salt, though when I went to visit him after Faris was born, he presented me with a fur coat which he said had, "fallen off the back of a lorry." That coat still exists today having travelled with me to Iraq and back; it is with my daughter, Suzanne.

Here are a few facts that I think you may find interesting regarding the news in the year I was born.

On the day I was born, Cuba recognised the State of Israel.

In the year I was born, Clement Attlee was the British Prime Minister. In February of that year the first president of Israel to be sworn in was Chaim Weizmann.

On 1st April, 26 counties of the Irish Free State became the Republic of Ireland, no joke there!

In May, Israel joined the United Nations as its 59th member.

In June, a rhesus monkey, Albert II, was blasted up in a V2 rocket 134 kilometres (83 miles) into space. I wonder what happened to Albert I and if Albert II ever made it back down to earth.

Oh, do not worry I just looked it up on Google – he died after a parachute failure caused his capsule to slam hard into the ground.

Another notable event in June was the publishing of George Orwell's novel '1984'. I did read the book many years later and it was also made into a movie. His story rings true in our modern era.

July saw the first flight of a jet-powered airliner, the de Havilland Comet, in England.

Brian

My brother had a selective memory. He often embellished his tales, like the time he told me he had been a twin and his brother (Michael) had been run over when he was a toddler. There was no evidence of a twin being born and registered; my brother's middle name was Michael. It was his alter ego that got killed.

Another time he told me that his puppy had been run over and killed. Also I do not remember ever seeing a puppy in the house though I knew he always wanted one.

Another habit of my brother, Brian's, was if anyone famous was mentioned in passing, he had met him or her when he was working here or there, or one of his friends was a friend of that person be it Lord or Lady Someone, Michael Caine, Bob Dylan, MP for Wherever. Brian had a wonderful sense of humour and always found a joke or two in his repertoire for visitors.

We looked alike, although he was my half-brother. His hair was light brown. Even into his 70's it did not turn grey and he still had his teeth.

He was a very heavy smoker, getting through 40 cigarettes a day. I was devastated when, in his 60's, he was diagnosed with lung cancer.

Thankfully, after several courses of chemo and radiotherapy, it went into remission. He also had COPD, a heart murmur, rheumatoid arthritis and a hernia!

My sister, Joyce, was 14 years older than me; my brother, Brian, was seven years older.

Joyce and Brian had a different father. Joyce's father was a previous husband of my mother who had died some years before I was born. Brian always told me that he did not know who his father was as he had been born eleven months after Joyce's father had died; some secrets went to the grave.

I sent away for a DNA test for Brian and placed the info on 23&Me and My Heritage, it was fun to watch the 'matches' pile up! Nobody was a close match. I guess too much time had passed to find his father even if that man had uploaded his DNA.

According to the records, my mother had been married at least twice in her life; through research, I have managed to trace those marriages.

She married David Bolland, Joyce's father, in 1932. He passed away in 1940. In 1944 she married Arthur Richard Roy Drury (who I later discovered on a census as a house painter and decorator).

Brian remembered him as being a nasty, violent man. My mother sure knew how to pick them.

Some people can remember so much about their life from the time they were toddlers. For me, many of those early days and years remain partly a mystery. Perhaps because I am now in my seventh decade, memory fades.

I have managed to jog my memory by looking up some of the histories of those years. Also, my children have passed on various tales I have told them throughout their lives about my family, myself and the life around me during my years growing up.

Family Home – London, Kingsdown Road

My brother, Brian, told me that when he came home from school one day, there I was, a new-born. He was only seven at the time but, as he says, his life changed dramatically from that moment on. Whenever I did something naughty growing up, if he was in the vicinity, the blame would fall on him.

I was born in North London; my mother was Vera – or Ronnie, as she was known. She had been born in 1912 in Middlesbrough, England, one of 9 children. Her mother, my grandmother, had died in 1915 when my mother was just over three years old, from complications following childbirth.

My grandfather struggled to care for such a large family alone. He met and married a widow, Elizabeth March, in 1916 when my mother was four years old. The new wife however was not about to take on such a mammoth task of looking after all the children. My mother, along with her elder sister Mary, was placed in an orphanage run by Catholic nuns.

She had a hard time there and would not often speak about it. One time, though, when I was older, she did tell me that if she were deemed to be naughty, the nuns would shut her in a cupboard in the dark for hours. She never liked the dark after that, nor nuns for that matter.

The windows of my attic bedroom at number 19 had bars on them, a safety feature in most of the tall four-storey houses in Kingsdown Road. Under my bed, there was a chamber pot. I used that during the night instead of the only toilet of the house which was situated in a brick-built block down at the bottom of the garden.

Inside the toilet the lavatory bowl was set into a wooden box, no lid on ours. A cistern high up on the wall held the water for flushing, a chain hung down with a ceramic knob on the end. This was pulled to start the flush.

There was no toilet paper like we have today. Instead, we had newspaper to wipe with, torn into squares and hanging on a hook. It left imprints of the newsprint on our bums. We could read the news while performing, if so inclined, getting educated in world affairs. It wasn't common practice to wash our hands when we had finished, nobody told us to, so we didn't. The toilet got very cold in the winter, so it was best not to spend too long in there. Inside there were lots of large spiders in their webs or scurrying around, so I would keep my feet off the floor for as long as I could in case one of them decided to crawl up my scrawny legs.

My brother told me I often wet the bed and walked in my sleep. The evidence of my sleepwalking would be found the next morning with the sight of all the shoes and slippers I could find during my sleepwalking lined up neatly in rows against the wall.

Some evenings, my sister would brush my long blonde hair for me before I went to sleep and twist it in rag strips to make ringlets. These strips were made from torn-up cotton garments that had seen better days.

A small amount of hair would be wound around the strip, this would then be tied to keep it in place. In the morning, before I went to school, the strips would be removed leaving bouncy ringlets which would be kept tidy with a ribbon.

Street Games

Street games were all we had to entertain ourselves. Squares for hopscotch would be drawn on the pavement, sometimes even on the road. There was little traffic in those days, if any vehicles did come along we just moved out of the way until they passed.

The game was played by each player having a pebble to throw. It must land inside the square and not touch the line. The player would hop to the end of the diagram, then back to the stone. The winner would be the player who had used up all the squares.

Skipping was another popular game for girls, we would skip and add as many girls into the rope as it turned until we stumbled over the rope and stopped.

We would gather up conkers from the chestnut tree when they fell to the ground. These were then pierced through with a nail and a foot long piece of string threaded through them knotted at the bottom to stop the conker from falling off.

This was mostly played by boys in the autumn when the conkers fell from the horse chestnut trees. The game, played in pairs, meant sharply smashing one conker against the other boy's until it broke. Girls usually shied away from this game, it was deemed too violent, and they could easily get hit in the face with a conker. What would mother say then?

Similarly, playing leapfrog, where one person bends down and places their hands on their knees while another jumps over their bent back, was not something girls usually did in case there was a glimpse of their knickers as they jumped.

Brian once made me a cart from some old planks of wood and four pram wheels. It was great to fly down the hill on it. The steering was done with the feet on the crossbar at the front. There was a piece of wood on one of the wheels for the brake. Sometimes this did not work too well and I would smash into a lamppost. Bruises were a common sight on my legs. We did not think too much of getting hurt as it was part and parcel of our daily life.

Guy Fawkes

In the run-up to November 5th I would gather old items to make a 'Guy' from some old trousers and shirt tied at the ends of the sleeves and legs then stuffed with newspapers. The head would be an old paper bag stuffed, with a face drawn on it.

After school, I would go home as quickly as I could, put my Guy in the cart and take him down to the corner of the street. Mother would not let me go farther. I found the best place and more profitable was outside the local pub. As people passed by, I could be heard saying, *"penny for the guy, penny for the guy."*

Some would drop a penny in my outheld tin can. On one occasion I even got a whole shilling! Later, when I had enough money, I took a trip to the local shop to buy fireworks. No 'over eighteen years old' stipulations in those days, I could buy them at will. They were not the fancy ones around today that light up the sky. These were simple sparklers, bangers, rockets, etc.

We gathered in the garden on Guy Fawkes Day, November 5th, lighting a bonfire of old wooden chairs and other bits to burn the Guy on and then light up the fireworks. The rockets were placed with their stick down into an empty milk bottle. The instructions printed on them said, *'light blue touch paper and stand back'*. This being done we watched the rocket as it shot up into the air while we all stood with our faces looking up to follow the trajectory and see the wonderful cascade of colours at the end - it was magic.

Brian's birthday was on the 4th of November so we combined the two occasions. He told me that, when he was little, he thought the fireworks were just for him.

Joyce

My elder sister, Joyce, was not around much as I grew up. As soon as she was able, she left home and went to live with her friends to get away from the toxic environment at home.

In 1957 she met and married Matthew Z Mardesich in Paddington. He was from Croatia, they moved to California after Vincent, their only son, was born.

Throughout my life, I have always tried to keep in contact with my siblings. When my sister moved to the USA, she left me her address and telephone number. We would write to each other regularly, or rather, I would write five letters to one of hers. One year when she moved house and forgot to let me know (she never was one for communicating and still is not), I received a letter I had written to her. It had been returned to me marked *'Return to Sender'* on the envelope – just like the Elvis Presley song!

This worried me a lot. I imagined that she was ill or worse. I had an idea. I was working on a large switchboard, so it was easy for me to make an overseas call, taking liberties, as it was in a hotel. There were many overseas calls made by the guests, one more did not make a difference.

I contacted the Los Angeles police department to ask for their help in tracing her. I gave them all her details and her last known address. They were extremely helpful in contacting her. One officer called me back after a few days, saying they had spoken to her and she had agreed for them to give me her correct address.

Her only visit to London was when I was about 16. We met up once for a meal before she went up to Yorkshire to see our mother and cousins, before flying back to California, USA. That was the first time I had met Vincent. He grew up to become a dentist, got married to Evita from Croatia and they have a daughter, Megan.

I was quite upset that she had not asked me, her younger sister, to come and live with her in the USA. I was a young girl living alone in London. I suppose she had her reasons; it was not something I let bother me too much later. She had left the family home when I was around eight or so. I had not even recognized her when she came to see me. Here was this petite, pretty woman with an American accent; she was almost a stranger.

On her trip to Yorkshire, she went to our mother's house; there was nobody in. After making some enquiries, she was informed by a neighbour that our mother was in hospital after having had a heart attack. Joyce visited her at the hospital, but it was not a good meeting.

She told me some years later that our mother had asked her for some cigarettes in the hospital! Joyce refused her request, telling her cigarettes and alcohol were the reason she had ended up where she was.

Chapter 2

Brian

My brother got away from the family home as soon as he could. He believed this was vital for his mental health. Brian joined the Territorial Army, he made many friends and enjoyed being *one of the lads*.

He worked in a grocery store in Hornsey Road, London. Sometimes he would bring home plastic strips of bushes and trees for us to sit and put together for the window displays.

Peter (r) and Brian going out for the evening in London 1963

He had a close friend, Peter. The two of them were like Siamese twins and went everywhere together.

He later joined P & O cruise lines as a steward so that he could travel the world. We would get postcards from such far off places as Australia or New Zealand. He went to see Joyce while his ship was in port in the USA on several occasions.

Joyce and Brian, Calif. the USA 1964

Home Cooking

We had a cast-iron range in the living room/kitchen. Each day the old coal and ash from the previous fire would be cleared out and the new fire lit. Mother would use a few newspapers twisted hard together and lay them down in the grate with some firewood on top and then coal. To help the fire 'draw' she would place a sheet of newspaper over the front of the grill. This would soon get it going. Sometimes even this paper would catch fire. My mother would quickly push it in between the bars of the grill.

The unit contained an oven with two hobs on top. I doubt if the heat could be controlled in any way. She knew how to use it, though. She was able to stoke up the fire enough to get the oven to the right temperature. There was no thermostat, working near the fire was a hot business indeed.

We would sometimes be lucky enough to get a roast on a weekend. The left-over congealed dripping from the roast would be smeared on thick slices of bread, cut from a loaf, for our evening meal; it was deliciously salty, something that would make the dieticians of today throw their hands up in horror.

Mother would also place large potatoes in the ashes of the fire to cook, washing the dirt off them first which seemed a bit pointless, these would then be brought out – the ashes dusted off and the potatoes split open to having salt and margarine (butter being too expensive) lathered on them. They were delicious.

Her apple pies were her speciality. Cooked to perfection with crispy pastry, we would have them served with Bird's Custard on Sundays.

She would clean the range with Zebra black lead polish and a cloth to keep it looking good, rubbing and wiping until she was satisfied with the result.

Bath Nights

Friday was bath night. The working week was over and my father had received his brown pay packet. The average weekly pay in those early days was less than £10pw.

Mother would bring the tin bath down from the wall outside in the garden. Spiders had to be tipped out first, she then filled it from the kettles and pots of water boiling on the range. It was a tedious and time-consuming process.

We did not have the luxury of hot water on tap in those early years nor was there a copper water heater in the house like some of our neighbours. When enough cold water had been added to the hot, father would get in and have his bath, using a bar of Lifebuoy household soap. When he had finished it was our turn, all in the same water. To empty and refill the tub would have been too much of a chore.

As children, we thought nothing of this procedure – it was normal in those times. When everyone had completed their bathing, my mother would empty the tub by using a bucket to scoop out as much water as she could before dragging the tub out into the garden to empty the rest down the outside drain.

She preferred to go to the local bathhouse and soak in the hot tub there.

Hornsey Road Baths – Islington (1956)

The local bathhouse was a much better alternative to go and have a bath when we could afford the price.

On occasion, a Saturday ritual was the trip to Hornsey Road Baths in Islington. Hornsey Road Baths were one of the biggest in London. It was first opened in 1892. It had two swimming pools for men and one for women. My school swimming was done there each week.

Mother gathered up all the dirty linen and clothes, wrapped them in a big bundle, placed them in an old pram and we would both make our way along to the baths. Once there she purchased a ticket with her name on it for the washhouse along with the time she could start to use the facilities, handing this ticket to one of the female attendants who would fasten it to one of the large drying horses. These were large pull-out metal affairs for hanging the wet articles on.

The ticket number corresponded to a number on one of the immense washing tubs, a bucket, a stick for moving the clothes around, a corrugated washboard for rubbing the clothes on and a large bar of yellow household soap.

There were three taps, one for boiling water, one for cold water and one for steam. After filling the tub and washing the linen by rubbing it along the washboard with the soap, the whole lot was transferred to the steam wringer. This turned at about 800 revolutions to the minute thereby drawing out the water quickly. The sheets were then hung inside the drying horses on racks, heated by steam pipes to dry the linen. My mother used the time waiting for her washing to steam by having a cigarette and a natter with her fellow washerwomen.

When the linen was ready, she gathered it all up and took it to the mangling and ironing room. The sheets were passed through the mangle first. This was a large contraption with big wooden rollers and a large handle. The sheets, towels or clothes would be placed, the handle hand turned to thread the material through the rollers pressing them. This saved the extra work of having to iron out the large items such as sheets or towels.

During this process, I would be sent off to the slipper bath cubicle with a clean towel and bar of hard soap. The bath was a strange affair. It did not have any taps inside, instead, the water was filled by an attendant, this saved wasting water. After I had soaked and soaped in the wonderful hot water I would get dressed. The tub would be emptied by the attendant and cleaned ready for the next user.

The 70-year-old washhouse was renovated in 1965 by Islington Council. It was turned into a modern self-service laundry with modern washing machines. In 1991 it was finally closed, along with the swimming baths, another wonderful building renovated to fit into our modern era.

The building today houses Platform which is an innovative venue for young people housing and study space, a music studio, venue hire and various other facilities, so at least it is useful again.

The Crown Public House

After the washing was taken home and put away, it was time to go along to the local pub, which was the Crown at 622 Holloway Road, N19 – just around the corner so not far for my parents to find their way home after a skinful.

My parents would be inside for hours, drinking my father's wages away, while I sat outside on the step with a glass of lemonade and a packet of plain crisps which had a little blue twist inside containing salt. This I would sprinkle on the crisps before eating them. There was no fancy flavoured cheese and onion or black pepper flavour in those days.

The cold step in the winter made my bum numb and my cheeks caught the cold wind as it blew. I rarely get a cold these days, probably due to my exposure to the elements as a child.

After a few drinks, Mother would sometimes do her bit of dancing, waving her arms akimbo, a bit like Mata Hari. I could see her whenever a punter came by and opened the door. This left me constantly embarrassed whenever I spied her.

Often someone would start belting out the old Cockney songs and everyone else would then join in. This usually ended in a knees-up. They were jolly times, people had their drink and had fun. Very little fighting broke out as everyone knew each other.

I went back and visited the area with Samer a few years ago just to see what I could remember. I went into the pub and spoke to the bartender, but of course, he had not been there in the old days. The house is still there. Here are some photos, go along one day and have a look.

Kingsdown Road, Upper Holloway, London N.19

Here are a few of the popular pub songs of that era:

My Old Man said Follow the Van – (1919) sung by Marie Lloyd
Daddy Wouldn't Buy Me A Bow Wow – (1892) sung by Vesta Victoria
Underneath The Arches – (1931) sung by Flanagan & Allan
Where Did You Get That Hat? – (1888) sung by Joseph J. Sullivan
Knees Up Mother Brown – (1938) sung by various artists

If any of the old Irish ballads like, *'When Irish Eyes Are Smiling'* were started my mother would suddenly remember her roots and usually end up in floods of tears.

This was in the year 1953 or 1954, I was four or five. When the closing time bell was rung it was the signal it was time to go home, usually at 10 pm.

Both my parents fought constantly. Irish mother and Scottish father – both with tempers, both alcoholics, what a wonderful combination! By the time we had gotten home, and I had been put to bed, mother and father would often continue their arguing, which started on the road back to the house. Their voices would get louder and louder. I never could remember just what they argued about, it's been such a long time past, but in my teenage and adult years, I cannot stand listening to anyone arguing. I enter flight mode and want to get as far away as I could from the noise, often just walking out of the house trying to put as much distance between me and the altercation.

There were times when my father would walk out, but he always came back after a few days. I never knew where he went. It was only when I was a bit older and he took me to the home of his lady friend – Kitty Flowers. She was a gentle, kindly soul, as different to my mother as chalk and cheese. I know that I enjoyed the calm of her home and company.

Father Left Home

One day he left for good. After that I rarely saw him and, on the occasions when I did manage to catch him, he would give me a few shillings, pat me on the head and walk away.

My one wish during those times would be to get him to come home again. How I longed for it, yearned for it, he was my father and I loved him. There were times that I begged him to come back, he could not be persuaded and would sadly walk away.

Mother and I moved around a lot after my parents split up, staying in different rooms in London, sometimes getting on a bus from Victoria Station to go up to Middlesbrough to stay with various aunts.

I was packed off at some point in my early years to Ayr, Scotland, to stay with aunt Elizabeth but it was not a happy time for me. I had quite a chest cough. She kept making me some home-made cough syrup for it, boiling it up on the stove; it tasted awful, thick and gooey and I fought against taking it.

Then she accused me of stealing some money that she had left on the mantlepiece. Maybe I did, maybe I didn't, I do not remember. I got sent straight back to mother.

Here is a photo of me (back left) with some children I think were cousins (notice I am standing on tippy toes to appear taller).

Chapter 3

School – Infants (1954+)

I attended many schools in my life. My memories are of Grafton Infants School, which was in Eburne Road, N7. I started there when I was four. There were no nurseries or pre-schools in those days.

I remember a teacher called Mrs Knight. We had a verse that we made up which I still remember as if it was yesterday.

'Mrs. Knight had a fright in the middle of the night. Saw a ghost eating toast. Halfway up a lamp post'.

Regular examinations of our head were done by the 'nit nurse' for any sign of fleas. She combed through our hair with a plastic nit comb and if any of the little creatures were found we would be sent home later with a letter for our parents for them to get us de-loused.

We were also given a lump of sugar that had been soaked with the polio vaccine. Measles, mumps and German measles were not yet vaccinated against. It was known that German measles could affect the baby in the womb so if any of the young girls got it, then it was not uncommon for their mothers to have a party for their girlfriends so they would get it too.

I did get measles, which kind I do not know but it was not very pleasant. My mother covered me in something called Calamine Lotion to ease the itching. I also contracted pneumonia (hence that cough up in Scotland) and ended up in The Royal Northern Hospital, Holloway Road, which was our local hospital.

The children's ward I was in was a mixed one. In the bed next to mine was a young boy of about my age, I think his name was Duncan. He did not get visitors very often and seemed quite lonely so when my mother came to visit me, I would ask her to go and say hello to him and give him some of my chocolate bars. I would also pass on any of my Beano comics; after I had read them of course. I felt sorry for him and wanted to make him feel better as he always looked so sad.

I was a very naughty child, always getting into trouble one way or another as I grew up. At school I was the class clown, getting a laugh out of my fellow students was my aim to cover up my shyness. For this I was mostly kept behind after school to write those awful lines of 100 'I must not' or 'I must' do this or that.

I have one photo from that time. It is a school photo, and I am amazed how I have kept it all these years. It shows me as an angelic, blonde-haired child, so far from the truth as John O' Groats is to Land's End.

My school photo at 6 years old

Getting rapped on the knuckles by the teacher or palm of my hand with a wooden 12" ruler was fairly common. I got my fair share although I tried to avoid the painful experience often by pulling my hand away at the last moment. This only prolonged the suffering as the teacher would double up more strokes to make up for it.

Times tables had to be learned by rote. We stood up in turn and recited whichever table the teacher asked us to. The mostly cursive handwriting we were taught had to be as neat as possible, and we were punished (with those awful 'lines') for sloppy letters. We used pens with nibs which we dipped into a small ceramic ink well containing black ink, set into the wooden desk. Our fingers would be ink-stained by the time we left class for the day along with streaks of ink on our face if we forgot and brushed our fingers along eyes or in mouths.

One year I received a present for my birthday, a small plastic cooking range. I was so happy with that toy and insisted on taking it to school with me in my bag to show my friends. One of the boys seemed quite interested in it; so interested that, when school was over and I was walking home (nobody to come and collect me) he came up to me, snatched it and ran off. I followed him running all the way to his home, which was nearby in a block of flats but was too scared to go up and knock on the door. I ran all the way home, bursting in, breathless and upset. I told my mother what had happened. To her credit she did not hesitate. Grabbing my arm she first slapped me with,

"I told you not to take it to school, stupid little shit, now I have to go and get it back!"

Marching me down the road to where I showed her the house, she stomped up to the door still wearing her apron and slippers to bang as loud as she could. The woman who answered was a small lady, rotund and wearing an apron over her clothes. She had rollers in her hair and a cigarette dangling from her mouth.

She looked shocked to see this wild-looking and large woman banging on her door. My mother said, *"Tell your lad to give my girl her cooker back or he will feel the back of my hand round his chops!"*

Her lad was duly called, and my cooker handed over pronto, my mother looked at him and said, *"You stay away from my girl or else!"* before turning and dragging me home again where I was sent to bed with no supper in punishment, which I wasn't too worried about. I had eaten enough at school. I always had seconds of dinner and even puddings to fill me up. I think I was the only child in the UK who enjoyed school food, I must have been mad!

The dinner ladies were nice and seemed to like me. My favourite meal was mince and tatties with gravy. The pudding was spotted dick (steamed suet pudding with sultanas) with custard or apple pie. I would eat as much as I could in those days as I did not get much at home. I even drank up the ¾ pint bottles of milk we got for free. If my friends did not want theirs, I would drink those too. Despite those meals, I was very thin and taller than most of the children in my class.

It was during these years that I was able to attend Girl Guides for a while and also took some Irish tap-dancing lessons at the Landseer Arms pub, Stanley Terrace, in their upstairs room.

In the Guides I had a smart dark blue uniform and hat. We had to say the Original Promise when joining, as follows:

On my honour, I will promise that I will do my best:
To do my duty to God and my country.
To always help other people.
To obey the Guide Law.

The short time I spent with the Guides was a happy one for me. I had a sense of belonging, friends and duties. I missed that comradery later. I had never been immensely popular, having but few friends, but the friends I had now, they were friends for life. It was unfortunate that, as we moved around like gipsies without a caravan, I mostly lost touch with any of the friends I made.

One of my best friends was a girl called Jacqueline Bond. She was shorter than me, lanky, with mousey coloured straight, thin hair. We bonded closely and went everywhere together. On one occasion I asked her to come home with me to play. When we got to my home, my mother took one look at her and said, *"Who in God's name is this dwarf you have with ye? Get her out of my sight now!"*

Jackie was duly turfed out of the house never to return. I thought after that she would never speak to me again but our friendship remained. I sometimes went to her home where she lived with her parents in a high-rise council flat near Arsenal football stadium.

On a Saturday we could sit on her balcony and watch the match for free, not that I liked football in any way, shape or form. Some years later when I went to see her, she told me her parents had passed away and she had sadly lost her baby to SIDS. She just found her one day in her cot, not breathing. Nothing could be done for her, she said, it was an incredibly sad occasion.

After that visit I lost touch with her. She moved out of the flat. There were no mobile phones in those days to store people's numbers and Facebook did not exist to keep in touch. In later years I tried to search for her on social media but had no luck.

Pocket Money

My pocket money consisted of 6d (in old pennies). To put it into perspective, the pre-decimal currency was as follows:

12 pennies = 1 shilling

20 shillings = 1 pound

240 pennies =1 pound

The money was mostly coinage, these were the denominations.

- Farthing = ¼ d
- Half penny = ½ d
- Penny = 1d
- Threepence = 3d
- Sixpence = 6d
- Shilling = 1/-
- Florin = 2/-
- Half Crown = 2/6d
- Crown = 5s

I walked to the shop on the corner of our road and got a Bunty magazine which contained a little gift and a bar of chocolate (2p) or gobstoppers, Fry's 5 Centre chocolate with the different flavours of strawberry, lime, orange and there was a mint one which I liked, and I have even seen it on sale today all these years later! Pink mice with a white cord for a tail, made of icing sugar, sickly sweet, I don't think I could eat one today – my cholesterol would be through the roof.

The shop is still there on the corner of Kingsdown Road. The current proprietor is Asian. The Crown public house also exists. I passed by, a few years ago on a nostalgic trip down memory lane. A packet of sweet cigarettes which had pink tips that I could pretend to smoke was on sale. Everybody smoked cigarettes in those days, unfiltered too, or roll-ups, it was fun to mimic the grown-ups.

There was a cigarette factory on Hampstead Road, London, opposite Mornington Crescent Tube Station. The Black Cat factory was built-in

1926 for the Carreras Tobacco Company. It was described at the time as 'London's most hygienic tobacco factory'. It had air conditioning units and a dust extraction plant installed. Two massive 8 ½ ft high bronze statues of Bastet – the Egyptian Cat Goddess, stand guarding the entrance. The black cat was the symbol on Black Cat and Craven A cigarettes which were produced at the factory providing jobs for hundreds of people.

The company took good care of the employees with an onsite doctor, dentist and chiropodist. They even had a convalescent home outside the city for those employees who needed to recover from an illness. A bomb shelter was installed in the basement.

Women had the task of stripping the leaves from the stems of tobacco, enduring the dust thrown up in their faces for eight hours a day. Nobody then understood that this was akin to 'passive smoking', or the effects smoking cigarettes would have on their lungs. I suppose they got a discount when they purchased from the factory. Whole families were employed at the factory, generation to generation worked there.

If anyone would like to go and see this wonderful building, the postcode is NW1 7QF. If you look on the pavement opposite the factory – which is today known as Greater London House, you will find a stone with the 'Eye of Horus' set into the pavement.

During those years smoking was seen as glamorous; in the movies of the day and, on television, the actors smoked like chimneys, even those who played doctors visiting their patients! Girls would come around with trays of cigarettes to sell to the patients.

My father rolled his cigarettes when he was short of cash, which was most of the time. He had a little machine that he placed his ciggy paper in, put the tobacco on top, even it out, licked the side of the paper, then pushed the edges of the machine together and rolled his fag. It would produce the perfectly rolled cigarette most of the time (unless he forgot to dampen the edges).

Both my parents smoked like mad, packet after packet, in the early days. A favourite brand of that period was unfiltered, high-tar Woodbine, known as 'gaspers' or 'Woodies' in packets of 5, 10, 20 or 50, they were advertised with the slogan:

'Light up life with a Woodbine! It's Britain's best-selling cigarette!'

Another popular cigarette was Player's Navy Cut, which had a picture of a sailor inside a lifebuoy on the front and I do believe the packets contained collectable cards, flags of the world or famous ships, etc.

Football Pools

Another habit of my father's was that he did the football pools as they were called. He would ask me to read out the scores for the teams while he checked them on his coupon. Sometimes he would win a few pounds, but the big prize always escaped him. His favourite was the Treble Chance, the lucky winner could get a £500,000 prize, a huge amount in those days, a large house could be purchased for the equivalent of around £2,530.

Liverpool Football Pools had 15 million players before the introduction of the National Lottery in 1994.

There was also a weekly game in the newspaper called *'Spot the Ball'*. A photograph was published each week in the paper of a soccer match with the ball removed. The reader was then invited to place an X on the area where they thought the ball had been. There was a weekly cash prize of £1,500 for the lucky winner. Of course, it was quite a feat to pinpoint the ball and very few would be successful. Quite a money-making con for those gullible enough to play, as most games of chance are even today. With our Lotto and EuroMillions, you have better odds of being hit by a bus than winning. I must admit though I do sometimes buy tickets for those games today, about once every six months. I might win the odd £10. Once I did manage to win £67 which I considered a great bit of luck.

Dentist

With all this sweet eating it is no wonder our teeth rotted. Nobody ever told me to brush mine and I cannot remember even having a toothbrush. At school, we had the dental nurse who would check up on our teeth regularly and give us a yellow card to match the colour of our teeth, which we took home for our parents to arrange a trip to the dentist if she saw that we needed work done.

The dentist I went to was a friendly old gent. He used to make plain little figurines out of white clay in the shape of Disney characters which he would give to the children after their treatment (if they were good) and tell them to paint them and bring them back next time so he could see how well they had been done. A good result would be put on a display shelf in the surgery.

He would place a mask over my mouth and nose, with gas and air in it, which I hated so much but tolerated as I loved getting those little figures to paint.

If a tooth fell out at home, this would be placed under the pillow for the tooth fairy to take and replace with 6d. Whenever I felt one of my teeth getting loose, I would wobble it with my tongue as hard as I could to make it fall out so I would get some money. There were occasions that the tooth would still be there in the morning as my mother had been too intoxicated to play tooth fairy and there was no money to spare.

Getting 6p a week pocket money was never quite enough. I liked sweets and magazines and found that, on the occasions when my mother gave me money to go and buy some milk for breakfast, I could just as easily put the money in my pocket and pick up a pint of milk from someone's doorstep instead. She never knew the difference and I did not take the milk from the same house each time, sometimes even going into the next street, always watchful of anyone looking through the window or down the street.

Milk in those days came in clear glass bottles, delivered by the milkman with his horse and cart, and left on the doorstep. Empty bottles were washed clean by the customer and left out for collection. If anything extra was needed, like bread, a loaf of bread cost four pence, or orange juice, a note could be left in the bottle for delivery the next day. Each week the milkman would knock on the door to collect his payment for the week's deliveries.

Different coloured foil caps denoted what type of milk the bottle held. Gold topped milk was for more expensive full cream milk, there would be about an inch of cream settled at the top of the milk. This was aptly named 'top of the milk' and was delicious. Many recipes normally included this in their ingredients.

Silver foil was for the basic milk, which still tasted more delicious than today's skimmed milk. I do not remember any separate cream being sold. For dessert sometimes we would have tinned peaches or fruit salad with Carnation condensed milk poured over it.

I found a humorous rhythm about the Carnation Evaporated Milk which may have been the result of a slogan contest run by the company, which goes as follows:

Carnation Milk is the best in the land,
Here I sit with a can in my hand,
No tits to pull, no hay to pitch,
You just punch a hole in the son of a bitch.

Scrumping Apples

My escapades as, for want of a better word, a tea leaf, were many. I was very resourceful even at a young age.

I brought my mother apples so that she could make her delicious apple pies, telling her that my friend's house had an apple tree and her mother had given me some to take home.

On one occasion I had gone with my friends up to Highgate Hill where we managed to climb into someone's exceptionally large garden. We had spied the apple trees through the fence surrounding it and decided it was a great opportunity to scrump some (steal, in other words).

I was up the tree picking the apples and throwing them down to my friends waiting below when a man came running out. "Hey you little buggers, get down from my tree," he shouted.

Of course, my two 'friends' ran off as fast as they could. He saw me up the tree and shouted, "You stay up there, missy," while he ran past me and chased after them. No way was I about to be hauled down and given a pasting, so I climbed down and took off as fast as I could, running down the hill.

Holy Joe's

Mother, being a Roman Catholic, took me to church with her on a Sunday, St Joseph's church in Archway, London.

It was there that I had my first communion and later, I would often go there as I had, quite by chance, discovered something very interesting - an alms box on the wall. People attending church would deposit their donations here, coins mostly. Nobody would put any notes in there unless they were completely bonkers.

Not much interesting in that, I hear you say, wait till you read the rest!

One day I noticed that there was a small gap at the bottom of the box, I could see some coins inside. The next time I came when the church was empty and quiet. Taking out of my pocket a small penknife which belonged to my brother, I was able to flip a few coins out of the box through that gap. This became a convenient source of extra cash for me until we moved away from the area.

Each Saturday a dance was held in the church hall.

In 1964, I was 14 but I looked a lot older. I was able to go to the church dance and sometimes wore my flared skirt with the pictures of Elvis Presley, Cliff Richards and other current singers printed on the fabric. I wore a wide belt at my waist, a plain top and flat shoes. My brother often got me clothes from the tallyman, paying a few shillings each week.

The 'Holy Jo' dances were wonderful. Soft drinks only were available. Some of the older lads brought spirits – not of the ethereal kind, either, but the DJ played records of the top hits of those days for us to spend a couple of hours dancing to.

I am going to digress a little here to tell you about some of the bands that were popular in the 1960s. Some are still going strong today.

The Beatles

The Beatles were a popular group from Liverpool. Formed in 1960, they played mostly in Liverpool clubs notably in the Cavern Club and Hamburg, Germany.

When they had their hit with 'Love, Love, Me Do' in 1962 they became wildly popular. Beatle mania was born and youngsters, mostly girls, would become hysterical at their concerts, fainting, crying and screaming for their idols.

They were known as The Fab Four - John, Paul, George & Ringo. With their pudding basin haircuts and snazzy clothes, the teenagers swooned at their concerts. 'Please, Please Me' was the first of eleven consecutive albums to reach number one in the charts.

Rolling Stones

Mick Jagger – he is now, at the time of writing, still jumping around like crazy at 77 years, I bet eventually he drops dead on stage.

Pink Floyd

Pink Floyd are a rock/blues band active in 1965–1995, 2005–2012, 2012–2104. English from London, the members were Roger Waters, David Gilmour, Syd Barrett, Richard Wright, Nick Mason, and Bob Klose. Their song 'Another Brick in the Wall' was extremely popular with my granddaughters, Sandra and her sister, Katya, who would often ask me to play it when we were in the car going somewhere so we could all sing along.

Led Zeppelin

Led Zepplin was a rock/heavy metal/blues rock band, active 1968–1980 in London, England. I was not a fan of the heavy metal or hard rock music genre; it gave me a headache.

The Beach Boys

The Beach Boys were a USA band. Rock, pop, surfing, psychedelic music, active 1961. Some of the members are still playing today in 2021, dragging themselves out to perform in concerts in the USA. The oldest member is Brian Wilson who will be 79 this year and wrote or co-wrote many of their hits, my favourite being 'Good Vibrations', though I am not a fan of the band.

Bee Gees

The Bee Gees were a pop, soft rock band. British guys born in the UK, their family then moved to Queensland, Australia. Active 1958–2003, 2006, 2009–2012.

Brothers Barry, Robin and Maurice Gibb had the whitest, largest teeth I have ever seen. They sang in squeaky voices, Barry's falsetto became their signature sound, which to my un-musical ear, sounded like cats being strangled.

They wrote all their hits as well as writing for other artists which went on to become major hits. Their soundtrack for the movie 'Saturday

Night Fever' starring John Travolta (1977) was a massive hit, catapulting them into fame and fortune. I bought the album when it was released. It went with me to Baghdad and was stored there until my son, Mohammed, brought it, along with some other LP's, over to the UK for me in 2022. Barry to date is the only surviving member of the band.

Cream

Cream were British Psychedelic Rock, acid rock, blues rock band. Active 1966–1968, 1993, 2005.

The members were guitarist Eric Clapton (formerly with The Bluesbreakers), drummer Ginger Baker (formerly with The Graham Bond Organisation) and bassist Jack Bruce. They had the reputation of being the world's first supergroup before their break-up in late 1968. Another band not in my fan book, though Eric Clapton is one of my favourite blues artists.

Simon & Garfunkel

American – (Folk Rock) with Paul Simon & Art Garfunkel, active 1956–1964, 1965–1970. Also they have had some reunions in 1972, 1975–1977, 1981–1984, 1990, 1993, 2003–2005, 2007–2010. Paul Simon is still performing today at 79. I like his album 'Graceland' released in 1986.

Creedence Clearwater Revival (CCR)

CCR were a band from El-Cerito, California, USA. They played roots rock, swamp rock, blues rock, southern rock, country rock and were active 1959–1972. The band consisted of brothers John and Tom Fogerty on guitar, drummer Doug Clifford and bassist Stu Cook.

They had many names before they settled on CCR. In their early days they were known as The Blue Velvets, Tommy Fogarty & The Blue Velvets, Vision, The Gollywogs (1964–1967), not a name that would be accepted in today's Black Lives Matter culture. 28 million of their records have been sold in the USA alone.

Jimi Hendrix

Jimi Hendrix was an American electric guitarist (Rock, psychedelic rock, hard rock, blues, R&B). Jimi, who began playing guitar when he was 15 years old, was regarded as one of the most influential electric guitar players in the history of rock. Throughout his short career of only 4 years, he played with such great artists as The Isley Brothers, Curtis Knight and the Squires and Little Richard.

He moved to the UK in late 1966, got a new manager in Chas Chandler of the Animals, then proceeded to earn three UK Top Ten hits with The Jimi Hendrix Experience. My favourite tracks of his are 'Hey Joe', Purple Haze' and 'The Wind Cries Mary'.

He passed away in 1970 after asphyxiating on his vomit. He had taken 18 times the normal dose of his girlfriend's sleeping tablets, a member of the **27 Club** (a phenomenon where people believe artists, musicians and actors die at 27 years old due to their drug-taking lifestyle).

If you are ever in Tel Aviv, Israel, you can go to see a graffiti depicting artists who have died at 27. It shows left-right Brian Jones (Rolling Stones), Jimi Hendrix, Janis Joplin, Jim Morrison, Jean-Michel Basquiat, Kurt Cobain and Amy Winehouse.

I hope you will take some time to go and listen to some of these bands' songs. I am sure you will like some of them, I do.

Teddy Boys

My friends and I eyed up the teddy boys at the dance hall on a Saturday, far too old for the likes of us. They had their motorbikes outside and got into constant fights. They wore their hair heavily coated in Brylcreem coiffed up into some weird shapes, the rear sometimes referred to as a 'Duck's Arse', never able to pass a mirror without stopping to look at themselves, whipping out their little plastic combs to comb it back if a hair or two escaped the style.

They walked with a swagger, right dandies they were, in their long drape velvet collared jackets with their tight drainpipe trousers which were short enough to show their usually white socks. A 'Mr. B' collar to the white shirt, a Slim Jim tie. Clothes are tailor-made, bought on credit from the tallyman and paid off in instalments each week. On their feet they wore suede, crepe-soled shoes, so quiet that they got the nickname 'brothel creepers' or brogues polished to a high shine, completing their fashionable look.

My friends and I liked one, in particular. His name was Bobby, he must have been in his 20s and was, to my young eyes anyway, extremely handsome.

A popular song out at that time by Susan Maughan was '*I want to be Bobby's Girl*'. My friends and I always walked home singing it at the top of our voices as we dreamed of our idol.

We girls danced together. A popular dance in those days was the '*Twist*'. Sung by Chubby Checker it was a great workout for us and we twisted the night away. The good thing about dancing the Twist was that you did not need a partner, you could just twist away alone, not touching anyone else. This dance became quite a craze.

There were other crazy dance moves too with equally crazy names. The *Mashed Potato* involved both arms being placed out in front of your body while twisting your foot and jiggling your arms, which was supposed to look like mashing potatoes. If you look at videos today you can see what a weird dance it was.

The Locomotion was a dance where the dancers would get in a line, like a locomotion train and dance. Little Eva was the singer, it was quite popular and got to number one in the charts.

It seemed like new dances came out every week, here is a list, perhaps you would like to look them up to see how they were danced:

The Watusi

The Hitchhiker

The Stroll

The Hully Gully

The Pony – quite popular

The Swim

The Jerk

The Fish

The Bunny Hop

The Madison

The Hand Jive

Elvis Presley was a popular singer of that time along with cappuccino, a drink which was a novelty to us.

A café in the Hornsey Road was run by a Cypriot man. He had an espresso machine, and my friends and I met up there one day to try the cappuccino.

Inside the café there was a jukebox where you could place your coin and choose a record. The records were arranged in alphabetical order. One of my girlfriends, who happened to have some money left over from buying her coffee, placed her coin and chose Elvis Presley singing '*Old Shep*', a song, would you believe it? - about his dead dog. We must have been avid animal lovers at that time because we ended up all sitting there crying our eyes out about this bloody dog! The owner of the café threw us all out, three hysterical teens crying in his café was not good for business!

Mother met a genuinely nice man called Joe Greenwood during these years. He had a second-hand shop in Hornsey Road and kept a horse and cart elsewhere. He was known as a ragman, rag and bone man or totter.

I used to enjoy going out with him in the horse and cart up to the posher area of Highbury where he would call out '*rags and bone*' or '*any old iron*'. People brought out their unwanted items and if he thought he could get some money for them later, he would take them. I got at least two particularly useful bicycles from him this way.

Rag consisted of any type of clothing or linen, mostly made from cotton or wool which could be sold for a few pennies per pound weight to be recycled into cloth or paper. Anything metal was collected for scrap; he would pay for some things but mostly the householder just wanted to get rid of their rubbish so gave him many items for free. Today the collector of scrap comes round the streets in a van, or you take any unwanted items to the local recycling centre. No need for a horse and cart, though I guess one would come in handy if you had a lot of rubbish to clear out.

Some of my best times were spent in his shop and looking through all the items that he had stored there. One day when I was sitting inside the shop I found a box-cutter. I decided to use it to cut up a piece of cardboard which I balanced on my lap, the knife slipped and cut my outer thigh deeply. Mother did not deem it necessary to get medical help. A large plaster was slapped on and it healed eventually, I have the scar till today.

One day, while I was at my Greek friend's house watching Pinky and Perky on TV, my mother came knocking at the door. She asked for me and when I went to see her, she was crying. She told me that 'Uncle Joe' had passed away in the hospital that morning. Being young I could not understand the concept of dying. My only thought was to get back to the program I was missing on TV. I told her, "Sorry Mother, he was a nice man, can I go back now and watch TV?" She looked at me shocked, and called me a few names one of which was 'Selfish bitch'. I went back and sat in front of the TV. We had never had a TV, and this was a novelty to me. What did I understand about her pain and grief? It is only later in my adult years that I experienced grief myself and understood what she must have been feeling.

Chapter 4

First TVs

The first TV set that I remember seeing was at a neighbour's house. Mrs Hedges lived on the other side of us in Kingsdown Road. She had a daughter called Lynn.

One day when I went over there to play with Lynn, I was amazed to see this box in her front room with a small screen that had a magnifying glass in front of it to make the picture bigger I supposed. It was only well-off families that could afford a television in those days, though I would not have thought Mrs Hedges was particularly well-off.

The screen was about 9 inches in size, the programmes were in black and white – no colour then, that did not come in until 1967.

The picture quality was not particularly good, though to us any picture at all seemed like a miracle. A cathode ray fired horizontal lines onto the inner face of the tube. 405 lines covered the whole screen. The magnifier was hung from straps over the screen (some were attached to stands). There was no remote control, so all adjustments had to be done manually. The ones used quite often were the 'vertical hold, brightness and contrast'.

The picture would often drift up or down and it was quite a feat to be able to fine adjust it to keep it steady. The BBC was the only channel in the early days.

The television sets had a series of valves that were expensive to replace when they blew, and this happened quite often.

A more practical option on the market then was a company called Radio Rentals. Despite the name, they were a TV rental company. To rent a TV a lot of paperwork had to be filled in and background checks are done to ensure the customer did not move away with the television. Renting would save you quite a bit of money because the company would undertake all repairs of the TV free of charge, though of course, you would never own the TV.

The BBC had a test card screened before the main programmes started. It was in various shades of grey with lines in different directions. This enabled you to adjust the brightness and contrast better. The programmes were at first only put out for a few hours each day. A little later a further channel, ITV (Independent Television) was added, with the first advertising, then a third channel BBC2 arrived in 1964. It broadcast in 605 lines – still black and white, and UHF.

The children's programmes in the early years of TV that I can remember were Andy Pandy, a marionette who lived in a picnic basket. He was later joined by Teddy and Loopy Loo a rag doll. When Andy and Teddy were away, Loopy Loo would come alive and sing a song 'Here we go Loopy Loo'. They all lived together in the picnic basket. At the end of the programme they would sing 'time to go home, time to go home'. Andy is waving goodbye, we would sing along with them each time.

Blue Peter was quite popular. It was the first broadcast in 1958 and I believe it is still running now in 2021, having the accolade of being the longest-running children's TV show in the world.

Bill and Ben, the flowerpot men, was one of my all-time favourite shows. It was part of the 'Watch with Mother' programmes. They were two little flowerpot puppets who lived down at the bottom of a garden. Their companion was Little Weed, which was either a smiley-faced sunflower or a dandelion that grew between the two flowerpots. Bill and Ben spoke their own language too. It was a version of English called Oddle Poddle (invented by voice artist Peter Hawkins later to provide the voice over for the popular Daleks in Dr Who). When the programme ended Bill and Ben would say bye-bye to each other and Little Weed with 'Babap Ickle Weed' and Weed would reply with, 'Weeeeeeeeeed'.

Muffin the Mule, also a puppet, who worked with visible strings, danced on top of an old piano as Annette Mills played. He was joined by other puppets like Zebbie the Zebra, Hubert the Hippo, Sally the Sealion.

Pinky and Perky, a pair of puppet pigs – they were also on my favourites list. Pinky wore red clothes and Perky wore blue ones. Of course on a black and white TV this did not show, so Perky wore a hat to show he was different. They spoke and sang in high pitched voices. Their show had other puppets such as Topo Gigio who was a mouse, Ambrose the Cat, Conchita the Cow to name a few.

The Sooty Show with Harry Corbett on BBC was about the adventures of a *glove* puppet called of course, Sooty. He had friends called Sweep and Soo. Each episode had a new adventure for the characters and was a popular children's show. When Harry Corbett retired in 1976, his son Matthew took over the programme until it was discontinued in 1992.

Most of my TV viewing in those years was done in other people's houses.

Radio

We owned a radio at home, one with knobs and valves and, when I was quite small, I remember I would listen to a programme on the BBC called Listen with Mother. It was broadcast at 1.45 pm every day. I can still hear the presenter saying, "Are you sitting comfortably? Then I will begin," before reading a story or saying a nursery rhyme. Her phrase became so well known that it was later entered into The Oxford Dictionary of Quotations.

My mother would sometimes listen to a daily magazine programme that followed, called 'Woman's Hour' which is still being presented today (2021).

Funfair

The funfair came to Hampstead Heath each year at Easter. My brother would often take me there when he could afford it.

I could ride the dodgems, 'fish' for prizes with a pole and hook, shoot at cans, go on the spooky ghost ride, eat some candy floss. Sometimes I would win a goldfish in a plastic bag which I would take home and keep in a bowl on the table, the poor thing would not last long. I knew nothing about aerating the water for the fish to breathe, eventually, my mother would just flush it down the toilet. Coconuts were also given as prizes. If we were lucky enough to get these hard, hairy nuts my brother Brian would crack it open for me at home and we drank the juice inside and ate the hard, white flesh. The funfair was a great few hours spent and a very fond memory.

Christmas

Christmas in the 1960s was quite a frugal affair for us. Today the whole thing is so commercialised with lots of fairy lights, tinsel decorations, lavish trees and expensive presents costing hundreds of pounds. A large family today would need the parents delving into their credit cards to cover the expense.

We had simple 'Christmas'. We made the decorations ourselves from brightly coloured paper chains bought in packs of multiple colours. these we licked on one side, passed through one already done and stuck together to make a circle until we had a long chain of them. That was looped along the walls with perhaps some foil decorations (sometimes made from milk bottle tops that we had saved up for months), or a couple of purchased ones in the shape of bells. We cut newspapers out into the shape of dancing dolls, purchased sprigs of holly and mistletoe to be hung on lamps.

Our Christmas trees were small affairs, we decorated them with glass balls, little sweets hanging from the branches and the inevitable fairy at the top.

A pillowcase, left at the bottom of the bed for us to find when we woke up on Christmas morning contained such delights as satsumas, walnuts in their shells which we cracked open later with a metal nutcracker, chocolate coins, a colouring book with crayons to keep us quiet or a book with a page showing a picture of a doll wearing just underwear which I could detach from the page. There would be paper clothes to dress this paper doll that had tabs to close around the back of the doll to keep her clothes on, this would keep me busy for ages. An A4 page of little stickers of angels with just their heads and wings showing which I could then lick and stick into a book. For some reason, even today, if I see these angels' stickers, I begin to feel slightly anxious and sick. I have no idea why and wonder what could have caused this bad memory.

Sometimes there would be knitted items from Aunt Mary like a hat or scarf.

If Brian could get one from work, lunch might be roast turkey, (whoever got the wishbone would make a wish for the coming year), with roast potatoes, cauliflower, peas or the dreaded brussels sprouts and lots of thick brown Bisto gravy.

Christmas crackers would be on the table to pull open with a 'crack' then the joy of finding a small present in each one, and of course the paper Christmas hat to wear.

If there was not enough money to get a turkey, mother would make 'toad in the hole' which consisted of sausages cooked in a Yorkshire pudding in the oven. Having money put away each week for a year in the Christmas Club was a good way of making sure the turkey would appear on the table. My brother Brian oversaw this. Working in a grocery store he could get us shopping which was marked down in price.

After lunch we would be allowed to get our main present from under the tree. Rarely was this something I had asked for and I was always disappointed not to find that doll complete with her pram or the bicycle I longed for.

Money was short in those days and my parents had to keep the pub open with their weekly donations.

My mother made the Christmas pudding weeks beforehand. She stirred a sixpence into the pudding mix. This encouraged us to eat as much of it as we could in the hope of finding the treasure, hopefully without breaking a tooth in the process.

One Christmas I received a special present from an aunt, a relative of my father, who had emigrated to Australia and sent me the most beautiful doll. I was so happy to finally get something I wanted, for Christmas.

Not having a TV, the radio was our link to the outside world. We listened to Queen Elizabeth II's Christmas broadcast on the wireless in the afternoon. The BBC broadcast it from Buckingham Palace. Her first televised Christmas broadcast was in 1957. Her message was given over the airwaves from her Norfolk Estate at Sandringham, UK.

At some point, we moved from one house in Kingsdown Road to another one further along the same street where we rented rooms on the ground floor. I think it was number 49. It was just mother and me at that time. Other lodgers were living in the house too.

One was a lady called Joyce. She had a 4-year-old daughter, Debbie. Joyce and I got on like a house on fire, she was a great mother figure, did not drink much and would often give me a few shillings for myself. She rented one large room on the first floor, and I spent a great deal of my time with her.

Debbie had a club foot; her mother did not initially want to put her through the pain of an operation but had agreed eventually for her to have it done.

Joyce told me that her husband was in prison, and she was having to manage on her own. She sometimes sent me to Shepherd's Bush market to get her 'tablets' which she told me were for her headaches. I went there on the bus from Holloway and back.

I did not know at the time that the 'pharmacist' was giving me drugs in the illegal sense. At that age how would I understand what they were? One time while I was waiting for the pills, I sat on a chair to one side of the door in the pharmacy. A lady walked in, very well dressed and coiffed, she walked up to the counter, did not see me sitting behind her. As the pharmacist was busy inside, she had to wait. Thinking she was alone she let out a massive fart which made me jump and I burst out laughing, this made her jump too.

Drugs

Purple Hearts were amphetamines. The pills themselves were blue, small and triangular. One tablet would cost about 6d. They were popular among the teenagers and Mods. The craze for this drug started in London's West End. Used as a pick-me-up for those who wanted to stay awake longer. Working all week meant the weekend was a time to party hard. Those little pills helped you speed up, dancing until the early hours in clubs and dance halls.

Dope or marijuana was another drug popular especially among musicians like Bob Dylan, the Beatles, Rolling Stones, etc. Jimmy Hendrix's song 'Purple Haze' has drug connotations. This drug put the user into a slowed down state. The world was at rights, all people were your friends and you just loved everybody. Popular among musicians, as were most drugs.

Lysergic Acid Diethylamide – 25, known by its other name of LSD or Acid was widely used as a drug in the study of psychosis. It is derived from a fungus that grows on grains such as rye. The user would go on a 'trip' sometimes with frightening consequences which could be terrifying. This hallucinatory state can last for several hours or just a few minutes, depending on how much of the drug is taken.

The CIA in America used it as a 'truth drug'. It was brought over to the UK by Michael Hollingshead, founder of the World Psychedelic Centre in Chelsea, London. Amazingly, at that time, drugs were not yet illegal.

The police only had the outdated Dangerous Drugs Act of 1920 to go by, which did not cover synthetic drugs. It was not until 1964, The Drugs (Prevention of Misuse) Act was brought in to try and control these substances.

Some people died from their misuse of drugs and this is still the case in this modern-day.

In the 1960's film stars such as Montgomery Clift, Dorothy Dandridge, Wynona Harris, Marilyn Monroe, Natalie Wood (supposedly drowned while under the influence of drugs) are a few of those unfortunates to lose their lives to addiction.

Musicians such as Keith Moon, Janis Joplin, Brian Epstein, Jim Morrison, Elvis Presley, Johnnie Ray, Dinah Washington, etc, etc. The drug scene was quite popular, especially amongst the artistic set.

A quote from Dr Timothy Leary – founder of the League for Spiritual Discovery: "Acid is not for every brain. Only the healthy, happy, wholesome, handsome, hopeful, humorous, high velocity should seek these experiences."

Pie & Mash

Mother, Brian and I sometimes went to the pie and mash shop in Archway for a mince pie, mash potato and parsley gravy called liquor. Mother had her jellied eels as well. (I had no idea even what they were but decided I would never touch them as they looked awful). Lashings of malt vinegar was shaken all over and the dish was devoured hungrily by all concerned.

Brian normally footed the bill for the meal so it must have been on a Saturday afternoon. Even years later I still can remember that wonderful taste and smell. Living in London then, I would often find pie and mash shops to visit just to indulge myself with this icon of traditional London food.

These shops are fast disappearing which is a great shame. The one on Broadway Market, F. Cooke, closed after 120 years. The shop in Tower

Bridge called Manze's is now the oldest pie and mash shop in London and frequented by David Beckham and Rio Ferdinand of football fame.

Cockney's Pie and Mash in Portobello Road, London has slightly burnt pies, which are said to improve the flavour!

I just must mention before I leave this subject. A.J Goddard is now to be found in Welling after a stand-off with the Manze family. There is a Goddards in Greenwich beside the market. They have an exceptionally large menu which includes a lamb and rosemary pie, chillies minced beef pie or chicken and ham.

Most of these shops also do a delivery service due to the current COVID-19 situation. So, if you have never had pie and mash, do find one of these places and try some for yourself.

Chapter 5

Aunt Mary

My aunt, Mary- Mary Philomena Ford (1910–1976) - and her husband, Norman Grant, lived in a council flat in Lambeth, and I often went there with my mother to visit her.

Her husband had a large port-wine stain mark on his upper forehead which I found fascinating to look at and often got chastised for staring. She also had something I had never seen before, an electric cooker. On one of our visits, she had boiled a kettle up to make us some tea and, although she had switched the hob off, the colour went dull grey but it was still extremely hot, curious to feel it I placed my hand on the metal - big mistake!

My screams could be heard for miles. My hand was quite severely burned on the palm area which my aunt held under the cold tap for the longest time before rubbing margarine over and wrapping it up for me.

She gave me a whole shilling for my pain. Then it did not seem too bad and eventually, the burn healed up leaving not the faintest mark today.

Green Shield Stamps

Green Shield stamps, first introduced to the public in 1958, were sometimes given to the customer when purchases were made from the greengrocer, butcher, fishmonger, confectionery, etc. These were duly licked on their glue coated backs and then stuck into a book. When enough books had been filled, they could be exchanged for goods.

One stamp had a value of each 6d spent on goods. The stamp company produced a nice glossy coloured catalogue which my mother sat and looked through to see what she could get after licking hundreds of those little stamps and sticking them into the books. This would sometimes be my job, the taste of the glue was awful.

A 9ct Gold watch could be got for only 39 ½ books, how about a motorboat for only 107 books? Or would you like to take a flight somewhere with BOAC?

Let me show you the basics of maths on this one; each book contained 1,280 stamps. One stamp was issued for each 6p spent. So, 217,600 stamps would get you the motorboat for £5,440 (without the outboard motor).

Want a TV? That would cost you £2,816 in stamps licked and placed into 88 books. A 19" Regentone TV in the '60s would cost you 64 guineas, one guinea was £1.1s in pre-decimal money, that would be £67.4s if you went and bought the set outright, saving all that licking. But then again, getting something for 'free' was probably worth all that work.

The scheme was withdrawn in the year 1991 and the company went into voluntary liquidation in 2002.

The Green Shield company had a new office block on Station Road, Edgware, Middlesex in 1960. After the collapse of the business the property was renamed Premier House. The Green Shield Catalogue shops, warehouses and vans were eventually rebranded into the Argos we know today.

Although the stamps are now part of our history, they have been incorporated into many songs: Genesis in their 1973 album *Selling England by the Pound* 'Dancing with the Moonlight Knight', Bonzo Dog Doo Dah Band in their song *Piggy Bank Love* have a woman with a Green Shield Library, Jethro Tull in their song *Broadford Bazaar* verse *'We'll take pounds, francs and dollars from the well-heeled, and stamps from the Green Shield'*, a song called *'Green Shield Stamps'* by Nikki Sudden from his last album *'The Truth Doesn't Matter'*.

In a 1979 episode of *Fawlty Towers*, one of the guests asks Basil Fawlty, "What do you get for living in a climate like this? Green Stamps?"

Saturday Cinema

A treat we had some weeks was Saturday Cinema Club at the local cinema. It had its very own organ which rose out of the depths in front of the screen to magically play a tune.

We had one shilling, 6p was to get the ticket and 6p for ice cream during the interval brought down to the front of the screen by the ice cream girls carrying their trays of goodies from a strap around their neck.

The programme started with a cartoon - Bugs Bunny, Popeye or Donald Duck. Then came the movie, usually a Western with The Lone Ranger with his horse Silver accompanied by his Native Indian companion,

Tonto. The Lone Ranger shouted out something like 'Hiya Silver Away' and off he would gallop, or the screen would show a film with Roy Rogers and his horse Trigger, or the Cisco Kid or a similar. Mostly these were in serial form so you could not wait to get back the next week to see what had happened to the hero or heroine.

If I could not get to the cinema the following week, due to lack of funds, I would be mightily disappointed and must go to my friends who had been lucky enough to attend, begging them to tell me what had happened in the serial. At times, a small bribe was needed in the form of a sweet or two before they would part with the information.

Street Lighting

For as long as I could remember the streets where I lived in London had gas lighting. The decorative iron lamps were lit by the gas lighters with their long 8ft poles. Each lamp had a mantle that would throw out a soft glow from the lit gas.

Some homes still had gas lighting even up to 1970 and there are astonishingly 1500 streetlamps still lit by gas in London, each one hand lit by a five-man team of British Gas engineers every evening. They call themselves 'The Guardians of the Lamps' and are proud to be part of English history.

The gas lamps are somewhat temperamental; each one has to be wound and checked, the glass regularly polished and the fragile mantles, tiny, bell-shaped silk casings coated in lime-oxide which gives the lamps their wonderful glow, are replaced. The glass must be kept clean of the London grime to enable the full extent of the shining light, so different from the harsh electric streetlights.

The lamps along the Houses of Parliament are serviced by their staff, for security reasons.

The long avenue of Kensington Palace Gardens is lit only by gas lamps. take a walk along there sometime and imagine what it was like in Charles Dickens' era.

The gas lights have survived thanks to English Heritage which have restored and protected them.

Chapter 6

Secondary School (1960)

My secondary school was Shelburne High School for Girls. On looking up the history of this school I was amazed to discover that it was first established in 1825 as a community Mission on the Holloway Road, London.

When I first started there, I was set upon by a group of girls because I answered their leader's question, "Hey what's your name then?" with "What's it got to do with you, bitch?" setting myself up for trouble. They chased me down the road after school and I almost did not get away from them.

The next day I was terrified they would set upon me again, but they seem to have forgotten about me by then – short memories of mentally challenged gang members. I managed to get through the school term without moving on their radar.

I made some friends although their names are lost to me today.

The classroom was rowdy while we waited for the teacher to arrive, the noise deafening until the door opened and there she stood to immediate silence and innocent looks.

The Religious Instruction class was one I remember vividly.

I was brought up as an RC, but then that is another story. I had read the Bible, well, bits of it anyway, been to church and listened, bored to death, to the sermons.

Our religious teacher was a Catholic priest. One day he was telling us about the Bible story of Cain killing Abel and being banished from the land of his father, Eden. According to the Bible, he took himself off to the land of Nod *'where he took unto himself a wife'*. This was like a red flag to a bull for me, immediately my hand shot up.

"Yes, Sandra, what is it?" said the priest.

"Holy father," says I, "there is Adam & Eve, right?" He nodded his head blithely unaware of the trap he was falling into. I continued: "Then there was Cain and Abel, right?"

Again, he nodded his head, "Yes correct."

"Cain killed Abel, so, father, tell me where this wife of his came from if the only people living on the earth at that time was Cain and his mother and father, seeing that the brother was dead?"

For some reason the priest just looked at me, he did not give me an answer – just told me to sit down and then moved on to something entirely different. I was ignored and confused. Why, if he did not know the answer, who did?

I went back home that day after school and dug out the Bible again. There I discovered in Genesis that the whole story is even more confusing, and no straight answer was to be found, so I decided that Cain, finding himself alone and abandoned in a strange land, found a Neanderthal living in the land of Nod and decided he would marry her and build himself a city. I had no idea how long this took him, working alone as he did as I guess his wife wouldn't have been much help.

I always questioned those things that, to me anyway, did not make sense. I had an inquisitive mind, much to the frustration of my brother whom I would often ask questions that he could not answer. But I digress; back to the school days of 1961+.

There was one teacher that I did not like, and the feeling was mutual. She was always pointing me out, criticising what I wore or how my hair was done or what I was writing. She taught maths, one of my worst subjects. Due to her teaching lacking any sort of structure I could not understand even the basics and failed my tests and therefore my exams constantly.

After one particularly harrowing experience with her where I was called to the front of the class for a ruling (across the hand) for being 'out of order, Sandra', she gave me several extremely hard smacks across my palm with the ruler – something that we do not allow these days – thank goodness, but it was a common punishment then.

I decided on a plan to get my revenge. The following week, just before the class started, I got a small hammer and nails (brought from home) and hammered the nails under her desk and up into the drawer. Then I left the classroom.

In those days we moved around to go to different classes, so when it was time for her class again, I filed in and took my place with the rest of the other pupils. I waited eagerly for her to make a move. She always opened her drawer to get out her tools, rulers, pens, pencils, etc. Of course, this time the drawer would not open. Miss had an awful time pulling at it and the whole desk moved this way and that. The entire class was in hysterics, tears running down our faces watching her antics. It is a memory that will stay with me, she never caught on to what had been done, not until the repair person had been called in to fix the stuck drawer and discovered the nails. I was never even suspected. I doubt she is reading this now. She will be long in her grave; I should be safe.

For one term we had a supply teacher to take over our maths class when Ms X was off sick. She was from Canada. It was the first time I had heard someone speaking with an American (to me) accent, and I was fascinated. I kept on jumping up to ask her questions just to hear her speak and thoroughly disrupting the class until she became quite frustrated, shocking me into silence with the words, "Sandra – sit down on your *fanny* and SHUT UP!"

I sat down gobsmacked – here was a TEACHER swearing in class! Of course, to us Londoners the word FANNY had a completely different meaning. I did not know that she was referring to my bum and as I looked around at my classmates, I could see that they were equally shocked.

It was a very silent class after that, but I must say that her teaching methods were far superior to our regular teacher. I learnt some maths during her time. Of course, when she left to go to pastures new and Ms X came back, we were back where we started, dumb as ever.

One exam I had in maths is a vivid memory. We were advised by Ms X to read all the questions and answer the ones we thought we knew the answer to first, then go on to the more complex questions.

I followed this advice to the letter. By the time I got to the end of the paper I was so confused, completely lost, I answered the first question 'how many inches in a yard with the answer '12'. After floundering around the rest of the paper it began to look like it was in Chinese – I gave up. I remember my exam result was 1/20.

There was a tuck shop in school. The pupils could buy their treats – chocolate, crisps, drinks, etc. It was an innovation.

One day in class I needed some paper to write on and asked the teacher for some. She directed me to the cupboard right next to where I was sitting. When I opened it to get the paper my eyes were drawn to some boxes stacked inside with Cadbury's on the outside. I had found the stock of tuck shop treats! Somehow, I managed, through the next few times I was in that class, to extract a few bars for myself and, of course, any of my mates that I deemed worthy of a bit of chocolate.

The stock was moved somewhere else after that. I think they realised someone was helping themselves.

The school was just near Jones Brothers (later to be John Lewis). I often spent time wandering around in that massive store looking at the goods for sale.

My best subjects during my school years were English, Spelling and Reading. In these subjects I excelled. No idea why I had this ability as I was mediocre in everything else. I did not imagine my parents to be very intelligent.

My brother Brian was also very clever in his life. He was offered a place at Grammar School.

One term the class was given a subject to choose to write an essay on, I chose Blues, not because I understood what it was (I thought it was about the colour), but because I liked the sound of the word. The other subjects available were History, Famous people in Science or The Roman Empire. So, Blues sounded a better subject to me.

Once I understood my subject was music, I went to the school library and found a couple of books on the history of the Blues. I was able to copy out quite a lot of information into my exercise book, along with a few pages of photos that I tore out of the books to get glued into 'my' work. I got quite a good mark for my efforts and kept that exercise book for many years later before it eventually got lost on one of my many house moves. In my adult years, I rediscovered Blues music and have been an avid listener ever since.

I tried the violin but discovered I was tone deaf so my 'Twinkle, Twinkle Little Star' was enough to make you run for the door, I gave that up. I always wanted to play the piano after hearing Tchaikovsky's piano concerto. Of course, that would cost money, they did not teach it in school.

We had career advisers who came to the school to advise us school leavers on job prospects. He asked me if I had any idea what sort of job I would be interested in, 'lavatory assistant' quips I. He misheard my answer and thought I had said, 'laboratory assistant' after all – who in their right mind would want to work in a lavatory!

The last year in high school I was advised to take a commercial course and learn such delights as touch typing, filing, shorthand and office procedure.

I managed to get through that alright except for the touch typing, the keys of the typewriter were covered in metal caps. I found it much easier to remove these to see the letters and type. To this day I cannot touch type and Pitman's shorthand was quite beyond my understanding; all those squiggles and curves were supposed to mean something and be readable, not for me though.

Thinking back on my school years there are times when I wish I had paid better attention and at least had some sort of ambition. My only goal was to leave school and get a job that paid me money to spend on myself.

I managed to secure a Saturday job during my final school year, in Holloway, in a pet shop. It was my task to clean out the cages and replenish the water and food. I liked animals and enjoyed looking after them. In those days kittens and puppies were stocked in the shop, also snakes.

The owner of the pet shop would not let me near the snakes, some of which were poisonous but one day he did hold one of the non-poisonous ones for me to touch and I was fascinated by the fact that it had smooth, dry scaly skin. I had always thought that snakes were wet. He showed me the ear holes and how the snake's tongue was forked.

When we moved away to another area, I missed that job.

I was not able to complete my last year of school due to my mother deciding that we should move out of Holloway in 1964.

Chapter 7

1964

Mother and I got turfed out of our lodgings in Holloway for not paying the rent. We went to stay with a friend of my mother's called Maude in East London.

Maude lived with her long-time partner, Frank, who I discovered later, was an absolute letch. I remember he had a gold tooth and would often sit jiggling one of his legs. In later life, I would always steer clear of these leg jiggling types, they reminded me of him.

Maude had an upright piano, she could not play it. I could not either though I spent many moments bashing down on the keys imagining I was a great pianist – until she would shout out for me to, "Stop that bloody racket Sandra!"

In the mornings Maude made Frank, who was usually upstairs in bed, a cup of tea.

One day, she asked me to take him his cuppa. She called up, "Frank, do ya want a cuppa, I will send it up with Sandra?"

He called back, "yes." By the time I had gone up the stairs with his mug of tea he had got himself up out of bed, I knocked on the door and entered to the sight of him standing there with his erection showing through his pyjamas. It was a sight I will never forget and it scared the life out of me, so much that the mug slipped and I spilt some tea on the floor.

It is my habit, even today, that if I do not like something I just ignore it – so that is what I did. I did not look at him or his appendage, banged what was left of the tea down on the side, turned my back and left. The next time I was asked to take him his tea I told Maude he could come and get it himself.

Another one of his habits was to wait until I was in the toilet. The toilet was a makeshift affair which had been installed at the top of the stairs. It had one-inch gap between the door and the frame.

The first time I went to use the toilet, I heard the sound of someone creeping up the stairs as I was inside, pressing an eye to look at me through the gap. I could hear heavy breathing. I knew it was Frank, Aunt Maude was clattering around downstairs in the kitchen.

If I needed to use the toilet after that I stuffed as much toilet paper as I could along the length of the gap, from the top of the door to the bottom, so that he could not see me, but if I could hold out until he went out, it was a better relief for me. It did not occur to me to tell either my mother or Maude about this.

After mother and I had been there for a short while, she went out one day and never returned. I had been abandoned. Aunt Maude kept asking me where she had gone but I did not know. As the days passed and she did not return Aunt Maude realised that mother was either dead or in the hospital and she decided to call the police.

Neither of us thought at first that mother had just plain buggered off. Looking after a 14-year-old teenager must have been cramping her style, I was getting a bit out of hand, talking back, being a pain, and she could not cope with me anymore, so she just decided to dump me. I was quite worried at first, wondering if she was lying dead somewhere.

The police came to the house with a social worker and I was taken away. I think Aunt Maude would have let me stay on, but I am sure she was more than aware of Frank and his antics. I was so happy to finally be away from that awful man and his tricks.

The word 'paedophile' was not in my vocabulary but I am sure that is what he was. I was lucky to get away when I did, who knows what may have happened. I never saw or heard from them again except for one year sometime later when I saw a photo in the newspaper. I was 100% certain it was him, same face, same crinkly hair and gold tooth showed in the photo. The article said that he was working with youngsters in a drug rehabilitation programme. If it was him, God help them.

Chapter 8

Children's Home (1964 – 1966)

I was taken by social services to a children's home somewhere in Brentwood, Essex. I stayed there until I was 16, I can honestly say that time was the happiest and most stable I had ever been in my life.

I was enrolled in a local school to complete my studies, had regular meals, outings to the seaside, clothes, pocket money, friends. I even got to join the RAF Cadets – what more could I want even if it was only temporary?

We had a house mother and father; they had a Doberman dog. I was terrified at first that he would bite me, but he was as gentle as could be.

There were about five girls in our house, we slept in a dormitory upstairs. An older coloured girl had the prestigious corner cubicle with her very own door and a key. Everyone else had just a bed and a side cabinet and a small wardrobe for their things. Her cubicle was on the side of the house which had a fire escape. Her boyfriend often crept up and climbed through the window to visit her.

There was a lot of whispering and giggling at odd hours of the night from them both. The other girls and I never let on about her clandestine meetings, we kept it quiet from the house parents.

When she left the house to go out into the world, as I was then the oldest, I was given her cubicle. Unfortunately, she had not let her boyfriend know that she had been moved. No mobile phones in those days.

One night while I was in bed fast asleep, he climbed up the stairs, through the window and got into bed with me, which scared the hell out of us both. When I managed to explain to him that she had gone, he begged me not to tell anyone and promised he would not be back. I kept my word as I did not want him to get into trouble. He seemed genuinely upset, dumped again. There was no way to lock the window, it was the only way out in the event of a fire.

The cubicle served me well especially on a Sunday when we had church services. I found, if I made sure I was sitting at the back, I could slip away from the church and go back to bed, locking my door and keeping quiet.

I got away with this a few times but then I was caught out and given a warning that I must behave myself. I was also able to help myself to quite a few of the lovely little white Bibles on display inside the church, which I then gave to friends.

My brother came to see me in the children's home. He looked so handsome in his army uniform with his hat on, the other girls were quite taken by him. He told me that he was sorry he could not take me out of the home and look after me due to him being in the army. I understood, he did not have the resources to look after a teenage girl.

I joined a penfriend club after finding details in a magazine. I would write to boys living in other countries. One lived in Italy and we would exchange letters describing our lives and the area we lived in. Sometimes I would send him a task such as how many seas are there in the world? Name them. Whoever got the most seas would be the winner.

Even in those days I was an avid researcher, loved to find out about the world we lived in or the universe.

A few days after my 15th birthday (1965) it was announced on the news that Sir Winston Churchill had died after suffering a stroke. There was to be a state funeral telecast on television.

Putney, London – Hostel For Girls

When I became 16, I had to leave the children's home. I was taken to London by my social worker, to what was then called a halfway house hostel for young girls in Putney. There she left me and I did not see or hear from her again.

I was able to get my very first full-time job at Woolworths. The large store had wooden floors and counters, they sold food as well as stationery and other stock. I was placed on the stationery counter where I was trained up in the use of the till. Lots of items were sold at an odd price, such as 99d or 1s 99d. This meant that the till had to be opened to give the customer their change, therefore the money could not be slipped into the worker's pocket.

I remember a customer who stood at my counter with a cigarette dangling from her mouth. I respectfully reminded her that there was a non-smoking policy inside the store. She told me to mind my own business and get on with serving her.

When she had finished paying for her purchases and was walking away, I muttered, "Hope you set yourself on fire, stupid cow!" Unfortunately for me, she overheard this remark and went to the manager to complain. I was duly called into the staff room to explain my remark. I told the manager that she had misheard me, I was only mentioning that there could be a fire from her discarded cigarette, I got away with it that time.

My weekly wages were about £7, not a lot in today's money but it was enough in 1966.

I shared a room with another teenage girl who was pregnant and waiting to go to a mother and baby home. One Friday night very late, I woke up to find her moving about the room. She told me she had been bursting for the loo and just come back. Thinking nothing of it I went back to sleep.

The next day was Saturday so I went out to do some shopping. It was then I discovered that my wage packet, which I had received on Friday, was missing from my bag. Immediately I remembered the girl moving around the room during the night and as soon as I got back to the hostel I rushed to the room and guess what? She was gone, the rotten cow had taken every penny of my wages and not left me with anything knowing she was being moved out. I cursed her and her unborn child to the ends of the earth.

The hostel manager lent me enough money for my lunches until the next payday when I was able to pay her back, but I had to walk to work instead of getting the bus and that took longer. After that I was less naïve and warier of people. I learned a hard lesson.

One night in winter I woke up from a deep sleep wanting to go to the loo. As I attempted to get out of bed, I discovered that I could not move at all, I was paralysed in my back. After trying for some time and getting more and more desperate, I called out for the manager to come and help me. I was alone in the room, nobody else had yet been moved in so I had no help in that quarter.

After what seemed a long time of me shouting, the manager finally came to see what I was making all the noise about. When she heard I could not get up, she was able to drag me up to my feet and I made my way to the toilet. When I returned, she helped me get back into bed. Before she left she said she would call the doctor in the morning and let my work know that I was sick.

The doctor came at about 9 am and examined me thoroughly. He could find nothing wrong so suggested that I had been in a very cold wind as I was walking home which had hit my back muscles causing them to spasm, hence my inability to get up. He left me with some pain killers, I was in bed for most of that day but able to get up after that, back to normal.

In those days GPs would come and visit the patient at home, not like today in 2021 where, because of the Covid-19 situation you can only call the surgery to arrange for a telephone consultation.

I stayed at the hostel for about 6 months, then I was able to rent myself a bedsit which was small and consisted of a bed, wardrobe, electric two plate hob and a washbasin. There was a shared bathroom that always had a black ring of scum around it where other tenants had not cleaned up after themselves.

In 1966 landlords were able to advertise their property, especially single rooms, in the windows of sweetshops or tobacconists. They could stipulate in their advert, 'no blacks, no Irish, no DSS, no dogs'. It was not considered racist or cruel to animals.

I had moved away from the expensive Putney area to the cheaper Fulham. I started another job as a junior at a travel firm, Blue Horizons or Blue Skies holidays, not sure which. My job consisted in making the teas, gathering up the post and taking it to the post office. It paid a bit more than Woolworths and I liked the people there, they treated me well.

I also got trained up in some office procedures including the use of the telephone switchboard and the telex machine. I had always been unfazed by gadgets or machines so quickly mastered their intricacies.

One afternoon, during my lunch break, as I was wandering around in a store, I looked up and saw a woman who was the spitting image of my mother. My heart felt like it had stopped, I stared at her for such a long time and followed her around the store. She was so nicely dressed in a posh way, with her make-up done perfectly and her brown hair curled.

Noticing me following her, she turned around, looking at me she said, *"Can I help you?"* Well, as soon as she spoke, I knew that her perfect accent was not something my mother could ever manage. Disappointed I mumbled, *"No, sorry,"* before turning away and returning to work. I was deeply affected by this occasion. She could have been a twin of my mother, I often wondered how some people look so much alike.

You would think after all this that I would never find my mother again, but I did. I often used to go back to her old haunts and roam around. Berwick Street market was one of those places. She had been married at some point to someone who used to have a stall there, so I would go back there sometimes and ask around to see if anyone had seen or heard of her.

One day I got lucky when one of the stallholders I asked said she had been around. She had mentioned that she was going up to Middlesbrough, back to the place she was born.

My brother wrote a letter to his cousin, Joe, who lived there and was able to get an address for my mother, which he then passed on to me. I was not about to rush up there to see her. I was still hurting about being abandoned by her so roughly. I just wanted to know that she was still alive.

Chapter 9

Switchboard

After being trained on the switchboard at work I was now fully able to work as a junior PBX (plugboard extension) telephonist. To explain how the switchboard worked: when a call comes through a lamp lights up on the back panel. The operator answers the call by placing the rear cord into the jack and pushing the front key forward. The operator can then speak to the caller who will indicate which person/extension they would like to speak to. The operator would then check that the extension requested is free by tapping the front cord on the extension jack. If it is, the cord is placed into the jack and the front key is pulled backwards to ring the number. Then both cords are left up and the keys in position while the parties converse. When the call is finished the supervision lamps light up and the call can be disconnected by removing both cords from the jacks. The cords are weighted by a pulley weight behind the switchboard which pulls it down into position to stop it tangling.

I registered with a company called Three T's in Central London as a temp. This way I could move around to different companies and fill in where needed. I could also get to use the different types of switchboards, the ones I did not know, the company would train me on for free. It was a win-win situation, I became a 'hello girl' and a member of Britain's first female workforce.

Automatic switchboards were taking over from the older, larger PBX type ones in some companies. These were smaller units that sat on a desktop. The call came in, a light flashed, a button was pressed to answer and when the caller gave the extension number another button was pressed to connect the two calls.

I liked this better than a permanent job, I got to meet new people, see new places, it suited me.

I had regular work, filling in as a temp whenever an employee was off or there was a shortage of staff to work the switchboards. I was reliable, rarely late, willing to stay on extra time to help and this was appreciated by the companies I worked in.

One hotel I worked at for a few weeks had three large PBX switchboards. There were two women operators and one man, James, who was our supervisor.

James was sight impaired, he operated the specially adapted switchboard by using certain aids, running his fingers over the lights when he heard a call coming in to feel the small pin in the centre of the light which popped up. It was amazing to me how fast and accurate he was able to answer the many calls that came through. He could also tell the time by feeling the dial on his watch which had braille numbers.

I admired him very much. One incident that I remember of those days was when I was late one morning, he had been on the night shift and was waiting for me to relieve him before the other operator came in at noon, and here I was 30 minutes late. Of course, he chastised me quite severely, so I lost my temper and stormed out, no way was I going to take his criticism.

I marched along the road fuming, how dare he, who did he think he was, etc? When I got a short way along the road I stopped suddenly and thought about it all, it was my fault, I was in the wrong. That man had been working all night, how could I just walk out and leave him without anyone to cover him? I felt so ashamed of myself. Turning around I marched back into the building and the switchboard room. By now I was quite breathless. Facing him I said, *"I am so, so sorry, it's my fault, please do forgive me for being so bloody rude."* He seemed to think about it for a moment before getting up, and lifting his white stick he said, *"Never mind, don't let it happen again. Now forget about it, I'm off home for a kip."* Gathering up his things he tapped his way out. I was never late if I could help it, for anything after that.

On another occasion, at the same hotel, I answered a call from one of the guests who was from Burundi in Africa. He asked me to put him through to his home number. To do so, in those days I would have to go through the BT international operator. The number he gave was unobtainable and as I had the guest on the line I relayed this information to him.

The overseas operator also informed us that there had been some sort of coup in the country, his home was in the capital and the international telephone lines were down. The guest was quite panicked by this information, but I had an idea. I asked him if he had anyone outside the capital that he could contact, they might be able to contact his home on the internal telephone lines and make sure that his family was safe. Luckily, he did have a relative's number to whom I was able to connect him, and all turned out well. In gratitude, he sent me an envelope with quite a sum of money in it which I shared with the other telephonists on duty with me.

Sometimes, in the evening, I would go out with my colleagues and we would have a meal in the local pub. Due to the experience of being brought up by alcoholic parents, I was not much into alcohol. My tipple was mostly a lemonade or a Babycham.

Babycham was a popular drink among the ladies, something I would have on occasion, tiny bottles of sparkling perry with an alcohol content of 6% which, as it was served in champagne glasses, looked like champagne and we could pretend we were 'posh'.

Drugs were not something I experienced, nor did I want to, even today I do not see the point of them. I did not attend parties or move around with a large group of friends getting into mischief even at 16.

I had been out with one or two lads to a movie or dancing at Hammersmith Palais but was not interested in the opposite sex, being quite shy. Even when I went dancing, I preferred to dance with my friends and rarely accepted invitations from the lads at the dance hall. I was told off one time by a young lad who had come over to ask me to dance on at least two occasions and became quite annoyed when I refused. He said to me, "Why did you bother to come here for then if you won't dance with anyone?"

Hammersmith Palais formerly known as Hammersmith Palais de Danse was the first Palais de Danse to be built in Britain in 1919. It was owned by the Mecca Entertainment Group from 1960 to 1990. Occupying a large building on the A219 at 242 Shepherd's Bush Road, London W6, it was near the A4 Hammersmith Flyover. On some Saturday nights, the place would be packed out with up to 2,000 people all dancing to a band playing on the huge revolving stage. The Palais was demolished in 2012, a new building constructed on the site was a luxury student Hall of Residence.

There is an interesting account of British nightclubs by Dave Haslam:

Haslam, Dave 2015 *Life after Dark: a history of British nightclubs.* **Simon & Shuster ISBN 9780857206985**

Chapter 10

London (1967) – Wedding & Pregnancy

I met Ahmed in 1967 when I was working in Kensington. He asked me where I was from, all the normal questions to ask a young girl. I was 17, he was in his 20s, he told me he was from Iraq – a country I was then blissfully unaware of – and was attending engineering college in London. He was my height, good looking with black hair and brown eyes, well dressed and slim.

He offered to walk me home, when we reached my place and I said goodnight I gave him a quick peck on the cheek.

"What's that supposed to be?" he said.

I looked at him, puzzled.

"That's not a kiss, this is a kiss," and he leaned over, clasped me to him and kissed me full on the mouth.

Shocked at the boldness of a man I had only just met, I backed away and quickly climbed the steps leading to my flat. Shakily I opened the door and with a quick wave goodbye I stepped inside slamming it shut.

We went out for a while and when he asked me to marry him, I agreed. I remember having to write to my mother at the time and ask for her to send permission for my marriage as, according to the law at that time, I was underage.

A day for the wedding was set in December at Kensington Registry Office after first having posted the intention to marry notice, which was and still is today, a legal requirement. If you are getting married in a Christian church then you post banns which are announced on three Sundays before the wedding, at the service.

A few days before the marriage it occurred to me that I did not have a wedding ring. Ahmed-to-be had not even thought to get me one so I had to ask him for some money to go and buy one for myself. He stipulated he would not wear a ring.

My friend, Marie, came with me to Shepherd's Bush so we could look for something within the budget. I remember her asking me a strange question. If I did not get the ring that day, could she borrow the ring money for a pair of boots she had spied in Dolcis! I bought a simple gold band for the money I had; she didn't get her boots.

On the wedding day, we turned up at the registry office with Marie and her parents, who were to be witnesses to the wedding. I remember Ahmed had an allergy and was constantly blowing his nose. The clerk who married us thought he was wiping tears from his eyes! I should have been the one crying.

I wore a green two-piece suit that I had bought for the occasion from Shepherd's Bush Market, (when I got home with my suit, I discovered my purse had been stolen).

Green was a colour that my mother would never wear saying it was unlucky for her. I found out that it was unlucky for me as well that day and wearing it at my wedding seemed to have put a curse on my entire marriage. I have never worn anything green to this day.

After the marriage ceremony, we went with Marie Ward, who was going out with a friend of Ahmed's, and we all went for a meal at a local restaurant. When I got up to go to the ladies', I found that, although the door to the cubicle locked when I shut it, the inside mechanism was missing, and I was locked in. I was so shy that I could not even think to call out for help. After waiting for ages for someone to come, Marie was eventually sent to see what was taking me so long and she let me out. We had fits of giggles just thinking about it later.

Ahmed and I lived in Kensington for a while as he completed his studies. I was by then pregnant with my first child, Faris. Marie Ward, who had attended our wedding, lived a short distance away with her parents. She would often turn up at my door, sometimes with a large bottle of cider clutched in each arm and tears running down her face as she sat with me lamenting the woes of her relationship with her boyfriend, who was also a friend of Ahmed's and from Iraq and often beat her up.

Epilepsy

One night when I was about 8 months into my pregnancy, Ahmed woke up to find me having a seizure. I had never had one before although

I had experienced throughout my life what I later discovered to be called *petit mal* episodes. When I came round, I found myself surrounded by a mass of tissues he had used to wipe my mouth. He called an ambulance to take me to the hospital. Once there I was left lying on an examination couch in a cubicle while waiting to see a doctor. It was there that I had another seizure. If Ahmed had not been by my side, I would probably have fallen off the examination table and on to the floor which could have killed my unborn child.

After having some tests, I was later diagnosed with temporal lobe epilepsy of the *grand mal* type. I was prescribed a drug called Epanutin combined with Phenobarbitone in a form of a capsule. Nobody explained to us that Epanutin could cause serious birth defects in my unborn child, nor that Phenobarbital may lower folic acid and vitamin K levels, increasing the risks of spinal cord defects. At 17 I did not know about the dangerous side effects drugs could cause in a foetus and Ahmed was equally uneducated in these matters.

Throughout my younger years, I had experienced what I later found out was a *petite mal* occurrence where I would feel a sense of *Deja Vu*. I would seem to know what someone was going to say or the place where I was, I had the oddest feeling that I had been there before. I could not explain what it was, but this was with me for many years until the convulsions occurred later.

If I remembered to take the tablets the seizures were kept at bay. If I forgot for one day, they would occur again, so I was careful to remember most days.

Toothache

One day I woke up with the most awful toothache which necessitated a trip to the dentist. Due to my pregnancy I was entitled to free dental treatment.

I made an appointment with a nearby dentist. He was an elderly man who had been recommended to me by my landlady. After he had examined me, he told me one of my wisdom teeth was the cause of the pain and needed to be extracted.

After numbing me with the anaesthetic he proceeded to place one of his legs on each side of one of mine, gripping me closely while tugging at my wisdom tooth. I could feel his erection pressing into my thigh while he was working on my tooth and could not wait to get out of his surgery as soon as I could. There had been no nurse present and I wondered later how many other women patients he had 'pleasured' himself with while they were being held captive! My intense shyness prevented me from protesting or mentioning this occurrence to Ahmed in case he decided to deal with the dentist at some point in his way. Keeping quiet was my best option.

Yorkshire

Before we met, Ahmed had previously been attending a course for Aeronautical Engineering at Perth Aerodrome in Scotland. His eldest brother, Abdul Hamid, in Baghdad financed him throughout his study years, but he had been thrown off the course in Perth, Scotland due to some bad behaviour and low grades. His one wish was to become an aeronautical engineer and he was quite upset about his dismissal. I offered to write to the college dean and request that he be allowed to return.

I wrote a letter explaining that he was now much more responsible with a new wife and child on the way and had seen the error of his ways, would they be prepared to offer him another chance? Amazingly it worked. He was offered a place on the course again for the coming new term. We now had to leave our small one-room home in Kensington and make plans to travel up to Scotland.

As I was almost due to give birth, Ahmed asked me to write to my mother in Yorkshire and ask if I could come and stay with her for the birth. I had not contacted her since I had got married so she did not know about the pregnancy. I received a letter back. She was so excited about the baby, saying I was more than welcome to come.

So, we gave up our bedsit, the landlady had wanted us out anyway as she did not want a baby in the room or a pram in the entryway, and we travelled up to Yorkshire in our old and creaky Austin. There was no GPS, Google Maps or Waze of course, no mobile phones, so I was given the job of navigator, with a road atlas spread open on my lap as we joined the motorway North.

We finally arrived at my mother's house. Ahmed stayed for one night there before travelling on to Scone, Perth, Scotland to attend the course.

Mother lived in a couple of damp rooms which I did not think were suitable for a new-born, so the next day I went to the local council and filled in a request for a council place for us. I knew I would not be staying long with her but the time I was staying I did not want to be in that place. At least she would have something better when I left. It was easier then to get housing, not like today where the councils are overrun with homeless families.

She was allocated a bungalow with two bedrooms. I helped her move her meagre belongings out of her current rooms. We received some vouchers for furniture from the council which we used to purchase beds, a table and chairs along with some other bits we needed.

I spent my time knitting a few little jackets and trousers, bonnets, mittens and booties for the baby. Not too many as I was superstitious, it might put bad luck on the birth. I also knitted a jumper for Ahmed in some colours I thought he might find interesting. He could wear it when he attended his course. That never happened. As far as I can remember, he never wore it and I eventually gave it to charity in Scone, he wouldn't be getting another.

Here are some interesting news events of 1967.

Donald Campbell was killed trying to beat his water speed record.

The first person to become cryonically-preserved, Dr James Bedford, with the hope of being revived in the future, is still waiting in 2021. I wonder if this procedure will be successful in the future, will we be able to revive those people who have had their bodies frozen in the hope that one day they will be revived, or is this just a pipe dream?

A tragic event occurred when astronauts Gus Grissom, Ed White and Roger Chafee were killed when the Apollo 1 Command module caught fire during a launch rehearsal.

In December there was a news article about a doctor in South Africa, Dr Christian Barnard, having performed the world's very first heart transplant. The recipient Louise Washkansky died 18 days later but, hey, it was a world first and they will always be remembered in history.

Sweden switched to driving on the right-hand side. For tourists from the UK who drive on the left this was bothersome as they kept going the wrong way at roundabouts.

The Rolling Stones Band had a new release, 'Let's Spend the Night Together', (I loved that song).

The USA entered the Vietnam War.

The first Boeing 737 made its maiden flight, from Boeing Field to Paine Field for 2 ½ hours.

Boxer Muhammed Ali was stripped of his boxing title for refusing to be drafted into the army. He cited religious reasons, but I suspect he did not want to go to fight in the Vietnam War.

There was a Six-Day war between Israel, Jordan, Syria and Egypt. We spent a lot of time listening to the tragic outcome of this conflict as it unfolded each day.

Mohammed Reza Pahlavi crowns himself as Shah of Iran and his wife as Empress.

Chapter 11

Faris (1968)

I went to Middlesbrough Hospital for my induction on 29th January. During the examination the nurse informed me that the doctor would perform something called 'sweeping the membranes'. I had no idea what this entailed but when it was done, boy did I shout!

I was in labour until the next day. In the final stages of labour my feet were put up into stirrups, the straps holding my feet had not been tightened correctly by the nurse and when the doctor decided I needed an episiotomy, numbing the area with a local anaesthetic, it was painful and made me jump, my foot shot out of the stirrup, hitting the doctor on the side of his face and almost knocking him to the floor. He wasn't too happy about that.

My son, Faris, was born and weighed about 10 pounds, quite a big baby. He was perfect, fair-skinned with big eyes and all his fingers and toes.

My mother came to visit during the visiting hours, and she was happy as Larry to see him. She asked me if she could pick him up, but I noticed that her hands were not too clean, and she had a cold, so I told her that the nurses did not allow visitors to pick up the new-borns. She was disappointed, but accepted it.

I asked her to call Ahmed from the hospital telephone box and let him know he had a son; he told her that he wanted to name the baby, Faris, after one of his best friends. I liked the name, calling the baby Gunner or Bernhard after my father might have not gone down so well with his family.

Public Telephone

The public telephones in the hospital were the same as the ones in the streets, few people had a phone at home. The call was made by lifting the receiver before placing 2d into a slot in a black box marked with 'A' and

'B' after the number had been dialled. When the call was answered the 'A' button (for answer) was pressed and the money could be heard dropping into the box. Only then could you be heard. If there was no answer, then the 'B' button was pressed and the money would be returned into a slot at the bottom of the box.

I was in the hospital for two weeks while the perineal cut healed, by this time Ahmed had managed to rent a place and drove down from Scotland to collect me. He took me to mother's while I got my stuff ready.

On the drive there I held Faris in my arms, sitting in the front seat of the car. No seat belts, those became compulsory in the UK in 1968 only on new cars and became compulsory to be worn in 1983.

I remember her making me some tea and toast while I held the infant on my lap. She did ask me if she could hold him while I drank my tea, but for some reason, I did not want her to. It has bothered me for most of my life when I look back at that incident, that I found that moment, which should have been such a happy occasion, to be so cruel to her, because of what she had done to me.

We said our goodbyes and left for the drive to Perth to the house Ahmed had rented for us. It was quite an exciting time for me, now I was a mother and would soon be with our son in our new home. Our Austin Minor was old, the windscreen wipers did not work and the rain began to pour down. Ahmed asked me to put my free hand (I was holding the baby) into the space on the dashboard and pull down the metal part to work the wipers. This was okay for a while but then my fingers got stuck under the metal as the wipers were moving and caused me to yelp with the pain. After that, I was more careful not to leave them in place.

I never returned to Middlesbrough. Only a few months after I left there was a strange and terrifying weather event called The Great Darkness.

On 2nd July 1968, Teesside experienced one of the worst storms ever known. A five-mile-long, thick blanket of cloud blotted out the midday sun. A steamy monsoon type rain fell heavy and fast, bringing with it hailstones the size of marbles. The town quickly became flooded, people were so terrified that some of them, convinced the world was about to end, fell to their knees and prayed for deliverance. My mother called me in Perth, terrified she would not survive. She told me that an elderly woman had been killed by a lightning strike as she was walking her dog. I advised her to stay home. She did not have a dog so there was no need to go out walking, the pub would still be there, it would soon pass.

By the afternoon the storm had worn itself out, the worse was over. Life went on as usual.

Perth

The city of Perth is in central Scotland on the banks of the River Tay. The principal church is dedicated to St John the Baptist. Close by is Scone Abbey which used to house the Stone of Scone, also known as the Stone of Destiny. It is where the King of Scots was traditionally crowned.

In 1296, during the reign of King Edward I of England, the stone was removed to Westminster Abbey, where it was placed into a wooden chair called King Edward's Chair, on which further English/British sovereigns were crowned. There are many rumours regarding the stone's origins.

On June 11th, 1914, Suffragettes protesting for their women's rights put a small explosive device near the Coronation Chair, which caused slight damage to the chair.

In 1950 a group of four Scottish students were able to remove the stone from Westminster Abbey-how they managed it is a mystery - planning to return it to Scotland. During their efforts to remove it, the stone broke into two pieces. After burying the larger piece in a Kent field where they camped, they then removed it and returned to Scotland. According to talk at that time, the stone was hidden in the basement of the American Embassy, unknown to them, a tall tale indeed. When the two stones were eventually recovered, they were given to stonemason Robert Gray to repair it before it was then returned to Westminster Abbey.

On July 3rd, 1996, seven hundred years after it was removed, the stone was returned to Scotland and now resides in Edinburgh Castle where it sits alongside the crown jewels of Scotland.

Perth was known as a 'capital' of Scotland as the Royal Court were frequently in residence. The first railway station was built there in 1848, the city became a key transport centre.

The house Ahmed had rented in Perth was on the outskirts of the city and very isolated. It was a cold winter, with snow all around. I had only one neighbour whom I did not know.

I think back on those early days, remembering how I used to wrap him up warmly and put my new-born baby out in his pram in the snow. Not for very long, just fifteen minutes or so while he got some fresh air.

Alone during the day when Ahmed was at the college, I struggled to care for the infant who often cried and threw up. I had not been taught how to breastfeed him so found this quite difficult. Making his formula helped to supplement his feeding but this upset his stomach. He always seemed hungry, cried a lot and there were days when I wanted to run away.

My only source of help during those days was Dr Spock's book of Baby and Child Care (1946) one of the best-selling books in history. His tome encouraged mothers to see their children as individuals.

In the 1960's it was recommended by GPs that babies be left to cry themselves to sleep, not pick them up to kiss or hug them because they would then be spoilt. Dr Spock encouraged mothers to interact with their babies. If my son felt hot, I would grab my Dr Spock book and check what was recommended, how to take his temperature, what level was too high. How to feed him regularly, how to burp him, bathe him, check for nappy rash or spots. When were his vaccinations due, how would he be after having them? What childhood diseases he might get and what were the symptoms to look out for. I am sure without the help of that book, being alone as I was with no one around to ask, I would have been lost.

Moving to Town

I was so alone in that house and kept on at Ahmed until he eventually agreed to rent another closer to the town.

This was in the centre of town and above a pub. At closing time there was always a ruckus as the customers wound their drunken way home, but at least there I had neighbours and could put my baby into his pram and walk around town.

We had a television in the flat, but the signal was awful due to the aerial having fallen, and Ahmed wanted to watch something, probably his heartthrob-Tom Jones- on TV.

Our flat was on the first floor; the aerial was outside the kitchen window along the end of a sloping, icy rooftop. Ahmed decided he could easily climb out of the window to make his way gingerly along the roof. However, at one point his foot slipped, and he was only just able to grab hold to stop falling off the roof and down into the street below. Successfully he managed to get the aerial upright again and make his way back inside, the TV tuned in, and we watched the programme.

If You See Me Walking Down the Street

One of Ahmed's stipulations was that, if I saw him on one of my shopping trips, I was not to acknowledge him, just keep on walking. When I asked him why, he told me that, he was not supposed to be married, had not told his family about me or the baby and was worried that his elder brother, Hamid, would be angry. If the news got to him in Baghdad, he might cut off his allowance.

He had fellow students with him who were from Iraq and they might mention the fact that he had a family in their telephone calls or letters home.

My blood boiled at this, why should the fact that he was married and had a child be kept a secret? Perhaps he was planning to finish his course and then run off back to Baghdad, leaving us here. I had been abandoned once before and would not let that happen again.

DJ in Scone

One day, as I was listening to the local radio, I heard it mentioned that a well-known DJ was coming to the local hotel, I think it was the Station Hotel, for the BBC to do a music programme and would be taking requests.

I decided to put my cunning plan into action. On the day in question, I dressed Faris, put him in his pram and went straight to the hotel. I knew, from something Ahmed had once mentioned, that the students working in the aircraft hangar had the BBC on during the day and listened to the music, so I knew that the programme would reach their ears. I had written down my request on a piece of paper and was able to get close enough with Faris to hand it to the DJ.

"Well, here we have a lovely baby and his mother, with a request for her husband Ahmed Al-Haddad (he stumbled a bit over that mouthful), who is currently studying at Scone Aerodrome, she says good luck in your coming exams sweetheart, from your wife Sandra and Faris, your son."

The music played was one of his favourites, the Animals singing 'House of the Rising Sun'.

The secret life was out, all the students with Ahmed listening to the radio had heard my request. He was inundated with questions about this secret family of his. When he came home, he was furious and spent some time telling me off in his loudest voice, how his family would be so shocked, his brother would cut him off without a penny etc.

I did what I felt I had to do and was not sorry about it.

When Faris was just over one year old, Ahmed was studying for his final exams, he had the brilliant idea that it would be best if I took a trip to Baghdad to meet his family.

They knew about me and the baby now so I would not be such a surprise to them. His brother had been quite annoyed when news had reached him of our marriage, but as time passed this was forgiven.

A passport was applied for me and the baby-in those days, children could be put on the parent's passport. He wrote his brother's name and Baghdad telephone number down on a piece of paper and gave it to me along with a letter for his family. He said he would call his brother when I had left and let him know we were on our way so that I would be met at the airport. That did not work out as planned.

Chapter 12

Baghdad (1969)

Sitting on the bus taking me to the plane waiting on the tarmac at the airport holding my baby son Faris, I was terrified. This was the very first time that I had ever been on a plane, the first time I had been out of the country.

Overwhelmed with emotion I buried my face in my baby's while the tears flowed. What on earth had I been thinking to agree to go to Baghdad, Iraq, alone with my baby just because Ahmed wanted me out of the way so that he would be able to study for his final exams in peace and a wife and baby would not be conducive to his plans?

I knew nothing about the country I was travelling to except that there had been a coup in July 1967 which Ahmed had told me about. The president Abdul Rahman Arif had been deposed and Ahmed Hassan Al-Bakr had taken over which brought the Ba'ath Party to power.

Arriving in Baghdad

The flight was just over four hours long, Faris slept most of the time in a bassinet set up into the wall in front of me, and was no bother at all.

On landing in Baghdad, I quickly got through customs and went to the arrivals' hall. On looking around I could not see anyone who was looking for me, so I took a seat with my suitcase and baby to wait, and wait, and wait.

Over an hour later I was still waiting, it had been noticed by one of the customs officers and he came over to ask me in Arabic, why I was waiting. I explained that I could not speak Arabic, did anyone speak English? Off he went to get another officer who asked me the same question in English. Relieved to be able to communicate I explained I was waiting for my brother-in-law to come and collect me and did not know why it was taking so long. I held out the paper with the name and telephone number of Hamid on it. He took it and went off to make a telephone call.

When he returned, he said he had spoken to Hamid, who did not know that I was arriving as nobody had even told him! I was astounded, so much for calling and letting him know I was coming then!

He told me that it would take a while for my brother-in-law to come, got me a Pepsi to drink and asked to hold the baby. The officer and his colleagues seemed to go all soft and fluffy when I handed him over. Both officers cooed over Faris and fed him bits of chocolate despite me asking them not to. He was only one year old and I did not want him to throw up, perhaps if he had they would have handed him back quickly.

Hamid finally arrived to collect me, he was very apologetic. He spoke English very well as he did a lot of business abroad. Lifting Faris out of my arms (he had been reluctantly passed back to me by the officers) we went out to his large American car, I think it was a Chevrolet Camaro. Anyway, it was massive, very comfortable seats, no seat belts at that time. It was the first time I had seen such a luxury car.

We drove to the family home in Adhamiya, Baghdad, a journey of 30 minutes or so. On the way he stopped off and bought me something that I had never had before, a fresh fruit cocktail, from a vendor by the side of the road. It was icy, tasty and refreshing.

I saw many things for the first time - palm trees, men in Arab dress, donkeys, women in black abayas, barefoot children in scruffy clothes, orange and white taxis, big double-decker buses, massive American Buicks, Camaros, Oldsmobiles and vendors with their carts of vegetables or other goods.

We stopped at the gate of a large three-storey brick-built house with three large living rooms, 6 bedrooms, kitchen, two bathrooms, front and back garden. My eyes widened with wonder.

On entering the large lounge area, I saw wall to wall women, all eyes were on me. Faris was taken and made into a 'pass the parcel' item. He did not seem to mind one bit.

A short, bow-legged elderly woman came up to me and, holding out her arms, hugged me. I assumed this to be Ahmed's mother Khairya and hugged her back, pleased that she was so friendly, but was informed later that it was the family servant. They called her BeeBee Metoo or 'parrot', she was originally from Iran and had worked for the family most of her life.

All the ladies present, some relatives and others neighbours started chatting amongst themselves, very loudly. I thought that they were having some sort of argument.

The family unit consisted of my widowed mother-in-law, Khairya, brothers-in-law; eldest being Abdul Hamid, Mahmoud, Ali, Saidi, Salah and one sister-in-law Suad. The three eldest were married and had children.

Hamid took after his mother, he was lighter-skinned with green speckled eyes. The other brothers were slightly darker, only the youngest one-Salah-was very dark. I often wondered where this colouring came from as he was so different to his siblings.

Suad, came up to introduce herself and hugged me. She spoke a little English which she had learnt in school, so she introduced me to the ladies, taking me along the line like I was the Queen inspecting the troops.

After the first two or three ladies I gave up trying to remember who they were. There were just too many and they all looked alike with their black abayas and head coverings. There were so many aunts, uncles, cousins and neighbours living in the area, it was such a large family.

I kept hearing her say 'Um Faris' and asked her what that meant. She explained that it was customary for a mother to be called 'mother of' and the name of her first son (daughters get left out). So, I was, therefore 'mother of Faris', Ahmed would be called 'father of Faris or Abu Faris', this was a mark of respect.

After most of the ladies left, a meal of rice and different sauces was brought out of the kitchen and I ate with them. Faris had his bottle made by some dried milk that I had brought with me. A room had been prepared for me and Faris to sleep in. We were both very tired so there was no problem putting our heads down. I changed his nappy and clothes and placed him into a cot in the room. The only thing that seemed disturbing to me in the darkness was a very loud buzzing whining sound that seemed close to my ear. I imagined it to be a huge beetle-I had a fear of flying insects, especially beetles. Ahmed had once slapped me to stop me screaming when I became hysterical over a flying beetle, which had landed on me in our bedroom in London. I kept jumping up like a jack in the box, turning on the light to find this monstrous flying beetle in my room.

Little did I know then about mosquitos, or how they would feast on me whenever they could, leaving hard itchy lumps behind. I experienced cockroaches for the first time. They would always be waiting for me in the toilet, horrid brown insects waving their feelers and scurrying around with their hairy legs. If anyone wanted to torture me, just put me in a room with a few of these and I would sing like a canary.

Hornets were to be found in the garden, orange-coloured flying hornets which had the most painful sting, so best run away as fast as possible while emitting a loud screeching sound, and hope they do not chase after you.

The next morning when I woke up, I went downstairs and had breakfast with my mother-in-law and Suad. After breakfast, I was asked if I would like to have a shower and I was shown the shower room.

The shower room had a stone floor that was heated by a paraffin pipe lit under the floor to heat it, best to leave your plastic slippers on as the floor got quite hot! There was a tap and a large bowl which I was told to fill with hot and cold water and use a smaller bowl to throw the water over my body while I washed. I sat on a small wooden seat called a 'tukhat', then I could wash with the bar of olive oil and herb soap, using a loofah made from the gourd plant. There was no shampoo and I had forgotten to put a bottle in my suitcase.

Undressing, I hung my clothes up on the peg then I sat down to wash, it was all new to me. After a few minutes, the door opened. I was horrified to see my sister-in-law, Suad and my other sister-in-law along with my mother-in-law, naked, all coming to join me in my ablutions.

This I found very strange never having been so close to another naked body whether it be woman or man except of course, Ahmed. I was extremely put out by this behaviour, covering myself as best I could, but it was normal for them, they wanted to see what the foreigner looked like and so they did.

I was glad to get dressed and out of there, making my way back up to my room where Faris had been sleeping, to feed him and change his nappy.

In the days following lots of visitors came to the house to see this foreign wife and child of the family.

Food

Food was always being cooked in the kitchen; the air was ripe with the aromatic smell of the special Iraqi rice called amber rice, which needs a lot of cleaning. The rice is spread on a large flat round aluminium tray for the little stones it contained to be picked out. The rice is then rinsed gently many times in cold water before being cooked. Huge pots of rice and sauce were always bubbling away on the stove to feed any visitors, as was the custom.

Iraqi food does not usually contain hot chillies, red or green, there are lots of tomato-based sauces made with okra or potatoes, eggplant, and other vegetables. Dolma is one of my favourites, a mixture of minced lamb, rice, tomato and parsley rolled in chard leaves to make small parcels. These are placed in the pot, the bottom of which has the stalks of the chard cut and placed first to prevent any of the parcels from getting scorched, and covered with stock, seasoning and some of the juice from the bitter orange trees.

When the stock has evaporated the dolma is done, turned out onto a large sineeya (tray) and eaten with pickles and Khubz (flatbread made in a clay oven). Huge amounts of herbs would also be served. When I first saw these dishes with green herbs of parsley and mint, I was amazed. I had never eaten herbs in any form, except for a jar of mint sauce at home served with a bit of lamb. Here people consumed large amounts of herbs, grabbing big handfuls and stuffing them into their mouths - parsley, mint, coriander - it was something I could not imagine doing so at first, I avoided them. I was not a cow I thought. Over the next few weeks and years though I realised how beneficial these herbs were for health and partook of them with gusto!

After food, small glasses of sweet, black tea would be taken to be distributed to the guests along with something sweet like baklava (layers of filo pastry filled with chopped pistachio nuts and drizzled with sugar syrup), then trays of different fruits - grapes, peaches, figs, apples from the north of Iraq, watermelon - huge, heavy and shaped like a baseball - depending on the season.

The house was buzzing with chatter and laughter where I sat amongst them all, not understanding a word. Iraqis, in general, speak very loudly, so I was sometimes deafened by the cacophonous din.

Sunburn

It was summer when I visited, the heat was intense at around 45-50 deg. I decided it would be a good idea to go up on the flat roof and get my pale body tanned before going back to the UK. No men were around, and the house was the highest one in the area except for the identical one opposite in which lived Ahmed's mother's relatives, but nobody would go up on *that* roof during the heat of the day. I lay under that full sun in my swimming costume for 30 minutes. It then got too much so I went back downstairs.

By the evening I had a bad case of sunburn. My head ached abominably. The next day large blisters had formed on my back which made it painful for me to lie down. I was lucky not to have ended up in hospital with sunstroke. When I think of it now, I wonder just what I was thinking, how naïve I was in those days.

Iraqi Customs

I noticed that boys and men often walked along the street holding hands. This was a typical Iraqi custom and quite normal. It did not imply that they were gay-just good friends or brothers.

When a guest visits it would be considered impolite not to offer them something to eat or drink. If they ask for some water then the glass must be as full as is possible, a three-quarters full glass would be considered an insult. I would get around this by taking a jug of water and some glasses and letting them fill their glass-just in case I spilt some on the way.

Guests can stay as long as they like, even if it is into the early hours of the morning. Yawning or making sleepy time noises are not acceptable. I found this custom particularly tiresome as guests would often want to chat the night away and I would gradually begin to nod off, how rude!

On some occasions, I felt like getting out the Vacuum cleaner as a hint for them to go home!

Cooking an English Meal

My mother-in-law asked me to cook an English dish for the family. She wondered what it was like and wanted to try it.

I decided a nice roast leg of lamb with roast potatoes, peas and gravy might be welcomed. I had seen a leg of lamb from one of the slaughtered sacrifices sitting in the fridge so got it out. After adding seasonings, I popped it into the large gas oven to cook while I prepared the potatoes.

After 20 minutes or so, my mother-in-law came into the kitchen to see how my meal was going. Looking through the glass door of the oven, seeing the leg of lamb she let out a screech that would have woken the dead. Yanking open the oven door she grabbed the tray with the leg and dumped it on the kitchen counter while shouting in Arabic.

Suad, my sister-in-law, hearing the commotion, came into the kitchen as I stood there with my mouth open wondering what was going on. The leg of lamb was put back still hot and steaming, into the fridge and Khairya stomped off muttering.

Suad explained as best she could that nobody expected a whole leg of lamb to be cooked, it is too expensive. She advised me to keep the English meal until another time. I made chips with the potatoes instead.

Gas Oven Pervert

That gas oven always needed maintenance, it never seemed to work properly. One day, a fitter was asked to come to the house to look at the oven. I stood in the kitchen and watched him as he worked on it. There was something wrong with the pilot light.

When he had finished, he lit the gas, beckoning me to come forward and have a look at the flame inside the oven, to confirm that it was on alright. I had to bend down to see properly, I confirmed all was fine, but he asked me to check it again for him. I wondered why he could not check it himself then I realised that, as he was standing behind me, each time I bent over he was looking up my dress!

Gas was not piped into the house like in the UK but came in large canisters of propane gas which were attached via a hose to the cooker.

These were bought from a vendor who came round once a week with his horse-drawn cart selling full canisters in exchange for empty ones. He would bang on the canisters as he passed with his horse and cart.

On the gas cooker, the canister would usually last for 30 days. We had five canisters outside the kitchen door so a plentiful supply. Sometimes the neighbours would come and borrow one when they ran out.

Poor Kitty!

There was a water cooler attached to the window in the lounge. This had a large rotating fan for the cool air which was produced by water dripping down onto the straw lined panels. It was quite an efficient piece of equipment; the fan part though was uncovered and one day there was an incident where a small kitten ran into the house from the garden. Frightened by people trying to catch it, it dived into the rotating fan of the cooler and ended up inside.

The gardener was able to remove one of the cooler side panels to retract it, but the little animal had damaged its mouth and the lower lip was torn.

I wrapped it tightly in a towel thinking I could sew it up with a needle and thread. When I tried to insert the needle into the kitty's lip of course the kitty struggled madly trying to get away.

I had an idea, I remember when Faris had been born, I was given gas and air for the labour pain, there was gas in the oven and I was sure there is some air in there too, so I popped it in the oven and shut the door, turned on the gas and sat watching it as it went at first crazy trying to get out, then settled down and went to sleep. Satisfied that it was now safely anesthetised I took it out and sewed up the wound, placing it nice and comfortable in a shoebox lined with a cloth. I left it for an hour then came back to find it quite dead, of course.

Baghdad Museum Visit

Abdul Hamid came one day and asked me if I would like to go to visit the Iraqi Museum, I did indeed!

He asked his mother to look after Faris for a while as he was taking me for an 'appointment'. When we were in the car, he explained that the women would not be too pleased for him to take me to the museum and asked me to keep it quiet. I was puzzled as to why, but he explained I did not have a chaperone with me, so tongues might wag.

I enjoyed the visit very much. The museum had been open for a few years and had many wonderful items excavated from various archaeological sites in Iraq.

The Iraqi Museum was originally built in the 1920s. The author, Gertrude Bell, was instrumental in its setting up. The building we visited had been opened in 1966 with the help of the German government. It had 28 galleries of artefacts from Iraq's rich heritage sites such as Nineveh, Ur and Babylon, among others. I have always been interested in archaeology and the sight of the huge human-headed winged bulls from the Assyrian Period (1350-612BC), the gold jewellery and pottery took my breath away.

Ghost in the Garden

The neighbour next door was a half-sister of Khairya. Her husband was a judge or Qadhi. They would often come in the evenings, his wife would go and sit with the women, and he would sit with the men, drinking tea and playing a popular game of 'tawli' or backgammon. I would be invited to sit with them as he spoke English and wanted to practise it more, my visit gave him the opportunity.

One evening he asked me, *"Um Faris-are you afraid of ghosts?"* When I said I was not, he then asked me what would I do if I saw one? *"I am not afraid,"* I said. Then he asked me if I were brave enough to go outside the front door and walk all around the house (it was very dark in the garden) and return to them, he would give me ten dinars. In those days that was a good amount of money.

I took up the challenge and went out the front door walking all the way around. When I got halfway, I noticed a large figure in white coming towards me making ghostly sounds. I immediately realised that it was somebody wearing a large sheet, so I jumped forward and smacked my hand down on the head. Everybody rolled up laughing, it was the judge himself who had decided to frighten the life out of me, but it had not worked. He still offered me the 10 dinars, so I made a bit of cash that night, though I learnt later that I should not have taken the money-it was not etiquette.

I discovered later that their son, who was studying to become a doctor, had been taken, imprisoned and tortured by the Iraqi police on some spurious charge. When he was finally released he suffered from a mental breakdown and PTSD. Who knows what horror he had been subjected to while in prison?

Being beaten or otherwise physically abused leaves marks that will eventually fade but the memory of that ordeal stays with the victim for the rest of their life. Rape, on the other hand, has a silent scar. The victim may never be able to come to terms with their nightmare experience, will bury it as far as they can to cover the shame they will feel throughout their lives. This burden causes many victims to commit suicide. Unable to seek any professional help they chose the only avenue they feel is open to them.

Orange Farm

A visit was arranged one day to go to the family farm. I went with Mahmoud and his family, Khairya and Suad came with Hamid.

Walking around the farm I saw many trees of oranges, tangerines, pears and date palms.

The women immediately began to help themselves. I have never seen such a sight as they grabbed handfuls of citrus fruit, sat together on the ground and ate them as fast as they could, there was no genteel peeling of the fruit, just ripping it apart as if it was manna from heaven and they had never seen such fruit in their lives before.

I felt shy and embarrassed, even though the fruit was offered to me, I did not feel that I could eat any. I just walked along timidly holding an orange in each hand.

Me on a visit to the orange farm 1971

Chapter 13

Leaving Baghdad

All too soon my first visit to Baghdad was over and I was due to return to Scotland. I would have happily stayed there; the family were so welcoming and kind, I had enjoyed my time spent with them.

Returning to Perth, Scotland I found that Ahmed was giving up the small flat we lived in to rent a bungalow on the other side of town. The owner of this house was going abroad for one year to work and did not mind who lived there as long as the rent was paid on time.

I suspected that Abdul Hamid may have been behind the move. I had mentioned to him in Baghdad how small and cramped our flat above the pub was. He had told me that he had plans to come over to Perth for a visit shortly, it would have been impossible in our tiny place.

We moved into our new rented bungalow and settled down again.

Baby Ouch!

Faris had started crawling around. He always made a bee-line for the radiator in the front room, which was near the window, I would spend ages just rushing over and dragging him away from it. It was hot and I did not want him to hurt himself. He delighted in all the attention he was getting. Whenever he made his way towards it he would turn around and look at me, watching to see what I would do, to him it was a game. One day I decided to let him go and touch it, I knew he would get a shock.

Looking over at me as usual he began to make his way over, closer and closer, watching for me to jump up as usual and pull him back, but this time I just said as usual, "hot, no, hot." He succeeded in reaching the radiator, stretched out his little hand and touched it. Then he discovered what the word 'hot' meant. He was not burnt, just shocked. After that day he always steered well clear of the 'hot' object.

Ahmed eventually passed his written exams and went on to the next stage of practical work. Abdul Hamid did come and visit us in Scotland. We took him to some of the popular tourist spots like Edinburgh and Scone Palace. He stayed a few weeks before travelling down to London to visit some friends, then flew to Austria to complete some business before travelling on to Baghdad.

Chapter 14

Return to Baghdad (1971)

On the completion of Ahmed's course, we had to leave. We packed up and returned to Baghdad. The property we lived in was fully furnished so we only needed to take our clothes and other necessary items for the baby. It was the day after my birthday, January the 19th. We went by Swiss Air so we had a stopover in Zurich. The plane had a problem and was placed for one night in a hotel, courtesy of the airline.

While we were there, I suggested to Ahmed that we go out for a walk and have a look around the area where we were staying. I had never been to Switzerland and I wanted to see what it was like.

He did not want to go out walking in the town, he preferred to stay in the hotel for one night. I was quite disappointed but knew it would be useless to argue about it. The next day we returned to the airport and boarded the plane for the onward journey to Baghdad.

I was quite happy to go to Baghdad again as I missed everybody and could not wait to see them all once more. I spent the next 27 years living in Iraq, the next chapter of my life was about to begin.

My second visit to Baghdad was not as good as my first. We had been there for only two days and had so many visitors already. It was as if the Sultan of Baghdad himself had returned.

Many gifts were brought, boxes of crockery, cutlery or other gifts for the couple-us. These items were swiftly accepted by Khairya and whisked away upstairs to the storeroom at the top of the house, never to be seen by me. I did not even know these gifts were for us, I assumed they were for the house. It was years later that my sister-in-law told me of them.

On the morning of the second day, Ahmed called for me to go out to the garden to see something. As I stepped out of the front door I was greeted with the sight of a sheep having its throat cut, the animal was bleating up till its last breath.

It was then hung up by one leg onto a branch of a nearby orange tree to have the skin removed. This was done by cutting a slit in one leg, near the hoof and blowing hard till the carcass was separated from the fleece which was quickly pulled off. It took only a few minutes.

The butcher cut the carcass up in no time. Trays of meat were then sent to nearby neighbours. The offal and some of the best parts of the animal were kept for cooking later in the day to feed the visitors. Opening the fridge later I was greeted with the sight of sheep testicles sitting on a plate waiting to be cooked for the men's breakfast.

I could not bring myself to eat any of the meat. It turned my stomach just looking at it. All I could see was the image of that sheep meeting its doom.

Ahmed was rarely at home being out all day visiting his friends in their shops. His brother, Abdul Hamid, also had a shop selling hardware, which was his business, and Ahmed often went to sit with him, nattering and drinking tea there for most of the day.

This caused many arguments between us. I resented being left at home, complaining bitterly. This fell on deaf ears. It was normal for the men to do as they wished and the women stayed at home.

One morning we had such an argument, the reason now I cannot remember. Ahmed lost his temper. Slamming open the door to the patio, I could hear him shouting outside in Arabic to his younger brother Salah who came and called me to come out into the garden.

Picking up baby Faris I went outside and was greeted with the sight of Ahmed standing aiming a rifle at me shouting that he was going to kill me. My body went numb. At that stage, I did not care if he carried out his threat, but I was holding his son in my arms so I tried to reason with him.

"How can you aim a weapon at me while I am holding your son?"

He turned to his brother, "Take the child from her"!

His brother moved forward to take Faris, I stepped back, went inside and closed and locked the big wooden doors, then ran to the back of the house to lock the back door.

Shaking like a leaf, I ran into the kitchen where Khairya had been hiding. She had heard everything but was too scared, knowing the temper her son had, to come out and help me.

Eventually, after banging on the door for a while, Ahmed gave up and left the house. I never forgave him, nor his brother Salah for that incident where either myself or my child could have been killed or injured.

If you are reading this and wonder why I did not leave Baghdad then, it would have been impossible. I had no money, no friends who could have helped me, spoke little Arabic. Even if I could have got away where would I go? I did not know anything about how to reach the British Embassy or how to even get there. I had nobody in England. My brother was on the seas, my sister was in the USA, my mother and father were not reliable and I had a small baby to care for. So, I stayed where I was, existing but slowly suffocating under the oppression of my marriage.

There was another occasion where I was threatened with a handgun because I was not complying with Ahmed, who wanted a partner who agreed with everything and kept quiet, not one who argued or complained. He knew I was trapped, he took advantage of that at every opportunity to treat me like a chattel.

1971

I was pregnant again with my second son, Mohammed, who was due in October. I needed to go for regular check-ups, but such a thing wasn't something that was done regularly in those days.

I found it difficult to get to an appointment and would have to continuously ask Ahmed to take me. I found that Abdul Hamid was my ally and I could ask him to intervene with Ahmed so that he would realise I needed to have regular gynaecologist appointments.

My brother-in-law Mahmood also lived in the house with his wife along with my sister-in-law Suad. He would often pack us into his large American car for a ride around town where we would go to the centre of Baghdad and drive around so he could show me the different areas.

We would sometimes stop and have kebab or falafel sandwiches.

I used to enjoy these little trips out as it broke the monotony of being at home all day.

Mahmoud was building his own house locally near the river. When it was finished, we would go and visit him and his family, sit in the garden to have tea or a meal.

Despite the elder brothers being sympathetic towards me, they treated their wives no better. Mahmoud's wife asked me one day if I could have a look at her little child. The girl had quite a fever and was breathing rapidly. Of course, being unaware of the restrictions placed on her by her husband I suggested she must take the child to the nearby Al-Naaman hospital immediately, I would go with her in a taxi.

She tried to explain that this was not possible, her husband would not allow her to leave the house. Even with me accompanying her, she must call him and get his permission. It shocked me in my naivety that in such an emergency she could not act on her initiative.

When she did speak to Mahmoud, he said he would be home soon and would take her himself. To me this was precious time wasted but it was the way and I had no right to intervene. I was learning about the culture within the family very quickly.

What Was That?

One evening as we were sitting having some tea in the garden of Mahmoud's new house nearby, close to the river, some other guests arrived - a friend of his wife with their children. Everybody was talking loudly as usual.

I had a slightly upset stomach being about eight months pregnant. I felt that I needed to pass wind. I didn't want to have to get up to go to the toilet just to pass wind. I thought as everybody was talking so loudly, I might as well just have a fart where I was, nobody would hear it above the conversation.

Just my luck, at that precise moment when I let out what turned out to be a very loud fart, everybody stopped talking!

On hearing the noise, they turned to face me and goodness gracious what a carry-on, my sister-in-law said, "Oh Um Faris, what have you done?" Everybody burst out laughing in hysterics including myself.

I believe that story is still being told today in the family, along with other incidences where I have got myself into trouble.

Chapter 15

Street Vendors

In Baghdad, street vendors would pass by at various times of the day selling their wares. Each week the hawker selling fabric would pass by with his cart loaded up with different bales of different coloured and patterned cotton fabrics. He wore the traditional Iraqi garb which consisted of a long gown known as a thawab, with a waistcoat. On his head he wore a black cap unique to Iraq. He had a gold tooth and a big smile. He came down the street shouting out something that nobody could understand. He always said the same thing, whether it was in Arabic or another language, nobody could make it out but we all recognised his cry.

The housewives were always happy to see him. They came out of their houses, looked over and felt the different coloured cloths, choosing a few meters here and a few meters there to sew up themselves or give to the local dressmaker to make their dishdashas or dresses. Some had their sewing machines and were adept at cutting out and sewing up the cloth.

On some days a salt vendor came around with his large and grumpy camel loaded with sacks of rock salt. He weighed out the requested amount with a handheld scale while his camel spat at you or tried to get a bite in if you stood too close to it.

Another welcome sight was Wadoud, the lablabi vendor. His cart contained a large aluminium container heated with a gas flame containing hot tasty chickpeas in water which he would place into your utensil, adding some lemon and salt. It was a tasty snack which we all enjoyed. We could easily have made it at home, but somehow, from him, it always tasted better.

The women of the house saved up various items of clothing, shoes, plastic items for the 'farfoori' (ceramics) man when he passed by. He exchanged your plastic goods for some nice china, plates, bowls or cups, etc.

The household rubbish was collected once a week by men in a lorry. Along with some money to give them, we always kept a bunch of cheap rolled cigarettes for the men when they came round and on some occasions, if it was lunchtime, Kharia would send them out plates of food.

Another essential worker we would often see was the drain man. If the drains backed up, which they often did, especially after heavy rain in the winter, he would be called for. Stripping down to his underwear, he climbed down into the drain outside the house to trace the source of the blockage.

It was a filthy job, he emerged covered in excrement. We would take out the garden hose along with a bottle of Zahi washing up liquid when he had finished so that he could hose himself down, then provide him and his fellows with some food. If we had any used clothing we would also offer those.

These were simple people, the job gave them a low wage which was better than nothing. Many of them had families to support. Our meagre offerings seemed much appreciated. They carried out a necessary job and we were always grateful to them for it.

Death of My Mother (October, 1971)

Ahmed had developed a nasty habit of telling me, *"Umich Matted"* which means, *"Your mother is dead."* He delighted, in his perverse way, in telling me this often and I could never understand why. He, with his twisted sense of humour, thought it was funny. I did not, and asked him not to say it. I told him, "What if the day comes that my mother does die, would you be upset at your jokes?"

That dreadful day came when I was 9 months pregnant with Mohammed when Ahmed once again told me, *"Your mother is dead,"* and, like the boy who cried wolf, I did not believe him. He handed me a piece of paper with a London telephone number on it and told me to call, all would then be revealed. I still did not believe him, thinking it was another of his twisted jokes. He called his mother and sister, Suad, to go with him to Hamid's house. They left me alone in the house to make that call, it is a day that I will never forget. When I called the number on the paper, it turned out to be the coroner of a hospital in London.

He confirmed that my mother had passed away from a coronary. I was devasted, not just because I had learnt of her death, but because neither Ahmed nor his family had supported me in my hour of need. They had run off, leaving me alone to grieve for my parent and I could not understand it.

That was the moment I realised my life had become unbearable. I had no friends and nobody I could turn to. I was alone in this foreign land.

Mohammed (1971)

My son, Mohammed, was born in Medical City Hospital in 1971. I was weeks overdue and did not go into labour until well into my 10th month. Despite asking Ahmed to take me to the hospital he refused as he said I was not in labour and must have gotten my dates wrong, although the due date was given to me by the doctor in England. Of course, the engineer knew best.

My sister-in-law, Suad, eventually persuaded him to drop us both at the hospital by telling him I should have an examination. When I explained to the doctor there that I was overdue he agreed that the baby was large and a little while later I was admitted, then put on an induction drip. This soon started my labour.

It took many hours, I was alone in the delivery room, could not speak much of the language to ask the nurse, who was absent for most of the time, what was happening. Suddenly, for some unknown reason, the pains stopped. I called the nurse and told her in my broken Arabic using hand signals for emphasis, that I had no more labour pains.

I did not know what to do and began to panic. She went and after what seemed like hours later returned with one of the doctors who speeded up the drip. Soon I felt the labour pains restarting.

Eventually, after some time, my son was born. When he was handed to me I saw that his head was the shape of a baseball. It was elongated like E.T in the movie. I was terrified but the doctor reassured me he would get the specialist to come and examine him.

When the specialist came and examined Mohammed, he said that his head shape was due to him becoming stuck in the birth canal at the time my labour stopped. He reassured me that the bones would return to normal in a short while, and the skull would be a nice round shape again. Thankfully that is what happened in the next few days.

Mohammed was a heavy baby at almost 12 pounds. I reckon if I had not insisted on going to the hospital when I did, I would still be carrying him today!

Chapter 16

Epilepsy 2

I still had my epilepsy and sometimes would forget to take my pills of Epanutin with Phenobarbital.

One occasion when I did forget, I had a fit while I was opening my wardrobe and my sister-in-law found me half in and half out the wardrobe with my legs flying. She ran and got my mother-in-law, and both managed to get me onto the bed.

Later on, when I came round, they told me what happened and we had a good laugh about it.

Isolated Visitor

One day Ahmed had been invited to his friend's house. Now I was still very shy and did not really like meeting new people. I was happy with the family because by then I knew everybody but around strangers I was extremely wary. I had to agree to go. It was not often that he would ask me to accompany him on social visits.

When we arrived at his friend's home, we were taken into a room full of people who were strangers to me. The introductions were made and I was directed to one of the chairs.

I noticed one of the ladies had her head wrapped in a white cloth, which for some reason, I thought were bandages. I asked Ahmed if she recently had undergone surgery on her head. He thought this was hilarious and explained that she just wrapped her head in that way up because she was deeply religious.

We sat in the garden and had some tea and for some reason, I remember I was sitting apart from everybody else, and nobody spoke to me much. Their English was not so good perhaps, and of course, my Arabic was next to nothing.

I was too shy to go up and speak to other people and so I just sat there on my own alone, Ahmed was off chatting with his friends. He did not think to come and draw me into any conversations or introduce me to anyone.

I was glad when it became time to go home but Ahmed was not incredibly happy with my behaviour. He told me that he would not take me anymore to see his friends. He said they thought I was arrogant in the way that I behaved. I tried to explain to him how shy I was, I did not know what to say when in strange company, my Arabic was not good enough to hold a conversation. It did no good to talk to him about it, he did not understand. He was an extremely outgoing gregarious person and would talk to anybody, anywhere.

I rarely went out after that except to visit family. Besides, I was not eager to repeat the experience.

Smoking

I smoked rarely but did sometimes enjoy a cigarette. Ahmed refused to indulge me. He smoked Rothman filter-tipped which he got from the airports on his trips abroad. He would bring home the cartons of ten packets of twenty and put them in the wardrobe.

My little trick was to carefully open the cellophane at one end, slip out all the packets, open each one up and remove one cigarette-just one, no more, then carefully replace everything, a dab of glue at the end and nobody would suspect anything.

Ahmed never did, though he did mention, *"Those Rothman people are crooks, they say it's a packet of twenty, but there are only 19 in the pack!"*

I noticed a foreign-looking woman one day while I was waiting in line at the local Alban shop (a government shop selling dairy products), so I went up and asked her if she was English and she said, "Yes I am." I mentioned that I did not know any English people in Baghdad, and I wondered if she would like to come for tea one day. I gave her my home phone number.

She called me up one day and we arranged for her to come to the house for a visit. She was genuinely nice, she worked for the WHO food program in Iraq. During our conversation she said one of the professors in the WHO was looking for a secretary, would I be interested in the job?

I would indeed I said, as I was bored at home all the time, and it was soon arranged for me to have an interview.

Ahmed wasn't very pleased about that, but I managed to persuade him. His mother said that she would look after the children along with my sister-in-law at home.

Chapter 17

Working for the W.H.O

I started working for the U.N food program.

My duties were to type up the reports dictated by one of the professors. Each morning a driver would come and collect me in the W.H.O car, bringing me back in the afternoon. The hours were from about 8:00 AM to 2:00 PM.

One of the perks I received, it being the World Health Organisation food program, were large boxes of fruits and vegetables to take home with me from the farm they had after they had finished with them. I gave these to my mother-in-law and she distributed them amongst the family.

Ahmed by this time was employed in Iraqi Airways as a ground engineer. However, his salary was less than mine at the time. When he discovered this it put his nose out of joint a bit, so he started making problems for me. He began accusing me of things that I hadn't done such as where was this driver taking me? Why did it take so long to get home? Where had I gone during the time from leaving work to the time I got home? Stupid questions, but he was only jealous because I was getting more money than he was.

Eventually, all the accusations and asides each day became too much for me. I had to give up the job although I loved it so much. The final straw was when he said that his mother no longer wished to look after the children so I better be home to do it myself, although she denied this when I asked her later.

In those days Ahmed and I were not getting on very well, I was mostly ignored, left at home with the women, and I resented that very much. I needed someone to talk to, someone who I could tell my thoughts to and there was nobody.

The Gun Incident

One incident I remember was the day I opened the wardrobe to get something out. Right in front of me I was shocked to see a handgun on the top shelf.

I had never handled a gun myself much less seen one, but I did remember seeing how the clip was removed in movies. Worrying that one of the children would get hold of it I picked it up and checked the clip. As I held it in my hand I could feel how heavy it was so assumed it was loaded with live bullets. I removed the clip and ejected all the bullets, then replaced the clip. I have no idea how I did it, just watching it in movies I knew how to do it.

A few days later Ahmed came in and said he was going out with his friends to their farm. He went upstairs, came down and left. I did not know that he was going to his friend's farm to practise shooting his weapon.

He returned, scowling and extremely angry to ask me who had touched his gun. Of course, when he had gone to shoot his gun with no bullets in it, he was embarrassed in front of his friends. I told him it was me. He was amazed that I would know how to remove the bullets from the clip and replace the clip in the gun. Do not underestimate me, I can do things you would not dream of.

Burda Magazine

Baghdad fashion in the 1970s was fairly liberal. Many women did not cover up from top to bottom in an abaya or even wear a headscarf.

Many women went out in public wearing sleeveless dresses. I did not own a sewing machine at that time, nor did I know how to use one, so I went to a local Indian dressmaker to have a dress made up from a pattern I saw in the Burda Moden magazine.

This was a popular magazine in Baghdad. It contained dress-making patterns for the modern woman. By 1968 the magazine had sold 1.5 million copies worldwide.

The dress was duly sewed for me, was sleeveless, and came to just above my knees. I was very slender even after my two babies and the dress showed my figure. It had a long black zip down the back which later got me into some fairly serious trouble albeit innocently.

The Black Zip Incident

One day when I went to put the dress on, the zip broke. I asked one of the aunties if she could get it fixed for me. She said she would go with me to the local market where I could buy one. We could then take it to a local dressmaker nearby to replace the broken one. Off we went to the haberdashery shop. I was eager to try out my Arabic language skills. It was a big mistake.

The shop was run by an elderly gentleman. He greeted me as I stood there, in all innocence. Then I asked him if he had a 'black penis this long' (using my hands to indicate the length as I had seen others do at home when showing measures, as I had not brought the old zip with me). Unknown to me at that time, the word 'zip' is colloquially used in Arabic, in Iraq anyway, to indicate penis.

His mouth dropped open, his face turned an odd puce colour. Jumping up waving his arms around he roared something which I did not understand. He was extremely angry and looked as if he was going to launch himself at me at any minute. I looked around for help from the aunt, only to see her already rushing down the road, her black abaya flowing out behind her. I decided it would be wise to follow suit.

I caught up with her. As we walked back to the house, she moved along at a fast pace muttering and tittering under her breath, words that I could not make out. When entered, bursting in through the front door, she threw off her abaya and collapsed onto the sofa. Smacking herself in the face and pulling at her clothes she told everyone at home who had come to see what the fuss was about what had happened. Mouths fell open in horror, eyes turned to me accusingly.

Suad explained to me that I had said something very inappropriate, indicating her genital area. I still did not understand what had happened, I knew I had said something wrong. Later when Ahmed returned he was able to explain it to me, I was mortified.

"Why didn't you tell me?" I asked him.

"Tell you what - that we have words in Arabic that are not the same meaning in English and you should not say them? Perhaps I should make a list, so next time you won't go and almost get attacked!"

We all had a good laugh about it later, but Ahmed decided that, until my Arabic improved, I should not practise it outside the home in case I caused a riot next time. It became a topic of conversation for some time later. Another word for penis that I learned later, as it was said often at home and outside, was the word 'ayr'.

I had great difficulty trying to tell a neighbour, who asked me to recommend an English classic instead of an American one and the one book I came up with was Jane Eyre by Charlotte Bronte! I stopped at the Jane part, changed my mind and gave him Charles Dickens' Oliver Twist instead. No need to get myself into trouble again or give him any ideas.

Chapter 18

Wheat Poisoning (1971)

Just a few months after Mohammed was born, in December, the word on the street was that no meat or wheat flour would be available in the market due to a 'disease'. What this disease was we had no idea, but for a few months, we had to become vegetarians.

The government began importing frozen chicken from Brazil and lamb from New Zealand. This was distributed from suppliers on the outskirts of Baghdad. Ahmed drove there to purchase boxes for both families.

We made tikka on charcoal from cubes of the delicious lamb, chickens too. The price of the boxes of chicken was quite low due to being subsidized by the government. If you could get hold of a box which was not easy, bribes were often passed over to the distributor to ensure a steady supply.

Long queues formed each day before the delivery, as soon as the goods arrived at the distribution centre and the lorries unloaded. Each family was allowed one box per item, approximately ten chickens per box came to about 15 kilos.

News soon began to spread regarding the lack of locally sourced meat and the reason behind it. We discovered that in 1969 there had been a drought. This led to a reduced harvest, so seed grain was scarce.

Saddam was at that time the No.2 to Ahmed Hassan Al-Bakr. It was he who decided to import seed grain to supplement the farmers. The grain was imported from Mexico & the United States. It was not for human consumption, only for planting. 95,000 tons of grain that had been treated with methyl mercury fungicide was imported into Basra and distributed to farmers all over the country.

The grain was tinted with a pink-orange colour which was a strange sight for the farmers. It contained 7.9 micrograms per gram of methylmercury. The bags had red printed poison warnings on them, in English and Spanish. Farmers in Iraq were mostly illiterate so a warning in any language would be beyond them, or those who could read English did not believe the warnings. There were even skull & crossbones symbols on the sacks, but that meant nothing to them. Distribution of this poisoned grain started late, well after the planting season, which meant that the farmers would have to hold on and store it for the next planting season.

Many farmers decided instead to mill the grain into flour, washing off the dye though this did not wash off the mercury, some did not bother to wash the grain, using it in the original state. Grain was ground into flour. This process alone caused dust contaminated with mercury to be breathed in by the farmers. The bread made from the flour was a nice unusual pink colour, and so the disaster began to unfold.

Contaminated grain was fed to the farm animals, cows, chickens and goats, it was given away to relatives for them to use. Symptoms of mercury poisoning began to appear within 16-38 days. At first nobody understood what was happening. People who had consumed the bread made from the ground flour experienced various symptoms depending on how much of the mercury had been contained therein.

Numbness of the extremities (paraesthesia) in the not so serious cases, worst cases had ataxia (loss of balance) or blindness. Death was the worst outcome.

There had been previous outbreaks of methyl mercury compound poisoning in Iraq in 1956, which had resulted in around 200 cases, and 1960, which saw over 200 deaths in 1000 cases. It was after the incident in 1960 that it had been recommended that any toxic grain should be coloured for easier identification.

Kirkuk hospital began to receive many patients with symptoms of mercury poisoning which the doctors recognized from an earlier outbreak in 1960. By late December the hospital, becoming increasingly alarmed, sent a warning to the government and in January 1972, decrees were issued of the dangers of eating the grain. The death penalty was imposed for anyone who sold it instead of disposing or returning it.

Farmers discovered the easiest and quickest way to get rid of the grain was to dump it in the rivers, particularly into the river Tigris, causing further problems with contamination of the water supply and marine life. Fish became contaminated with the methylmercury compound.

Those victims with mild symptoms recovered completely, others were not so lucky. Many were left with brain damage, blindness, pregnant women passed the poison to their foetuses in utero resulting in babies being born with brain damage. It is reported that 6,500 patients were admitted to the hospital with symptoms. One-third of these were under 10 years old. The death rate was 459 deaths. By January cases had peaked. They began to subside by early March.

These figures may have been an understatement. Many farmers did not believe in hospitals or doctors. Those with symptoms who then recovered at home or deaths that may have occurred at home would have gone unreported.

There was little information released by the government after it issued a news blackout. The W.H.O organised distribution of medicine and equipment to help in the outbreak. I do recall some years later seeing a documentary about the occurrence.

Chapter 19

Crime, Abu Tobar (1973)

I was having tea with one of my neighbours one morning when she told me about someone called **Abu Tobar**. It was 1973. This person had been going around places in Iraq committing murders and robberies of whole families.

My neighbour was terrified he would come and murder her in her bed. She urged me to keep all the doors and windows locked.

I asked my son Faris about Abu Tobar, he said the name meant *Hatchet Man* or *Father of the Hatchet*. This man, who was an ex-police officer, had killed a Jewish man in his home. Then a few days later went on to kill a woman and her husband in their home.

As time passed we heard of many more of his heinous crimes. He killed a police chief and his wife, along with their 12 years old son and nephew.

By this time, he was joined in his killing spree by his nephew, his wife and her two brothers. The gang went on in late September of 1973, to kill a man, his wife and their two daughters in Karada Mariam, close to the Republican Palace.

Baghdad became gripped with fear, imaginations running riot, any noise we heard outside the home had us shaking as we wondered if the dreadful Abu Tobar was climbing over the gate to get us.

Those who hated the idea of having a dog in their home promptly went out and got one to keep as a guard dog.

A city-wide curfew was in place, extensive searches carried out by security forces (in which the murderer himself took part), confusion reigned for months.

We got the news of yet another murder - this time of a barber, who was bludgeoned to death, his carpets and furniture audaciously removed from his house.

At last, we heard that Abu Tobar-who incidentally did not use a hatchet but preferred an iron bar as his weapon of choice-had been captured. Everybody breathed a collective sigh of relief.

The authorities sentenced him to death by hanging on 5th October 1974. After the first two attempts to carry out the sentence failed, success was achieved at the third.

His name was Hatem Kazem Al-Hadum, his nephew was Hussein Ali Hassoun.

Chapter 20

I Return to UK (1975)

When the boys were about 4 and 7, I had to return to the UK. They stayed behind with their father and grandmother. My mental state was not good, I had suffered a complete mental breakdown. Going back to England to recover seemed the wisest decision.

I started working again in London as a live-in hotel telephonist in the Mount Royal Hotel in Marble Arch on a large switchboard. I was able to recuperate, the work kept me busy, and my mind began to settle. I kept in touch with the children through the switchboard I was working on, calling them in the late evenings. Some jobs are useful.

I made a few friends there, one of whom was Rita. She had lovely red hair and was quite slim. We got on so well that we decided to rent a flat together. We found a three-bedroom flat in Edith Road, Kensington, walking distance from Baron's Court underground station, and moved in.

These days a three-bedroom flat in the area would cost you an arm and a leg, but the two of us received fairly good wages and could afford the rent.

The Exorcist

After work one day we decided to go to see a new popular horror movie in the cinema called 'The Exorcist' with Linda Blair playing the part of a young girl possessed by a demon. A priest is called to perform an exorcism. Her mother was played by Ellen Burstyn, the priests were Max von Sydow and Jason Miller.

The reviews were exciting. It was reported that some viewers had severe reactions such as vomiting or fainting at some scenes. We read that people had even had heart attacks or miscarriages on viewing the movie, so we simply just had to go and see it.

Most horror movies did not bother me. I asked Rita if she was scared by them, and she said she was not. So, we went to the cinema, bought our tickets and sat through the scariest movie I had ever seen. I was mesmerized by the scenes of Linda Blair's head turning 360 degrees and at one point she violently masturbated with a crucifix! What stuff was this!!

Several times during the movie I had asked Rita if she was okay. She had been noticeably quiet throughout the showing. Each time she answered that she was fine.

When the movie ended, we stood up to leave the cinema. As we got into the aisle she keeled over, face down on the floor, out like a light! So much for being 'not scared of horror movies'.

Luckily, the cinema was prepared for the possibility of someone fainting and had St John's Ambulance staff out in the foyer ready for any emergency. They came and got her up, sat her down in a seat, and gave her some water to drink. When she had recovered we made our way home on the bus.

I always got her riled up when I mentioned the incident later. We were friends for many years until she passed away from breast cancer.

That movie became the highest-grossing R-rated horror film until the film 'It' in 2017, watch it sometime, I dare you!

Return to Baghdad

I eventually felt that I had recovered enough to return to Baghdad. I missed my boys immensely and just wanted to get back to them.

I had received word that Ahmed had married again. He could have four wives according to Islamic law. I wrote him a letter congratulating him on his wedding, it meant nothing to me now. It was somewhat of a relief as I felt the pressure would be lifted from me. He would now have someone else to bully.

Mushtamil Adhamiya

Before I returned it was arranged that Ahmed's sister, Suad, would move out of the small house she was living in, near to the main house.

She was persuaded to move out, quite forcefully I might add, she was not happy about it but had no choice in the matter.

I say 'small' but that is just comparing it to the much larger family home. It was a two-storey mushtamil (maisonette) made of brick. There were two double rooms upstairs, two double rooms downstairs, a lounge area, kitchen, and a bathroom with a toilet. There was a small balcony upstairs and a small patio downstairs which had a palm tree growing in it. The main gate led out onto the street. There was no garden at that time but Ahmed cordoned off some of the lands outside the house to make a garden later on.

The toilet was quite small and of the 'eastern' type, basically just a hole in the floor. Ahmed had it extended and a 'Western' toilet with a bidet and a small sink put in. This got me into trouble later with Mahmoud, Ahmed's brother, when he was visiting. He said he felt tired and I suggested he could take a nap in our new toilet! I don't know what I was thinking to come out and say that. He did not speak to me for at least 6 months afterwards, he was so offended.

The floors had patterned light brownstone tiles, very cold in the winter but nice and cool in the summer. The doors upstairs and downstairs were heavy metal. The whole area around us was once farmland, it had once been a farmhouse.

All the improvement work was done before I arrived, I was not asked what I would like, which would never occur to him. He bought furniture, kitchen utensils, everything one would need.

I lived there for some years with my children. The girls were born there, then my youngest son, Samer.

We were happy there; the children thought the house was haunted. Over the time we lived there many occurrences happened that could not be logically explained.

Fairies & Stranger Things

Sahar, as a small child, would often point up to the ceiling and laugh or talk to some unknown entity. As she got older, she was able to tell me that she saw 'fairies' flying around the neon lights. I explained it away by telling her it was moths, but she was adamant.

One of the twins, at age three, was passing by me as I sat on the sofa. She was going into the downstairs bedroom, suddenly she pitched forward and smashed her face onto the steel door frame. It looked to me like she had been pushed from behind. Luckily there was no lasting damage. There had been no obstacle such as a stray shoe or toy.

Samer & The Black Cat Incident

Samer recently mentioned a few times when strange things happened to him.

Once when he was about five years old (he was 36 when he told me this tale), he was sitting at the large dining table in the lounge when he noticed a black cat sitting on the chair next to him. We did not have a black cat at that time-the cat was looking at him, then it spoke to him in English,

"Get some matches from the kitchen," the cat said. *"Come with me, into the garden."*

Ahmed had previously taken some of the lands outside the front gate and made a small garden with a fence and a gate.

Samer got the matches from where I kept them in a tin in the kitchen and followed the cat into the garden.

"Now," said the cat, *"light a match and throw it on the fence."*

The garden fence was temporary and made of dry palm fronds which were inflammable.

Samer duly lit up one of the matches and threw it onto the fence, which then burst into flames. He looked at the fence burning, then looked at the cat, he could see the flames in the eyes of the cat.

"Look," said the cat, *"isn't that beautiful?".*

When he next looked, the cat had gone.

A passing neighbour came and knocked loudly at my door to inform me that my garden was on fire!

I always thought one of the other children had done it-especially Sindus. She was always getting into trouble.

Samer never told me about the cat until recently.

Another time he sat in his bed and lit a match, put it to a box of tissues which then caught fire. He quickly ran with the box and dumped it into the sink. I had noticed the light flickering while I was sitting in the lounge and quickly went to investigate. He got a clip round the ear for that, he could have set the whole bed on fire.

My son was a budding arsonist!

Chapter 21

Samer & The Chillies Incident

I had some plants in pots at various places around the house. One of them was a red chilli pepper variety with some small fruits on them. Samer thought they were something nice to eat. He was about four at the time. He picked one and popped it into his mouth and chewed on it.

The house reverberated from his terrified screaming as the peppers burnt the inside of his mouth. Sindus ran and got ice from the freezer, I got a bottle of Pepsi and filled his mouth with it along with the ice. It took a while for him to calm down. When I looked in his mouth it was slightly red, but the pain had gone. No wonder I was going potty!

Just to be on the safe side I took him to the local clinic for them to check him over. The doctor took one look at my boy and asked me,

"How long has he been disabled?"

I was amazed, *"What on earth are you talking about?"* I said. *"What makes you think that he is disabled?"*

I must admit I was quite put out by his remark. Samer did have quite wide-open eyes, perhaps this is what made the doctor think he was in some way mentally disturbed.

Later I found it quite funny. He is a lovely man today, with three boys of his own, a great sense of humour and loving nature.

Samer & The Lady in Black & Other Incidents

On another occasion, when he was a few years older, he said he had seen a woman in the lounge one day, all dressed in black. As he stood looking at her, she had turned towards him and smiled the most beautiful smile before fading away. He thought that it was quite normal and carried on playing.

There was also the time when he had been naughty, so Faris had not allowed him to come and sit with us at the table during dinner. He had banished Samer to sit on the stairs.

The stairs were made of stone, quite wide with eight steps up, a small landing area, another four steps up to the bedrooms. The door to the balcony and roof was at the top of the stairs.

Samer took his plate of food and sat on the four steps with his back to the door. He said something made him turn and look behind him. He saw a strangely shaped shadow on the door behind him. This scared him so much he ran down the stairs and refused to go up again.

Ahmed left us mostly alone, he was living with his other wife in the main house and would come for a visit to see the children, or stay overnight whenever he felt like a 'change'.

He would often entertain visitors at the main house, friends of his from the airline or family.

He had a further four children with his wife, Amina, so quite a large family. There were still times when I was driven to despair by his behaviour, but my children were my rocks, we were very close and supported each other.

We began to call Amina a nickname, Mary Fisher, after a character in a series we had watched on a video called *'She Devil'.* The name suited her, we still call her that today, although sadly we have discovered that she has early-onset Alzheimer's.

I Felt The Heat

One winter, Mohammed had gone to school early to get his exam results. I had lit the gas heater (which had an open front) to warm up the living room.

When I heard Mohammed return, as I was feeling cold, I went and stood with my back to the heater while I asked him how he did. I soon felt much warmer it was getting positively hot.

Turning around I saw that my dishdasha (long nighty) was on fire! Thankfully, it was made of cotton, not flammable material.

Faris ran to the kitchen and filled up a bowl with tap water but I foolishly would not let him throw it over me saying it was too cold. I quickly sat on the nearby sofa wrapping myself in one of the throws draped over it. This caused my buttocks to get burnt.

Ahmed came soon after and said he would get me some burn cream from the pharmacy. He flatly refused to take me to the hospital as the doctors there would see my arse.

The blisters which formed later soon went down and today nothing can be seen in that area, I think, though I can't quite see it!

Walking to Kathumya

The best times we had were when Ahmed, now promoted to flight engineer, would be off flying to London, Paris etc.

If he was around, I was not allowed to go out unless I had his permission and told him exactly where I was going. Of course, if he felt it was not a necessary trip, then I could not go.

One day when the girls were small and Ahmed had left for a trip abroad, I decided to put them in their pram and walk to Al-Kathumya, about 10 kilometres away. It was a lovely day, the walk was so refreshing. If I remember correctly it took about 45 minutes.

We wandered around the souk for a while looking at the various goods for sale, the lovely materials, gold in the gold shops, various items of clothing for sale, then started walking back. Halfway back my shoes were hurting so much from a blister that had formed that I removed them, walking the rest of the way barefoot. Nobody batted an eyelid but my feet were black as soot from the dirty ground and needed a good scrub.

I would sometimes take the children after school to Mahmoud's house, or the local shops where we could look at the goods for sale.

The shoes in the Bata shoe shop, gold in the gold shops, material in the haberdashery, if I had any money (which was very rare) I would get the children something small, a cake or bun.

Unbelievable, a trip to the hospital to get the baby vaccinated was not deemed necessary by HRH. I would have to gear myself up for a long and arduous request procedure, continuously asking and explaining why it should be done.

It was the same wherever I wanted to go out. As I did not want my children to go through a life of arguing and shouting, I mostly gave in and waited for a better opportunity.

Ahmed's temper was well known, he could fly off the handle at the drop of a hat and for no reason. His mother often told me stories about him and his temper, how he would always throw a fit if he did not get his way throughout his childhood and into adulthood.

I mostly left the vaccinations until he was away on a trip, then I would be free to take the children to the clinic or hospital.

On one occasion it was time for Sindus to have her vaccination, she was about 3 or 4 years old. I took her to the local hospital, AL-Naaman. As I sat her down in the small clinic there, the nurse came and prepared the syringe in front of us. Sindus took one look at that needle and dived out of the door. The nurse and I spent the next ten minutes chasing her round and round an ambulance before eventually one of the other doctors who was passing by and observed us managed to grab her. Then the nurse was able to jab her. She glared at me accusingly for quite some time afterwards.

Chapter 22

Islam

I became a Muslim of my own free will, nobody coerced me into it. I had studied the Bible and other religions. The one I thought made the most sense to me was, and still does, is Islam.

All my children have been given the choice of choosing their path as regards religion. All of them have followed Islam.

My grandchildren have been free to follow whatever they wish, if they are happy, I am happy.

Shopping

Grocery shopping was a nightmare. Ahmed did all the shopping for both houses, but he would get the same amount of food although we were the larger family with more mouths to feed. If I ran out of something before Mary Fisher did, there was hell to pay.

I remember one incident when I discovered the meat had finished. I would have to put in an 'official' request to HRH to get us some more.

This had to be done in a certain way, an appropriate time would have to be picked in order not to set him off. I preferred when the children were at school if he were in the house then I could ask him and manage any backlash.

I stayed awake most of that night going over the scenario in my mind, what would be the best way to broach the subject? I knew that there was no easy way out, but I delayed it as long as I could by making our food without meat for a while, just hoping 'Mary Fisher' his other wife (Amina) would finish hers.

It did not work, he decided to come for lunch! It was as if he knew something was up. I had made some soup called *Teshrib*. I put chickpeas in it, onions, a little bit of chicken I had left in the freezer, some potatoes and Maggie stock cubes for flavour. I served it with rice and salad.

Normally Teshrib is made with lamb. As he sat at the table and I served him the meal, *"Where is the meat?"'* was the first thing he asked.

Everyone went dead quiet, you could hear a pin drop, the kids knew I had none left, we looked at each other. The cat was out of the bag!

"It has just finished yesterday," I replied, (three days ago would have been the truth).

"Why do you finish everything before Amina? Do you know how much meat I buy here and there, but she doesn't finish it as quickly as you and we have visitors all the time." His voice was getting louder and louder as he got up from the table, throwing his chair back.

The kids scattered and I could only stand there listening to him going on and on about money and waste-then his face changed as he thought up another idea, the cats! I had at least two cats. Turning to look at me he said, *"Have you been feeding my meat to your bloody cats?"*

That thought set him off to go and look for the cats to give them a kicking before he left. They were wise to his tricks though and made themselves scarce, hiding under beds or cupboards until it was safe to come out.

Housekeeping Allowance

One year I managed to persuade Ahmed, with the help of Mahmoud, his brother, to give me a housekeeping allowance.

I was instructed to write down everything I spent the money on, in an exercise book which he would go over at the end of the month before he gave me any more, to make sure I was not wasting his money on frivolous fancies.

The scheme soon fell through, it became too much for me to listen to the continuous questioning about why I had bought this or that so I gave it up. It was like being in a refugee camp where everything must be accounted for. I would not have been surprised if we had ended up queuing for our rations!

Weapons

I learnt the art of the slipper which is well known in the Middle East. Kids are fast, faster than I could run. Knowing how to reach them as they were streaking away into the horizon, one must know the art of slipper throwing.

Most women in Iraq and some men, wore plastic slippers, different styles and colours, all worn on their bare feet.

Like lightning a slipper could be quickly removed, aimed at the retreating figure, and launched, twirling through the air, until it found its target. There were other times of course when I missed and the little buggers got away but they were never hurt much.

I discovered that some of my neighbours were much more abusive towards their children, heating a spoon on the fire and pressing it onto their child's arm (not red hot, mind you) now that is just plain wrong, maybe locking them in a cupboard or beating them with a wooden stick.

Contrary to what goes on these days in the West where babies and children are regularly beaten and abused for sadistic reasons, in Iraq the children were chastised because they disobeyed their parents in one way or another. I never heard of any child having broken bones or being murdered by their parents. I am not saying it did not happen, just that it was not something I came across.

Children grew up with respect and love towards their parents, most families doted on their children and spoilt them.

I remember one incident with the cousin opposite where her son, Amjad, had been allowed to go out with his friends. He was about 14 years old, his father had stipulated a time for him to be home. When the lad came home he was well late, to make things worse he smelt of cigarette smoke. It was considered *ebb* (shameful or disrespectful) to smoke at such a young age and especially in front of parents. His father was waiting for him at the door, I was upstairs and heard shouting so I looked out the window to see his father grab him and slap him in the face before dragging him into the house.

The next day I asked Sabiha, the cousin, what had happened after they went inside and she told me the lad had been sent straight to his room and grounded for a month.

Another handy trick with the slippers before I go - write the name of your enemy on the bottom of your slippers and walk on them all day long! It does wonders for your mental health, maybe I should patent the idea.

Cats

Faris found some kittens which had been abandoned in the street near a pile of rubbish. There were four of them, so he brought them home for me to look after.

They were so small and full of fleas that I managed to get rid of the little buggers using head lice treatment meant for the children. It did not seem to hurt the kittens. I kept them upstairs on the balcony, out of the way where they would not be seen by Ahmed. The children would go to feed them and enjoyed spending time playing with them.

I had taught the children to always be kind to animals.

One day Ahmed came on his usual visit. As he was sitting having tea, he suddenly cocked his head to one side, listening. There was the faint sound of mewing.

"What's that noise, have you got more bloody cats?"

He rushed upstairs, following the sound of the mewing and opened the door leading out onto the balcony where he saw the small kittens huddling together in one corner. Picking them up one by one he hurled them off the balcony and into the street below, a distance of about 20 feet. Only one of the kittens survived, but not for long, it was paralysed, the rest died instantly.

The children were devastated and spent a long time crying and asking me why their father had done what he did. I had no explanation why he did anything, this was the life we had.

I think it is time to move on now with my story by introducing you to my children, your relatives, cousins, aunts or uncles and if this book lasts well into the future-your ancestors.

Chapter 23

Faris

Faris as you will remember was born in Middlesbrough. He had blonde hair and blue eyes with fair skin, just like me. He had none of his father's tanned complexion or dark hair.

He was the apple of Ahmed's eye. When we returned to Baghdad, he would often take Faris around to visit his friends and show off this beautiful boy he had, like a prized pedigree pet.

Faris was a calm, quiet baby (thanks to Dr Spock), he slept early and had a good appetite. As he got older, he made friends easily and was well-liked.

He inherited his uncle Brian's knack of embellishment and never missed an opportunity to talk his way out of any troublesome situation. As a teenager, he had his father's argumentative habits which would make me want to murder him at times, but of course, I loved all my children to bits and, as a child, he was no exception.

He is one of the jokers in our pack, with a great sense of humour. One day, when he was about 12, he jumped up in the air, trying to see how high he could go. Unfortunately for him, he did it right underneath the steel door to the bedroom, smashing his head on the frame which resulted in a nasty cut needing four stitches at the local Al-Naaman hospital.

Growing into his teenage years he found the restrictions imposed by his father hard to bear. On one occasion he had brought home a bicycle which he had borrowed from one of his friends for a while. He kept this item upstairs on the balcony, out of the way. Unfortunately for him, one day when he was bringing it down to go out for a ride, in walked Ahmed.

When he saw the bicycle, he asked Faris, *"Where did you get that from?" "It belongs to my friend, Dad, I have borrowed it for a while."* Ahmed did not believe him, he went and got a hammer from the toolbox, came back and before anyone realised what he was about, he smashed the spokes and wheels of that bicycle, leaving us all shocked.

Turning to his son he said, *"I have told you before not to tell lies, this is the consequence of your lying."* Then he turned and left, leaving Faris in tears, because of course now he must explain to his friend what had happened to his bicycle.

For most of his life, Faris has tried to prove himself to his father.

His relationships with women have been disastrous, he has been married three times. His first wife, Louise from Norfolk divorced him after two children - lovely boys named Adam and Nathan.

Adam was diagnosed with juvenile arthritis when he was young. He has spent most of his life going through one treatment or another for it and often has days of pain.

Nathan has taught himself to play the guitar and often joins in jamming sessions where he lives, in King's Lynn.

Faris' second wife Reem, from Syria, also obtained a divorce after two children - also lovely boys, Ahmed and Amir.

To date, he is now married to Mona, from Iraq and they have two children, a son, Aymon, and a daughter, Jenna.

He is a commercial airline captain and lives in Baghdad. Now he feels that he is at last able to prove to his father his worth, but at a heavy price.

His relationship with his previous children, all four of the boys, is not very good as he has had very little contact with them since the divorces. They have, for much of their lives, grown up without a father. This has affected them in many ways one of which is that some of them do not wish for any kind of contact with him.

Adam and Nathan's mother changed their surnames to her maiden name of Jones after the divorce. She told me at the time that it would be better for their school years.

My attempts at urging him to keep in contact with his sons fall on deaf ears. He is now a grandfather, after Nathan's partner gave birth to their baby boy, Theo Noah Jones.

Mohammed (1971)

Mohammed was born in Baghdad's Medical City Teaching Hospital, which was new, having opened in 1970. He had curly black hair and brown eyes. He was also a placid baby, cried little and was always smiling. Faris was just over three when Mohammed was born. He liked to sit with his little brother while helping me feed him.

Ahmed gave him the nickname of Kabobi after the fact that, even as a child, his favourite food was kubba made from rice and stuffed with minced lamb.

He was a gentle child with a rare temper which, even today, is not often seen, but when he does lose it, you know about it.

Let's see what incident I can remember for him. When he was 13, he went outside to wash the patio using some washing-up liquid and a hose. With no slippers on, he ran back into the house to get something, slipped on the wet tiles, fell backwards and knocked himself out. He was out for a short period. I helped him up and made sure he was okay while sitting him down and getting him some water. There have not been any side effects to date thank God.

Mohammed is in a stable marriage with his wife Noor, from Baghdad, Iraq. They have three children, two girls and a boy - Sandra, Sarah and Mustafa.

Sindus (1976)

My eldest daughter, Sindus, was born in Red Crescent Hospital, Baghdad, Iraq.

Ahmed was away in Seattle to take delivery as a flight engineer with Iraqi Airways of the country's first Boeing 747, so I went to the hospital with my sister-in-law, Um Nidal, Mahmoud's wife.

Having a girl was frowned upon in the families' eyes, so they got a shock when, after two boys I had now produced a girl. After I had been moved back into the hospital room from the delivery room, I made sure to put on an incredibly sad face. The world was coming to an end and I had birthed a female, what could be worse?

My hospital bed was near the window which was on my right-hand side, and Um Nidal was sitting with another relative of the family on my left.

Nobody congratulated me on the birth of my daughter, I turned to them looking as sad as I could before turning my face back to the window and grinning. I was so happy that my daughter had been born healthy.

Perhaps if she had been born a few hundred years earlier, the family would have taken her out into the desert and buried her alive!

Sindus had blue eyes and blonde hair like her elder brother, Faris, but she was a loud and difficult baby and later, a naughty child. As a baby she would have the loudest, piercing scream for no reason, even though she was clean, fed and not too warm or cold, but she would not settle.

She is the second joker in the pack, she is very clever, wants to know about everything, thinks she knows about it too. She can have a heated discussion with anyone about almost any subject. Her personality is strong, you will hear more about her later in my story, things are coming that will make your hair stand on end. Her adventures growing up need a separate story all to herself!

When Ahmed returned with the brand new, Boeing 747, the aircraft he was delivering had been empty so the crew made the most of this by spending their allowances on US goods and loading them onto the flight.

He brought a white and gold wooden bedroom set for me from the USA to make up for the fact that I had not had one when we got married as was the custom, and some other bits of furniture. The children spent many happy hours jumping up and down on that bed throughout the following years until the wooden slatted base broke.

Suzanne & Betul (1978)

My twin daughters were born in Baghdad. There is a story, well more than one story, behind their birth.

My pregnancy had gone well but I was large, much larger than my other three pregnancies. I suspected twins due to the number of little feet or elbows which I could often feel through my abdomen kicking or pushing outwards. Finding this uncomfortable I would often push them back.

I had two scans during the pregnancy. In both, only one baby could be detected. In 1978 the scanning procedure was done with machines which were nothing like the modern equipment we have today. The technicians operating them had not been trained properly so it was no surprise that only one baby could be seen. I wondered about the heartbeats, surely two must be heard? They were in sync with each other on those days.

On the day that I realised my labour had started, I got one of the boys to take me to the hospital. While I was in there I became friendly with one of the other mothers-to-be, an Iraqi lady. We walked up and down the corridor outside the labour ward, holding on to our bumps, moaning with each wave of pain, like sumo wrestlers sizing each other up.

None of the nursing staff seemed interested in giving us any painkillers, the toilets were not fit for pigs to use, there was blood on the floor and the toilet seat would have to be very gingerly wiped down before being used. We had been there for hours, left on our own.

My companion began to get quite annoyed. Turning to me as we passed yet again in the corridor, like trains on a track, she said to me in Arabic, *"This place is awful, I am going home-how about you, lady, would you like to share a taxi with me?"*

This remark was from a lady who had been in labour for some hours and could give birth at any moment! What was she thinking?

I would have loved to go home, away from this dirty, germ-ridden place, back to my tea and biscuits, but I declined her generous offer. The last I saw of her she was waddling off to gather up her belongings and leave. I hoped she made it to wherever she was going and did not birth her baby in the back of the taxi.

It is a good thing that I decided against that taxi ride home because, within the next 40 minutes, I gave birth to my daughter Suzanne, easy peasy. The nurse took her away to be weighed and checked over.

Ahmed's friend, a well-known and respected paediatrician who worked at the hospital, Dr Laith Al-Kindi, was there on that day. He came and checked my daughter over, reassuring me that my baby was a healthy baby at around seven pounds in weight.

After approximately 15 minutes, as I was settling down nice and relaxed, glad the whole procedure was over with, the midwife returned. Pressing on my tummy to help expel the placenta she frowned, looking up to the ceiling as if there was the information written there that could help her, she said, "*What is this?*"

I looked up at the ceiling too, thinking there was a leak or something, then I looked at her as she proceeded to press some more, how did I know what '*this*' was?

Looking at me with her eyebrows raised in little arches she said, "*I think we have another one in here!*" My heart almost stopped, what was she talking about, no way! That was the signal for a state of pandemonium. Quickly a gynaecologist was called to confirm her diagnosis. I had no labour pains, an IV drip of Pitocin was set up for me, this helped to start my labour again.

Unfortunately, after more examination by the doctor, I was informed that my baby was in the breech position, there was no time at that stage to attempt to turn her. Things had just gotten a lot worse. Using all my remaining strength to push as hard as I could when instructed, I attempted to deliver her. To top it all a whole crowd of medical students had appeared who had been quickly ushered in to witness this rare event. They stood around watching my nether regions closely like I was about to produce the next heir to the throne.

Eventually, after a huge amount of effort on my part, my daughter was born, bum first. It felt like I had birthed a rhino.

She was a healthy baby also at just over six pounds, blimey-no wonder I was so big and heavy while pregnant.

I was super happy, both my babies were healthy and strong, what more could anyone want?

They were weighed, checked over by Dr Laith, dressed in whatever clothes I had brought with me, not enough for two babies so each one wore something before being swaddled in small white cot sheets.

Coincidentally, the day they were born was a day celebrated in Iraq as Women's Day.

I had a visit later that day from a group of women coming from a popular women's magazine called 'Al Mura' (The Woman). They interviewed me and took some photos of my precious twins. I was presented with gifts of a nightgown and some clothes for the babies, which they sorely needed. We were due to be published in their next issue. I never did get a copy of that published article. I wish I had, the twins would love to see it today.

Ahmed, now that was another matter, his world had just come crashing down on his head.

When he was informed, I had given birth to not one but two GIRLS, he was in a state of collapse. What a tragedy, now he had five daughters (two from Amina). He refused to come to the hospital for days, sending one of his minor female relatives to stay with me in the hospital to give me a helping hand with the girls.

Her name was Medeha. She was as useless as a chocolate teapot. She spent most of the time complaining that she had a stomach-ache due to her period being expected 'any day now', lying down on the couch in my room, drinking tea and stuffing her face with whatever food was brought in meant for me. I had to see to the girls myself. After a couple of days I sent her home to be useless there.

Ahmed would not name the babies. Each day the hospital administrator would come asking me to give him the chosen names for the birth certificates. Each day I would have to ask him to come back another time. Eventually, I got fed up with all this fuss about the girls being born and spoiling the rest of their father's life so decided to name them myself.

I called my firstborn, Suzanne and my second born, Betul (one of my neighbours was named this and I liked the sound of it, thinking that later if she wanted to, she could be called Betty. I was not aware at that time that the name meant 'virgin', not anything to do with Richard Branson though).

Ahmed wasn't happy that I had taken the initiative and named them, he later changed their names at home but not officially, by calling them Sahar and Summar, so they now had two names. This caused a lot of confusion in later years when they attended pre-school. Betul officially changed her name to Summar when she became an adult. She said she did not want to be known as a virgin all her life, especially when she got married.

They were not identical twins but looked so much alike it was hard to tell them apart. They had brown curly hair and large brown eyes, just like Mohammed, with slightly deeper tanned skin.

When I was discharged home, we had many visitors come to see the babies. One of the aunties, when she came to visit, shocked me with the suggestion that she take one of my babies and bring her up, as for sure I would have too much work to do looking after them along with the other small children. I knew that Amina had given her third daughter, Mayson, to her sister, their aunt, to bring up but I would not even think of doing that, passing them out like kittens. I politely refused the offer.

Ahmed's youngest brother Salah, as usual, had nothing good to say about the girls. Everyone else wisely kept off the subject.

They were quiet and calm babies, only crying when they were hungry or needed changing. I did not have a cot for them, so until these items could be brought, they slept together on two large armchairs pushed together. They woke each other up very early in the morning by cooing and stretching, then spent the next moments bashing each other in the face or chatting in their special language.

One day Hamid came with beds for them, which gave them more space to move and less boxing.

After I would bathe them, I would hand one out to Faris to dress, before bathing her sister. The boys learnt to help me look after them and even Sindus helped by shushing them when they cried. She was not trusted to feed them later with their baby food though, it would be one spoonful for them and two spoonsful for her!

They have a very close relationship even today.

Yasmina (1979)

Yasmina was born one year later, in Medical City Hospital. When I went into labour, I took some sedatives to calm me down. These were easily obtainable from the chemist, no prescription needed in Iraq, any chemist would dole out whatever you asked for. I took some more just before going into the delivery room. I thought the medication would help me get through the labour better.

She was born fast asleep, she breathed okay but did not wake up till hours later. Some mother I was, not realising the sedative could be passed through the placenta to the baby.

I was also sleepy and slept deeply when I was moved back into the ward. My new-born baby was looked after by another kindly mother along with her new-born until I woke up. She had noticed me, out like a light, and had changed my daughter's nappy. I was so grateful for her thoughtfulness and care.

The nurses on duty were not much good, preferring to spend their time in the nurse's station chatting and drinking tea together. Patients were left to look after themselves most of the time.

Yasmina had blacker, thicker hair than her sisters but was fairer-skinned, with brown eyes. As usual, her father was away at the time of her birth which was a good thing as I doubt, he would be pleased with yet another female, (Amina had already had three girls by this time).

I named her Yasmina after a blackbird in an Arabic cartoon about Sindbad that was popular on the TV. She has dropped the 'a' at the end, now it is just Yasmin.

When her uncle, Salah, and his wife came to visit us at home, he could not contain himself and just had to say something nasty, "I see you have given birth to yet another *shoe!*"

To him all girls were *'Kundera'* (shoes). He was newly married and his wife was pregnant with their first child. I prayed that it would be a girl. Calling someone a 'shoe' in the Middle Eastern culture is an insult, just as bad as if you were to call someone a dog. Dogs are considered *'negus'* or filthy, and shoes come a close second. I vowed that when his wife did give birth if it was a girl, I would go and say the same thing to her.

As it turned out, his first child was a girl, quite a disappointment for him and the family, but when I went to visit them, I found that I could not make that same nasty remark, it was not in my nature. I congratulated her on her healthy baby instead.

Someya, the mother, had problems with the baby at first. She could not feed her and the baby, Kawther, would not take the bottle. She became very hungry so she screamed most of the time. The mother was exhausted from lack of sleep. Salah took her and the baby to a doctor who prescribed a sedative for Kawther. What doctor in his right mind would give a new-born baby sedatives?

Each time the baby started crying, the mother would dose it up with this stuff until eventually, the poor mite overdosed. I was asked to go to see them. The mother desperately needed some sleep so I offered to take the sleeping baby home with me, not knowing about the sedative she had been given. When I realised what had been given to the baby, I was worried about her state. I arranged to take her to the local children's hospital. By the time I got the baby examined in the hospital, she was unconscious.

The doctor arranged for a saline drip, not able to bring up one of her tiny veins in her arm he had the drip inserted in a vein in her scalp. I could not stay in the room while this was happening and stood outside, tears rolling down my face. The parents turned up at that moment with the grandmother. Seeing me in that state they immediately assumed that the baby had died. Wailing loudly, they began to beat their heads and breasts in the corridor. I had to quickly reassure them that she was fine, just having the drip set up. Finally they calmed down.

It was arranged that I stay overnight with her in the hospital, during the night she eventually came round. I was able to get her to take the bottle at last.

Cats roamed freely around the hospital, there was no thought of the health of the babies. The cats were disappointed they could not get some of her milk. They had a habit of climbing on the babies' beds to lick the milk dribbling from their faces. The night staff never bothered to shoo them away. Their time on night duty was spent all night sitting on the floor drinking tea, eating and gossiping. Several times I had to go and ask them to keep their noise down or come and clean up some cat poo. I was not popular, I am sure they were glad to see the back of me.

Kawther is now married, she lives in Canada with her family.

Chapter 24

Circumcision (1980)

It is normal practice to circumcise boys in Iraq according to the Islamic religion. Faris was circumcised when he was young along with his cousin, Haitham.

There was a party afterwards. The boys wore white dishdasha or gowns and received gifts of money to appease them after their ordeal.

Mohammed was another matter. Despite me and his brothers encouraging Ahmed to circumcise him as a baby, this was never done. Only when he was about nine years old and Ahmed was away on a trip, did his uncle come to take him for the procedure.

As he was older this now had to be done in the hospital by a surgeon. He was given a light anaesthetic for the operation. All went well and by the time Ahmed returned it was all over. He wasn't pleased to have had no control over the matter but there was nothing he could do about it.

Vacation to London (1980)

Most years when the school holidays started we dreaded them. It meant nearly three months under what seemed like house arrest in the 50+ degree heat of summer. Getting through the day for us was spent mostly doing housework, sleeping long hours in the afternoon, reading or playing with the cats. It was too hot to go out anywhere. We could only do that in the cooler evenings.

We always had cats, some were allowed inside the house, others were kept in the garden. For some reason, my neighbours seemed to be under the impression that I needed even more cats in my collection. Any kittens they came across in the street were picked up and thrown into our garden. One poor mite had been twirled around by the tail until it detached before being lobbed over our wall. I found it in the morning when I went out, lying in the grass with a bloody stump. I took it inside and bandaged up what was left of the tail. The children called her 'Shrougy' which meant 'peasant' in Arabic. She was with us for many years. When she got diarrhoea one day I tried giving her half a tablet meant for humans. She wasn't having it and struggled so much I decided it would be easier to give it as a suppository, so I shoved it up her bum. Thirty minutes later she was running around like crazy, bumping onto the wall and the furniture-she had gone blind.

I was upset when I saw her like this, blaming myself for causing her blindness with my thoughtless action. After a few hours, the medication wore off and, to our relief, she was back to her normal self.

Misha was one of our first cats. He was pitch black with beautiful green eyes. He looked like a cross between a Persian and a moggy. He loved watermelon. Whenever I cut one open and he picked up the scent, he would come rushing over for his share.

Other fruits he liked were plums and bits of apple. He would go for the sand-coloured lizards that ran along the walls, they sometimes got into the house. Whenever he saw one on the wall, even if it was high up, he would launch himself like a flying fox, grab it and gobble it down, eww.

When the school holidays started this year, Ahmed arranged for us to go for the long hot summer weeks to London for a very rare holiday. He was entitled to concession flights from Iraqi Airways each year but rarely used them for us. We had not been on holiday abroad for years.

He was the flight engineer on our flight to London. Before we boarded, he took me aside and told me not to mention that I was his wife, or that these were his children. Of course, such a request did not go down very well with me. As soon as we settled into our seats, buckled up and took off, the air hostess came with the in-flight meals. I informed her that Ahmed Haddad, who was the flight engineer on board, was my husband, we were his family. Pointing to the children I told her the names of each one and asked her if the two eldest boys could go and see their father in the cockpit.

She looked at me in amazement, what a dark horse indeed was Flight Engineer Mr Ahmed, keeping his lovely family a secret. She promised to take the boys after the meal distribution was over.

True to her word, she came and took them to see their father, who was not too pleased that, once again his plans to sweep us under the carpet had been thwarted.

Ealing, London (1980)

A flat in Ealing had been rented for us by one of Ahmed's friends. He took us there and returned to Baghdad after a few days with the returning flight.

We settled down to relax. My brother, Brian, came to see us, he had not met the children before, and was so happy to meet them all. We went to the funfair on Ealing Common.

I was able to contact my father who promised to come and visit us. When the day came, we waited and waited, he did not appear.

As time passed I became concerned, I asked Faris to watch the children while I walked down to the tube station to see if he were there, maybe he could not find the address I had given him.

On instinct, when I passed by the pub near the station I decided to go in and check - lo and behold! there he was at the bar, drinking with his lady friend. He never was one to be able to pass up a pint.

When I managed to get him back to the flat and make him some tea, he, at last, saw his grandchildren. He was overcome with emotion. That was the first and last time that they saw their grandfather.

During this time Yasmina had her first birthday in Ealing. We did a small party for her with a single candle on her birthday cake.

She slept with me in one room while the rest of the children slept in the other. Early one morning she had woken up, climbed out of bed and gone to see her sisters. She got up onto one of the beds in their room, standing up she somehow fell backwards onto the floor, flat on her back.I was woken up by Faris shouting for me. Running into their room I found her lying on the floor. Her lips were blue, she was not breathing. Faris at that time was 11 years old. He did not panic, just bent down and started giving her mouth to mouth resuscitation while I phoned the emergency services for an ambulance. Crying and hysterical as I gave them the address, they arrived within minutes and started checking her over. By that time, she had come round and was sitting up. I went with her to the hospital where she was examined by the doctor. He said she was fine but told me to keep an eye on her in case she vomited or slept a lot.

It was after that incident, whenever she got upset through someone taking her toy or annoying her too much, she would collapse and have a seizure.

Dr Laith Al-Kindi, a paediatrician friend of Ahmed in Baghdad, arranged for her to be checked over when we returned to Baghdad. He told us that she was quite healthy and would grow out of the seizures, which she did when she was older.

Chapter 25

Breakout of the Iraq-Iran War

On 22nd September 1980, while we were still in London, we heard the dreadful news that Iraq had invaded Iran. I was mortified. All flights were grounded, airports in Iraq closed, how would we get back? At first, I wanted to stay in the UK. Taking the family back to a country at war did not seem a wise choice. I went to the council and asked if they could help and explained the situation that we were in. They were trying to help us. Being in London, which was and still is very overcrowded, it was not easy to get housed.

We could not stay in the flat as we did not have the money for the rent. The landlady tried to be helpful by offering us another property she had in Devon, but I knew we could not stay there either; it was too far and we would still not have any funds.

Ahmed's friend came to see us and gave us some money to help.

The council was able to put us into temporary accommodation in a seaman's hostel in London. It was not a good place. Each night the police would be called when fights broke out between drunken residents.

I manage to get some of the children into a school nearby for a while, it was not ideal. I knew we could not stay there, looking after six children on my own with no funds and no support just was not possible. I knew as soon as we could, we would have to return to Iraq, even though there was a war on. Ahmed reassured me the fighting was all in the Faw Peninsula, a long way from the capital.

Amman – Baghdad by Bus

Eventually, Ahmed was able to arrange for us to return. There were no direct flights into Baghdad so we had to fly first to Jordan's capital Amman, then get a bus to take us to Baghdad, a journey of 22 hours or so.

Ahmed was already in Amman attending airline business. When we arrived we were all tired from the long journey. It had not been easy especially with a one-year-old baby. He met us at the airport and drove us directly to the bus station where he bustled us onto the next bus to Baghdad.

He brought us some sandwiches and water for the journey, it seemed that the quicker we were gone the better, his colleagues (?) might have seen us otherwise. The two older boys were such a great help to me on that journey. They helped make sure the little ones (twins) were not frightened and helped to feed them. Even Sindus did her bit to help and she was only four.

The bus we were on did not even take us to the bus station in Baghdad, the driver dumped us in someplace on the outskirts of the city. He muttered something and drove off; the children needed the toilet badly so I went to one of the houses nearby and knocked on the door.

The family was so kind, they let us use their toilet, gave us some water and sweets for the children and when I asked them to call a taxi for us to continue, they kindly did. Squeezing us all into the taxi was a feat but we eventually managed to make it back home.

What with all the kids and their various bits of luggage to load up into the taxi, we forgot one of our plastic bags in the street. It contained some of the children's clothes and the baby's new shoes.

It was good to be home, at last. Dumping all the suitcases in the middle of the lounge, we all lay down and slept right through till the next day, exhausted.

There was nothing to eat in the house, so I sent Faris to the main house to ask Amina for some supplies. Later, Mahmoud passed by and got us some shopping to tide us over until Ahmed returned.

Switching on the television we watched the scenes of continuously uplifting music and songs, men, women and children all singing the praises of Iraq and President Saddam Hussein. *'By our soul, by our blood, we sacrifice ourselves for you, Saddam'.*

The news we heard from neighbours was that Saddam wanted to capture the Shatt al-Arab waterway-the two rivers of Iraq meet at Qurna - Iran on one side, Iraq on the other. His idea was to capture the oil-rich border region, of Khuzestan, he thought that Iran's army was weak. His troops advanced and captured the city of Khorramshahr. They attempted to take the oil refining centre of Abadan but were not successful.

The Iranian army was boosted up with the Revolutionary Guard. They fought back, forcing the Iraqi army back across the Karun River.

In 1982 Iran re-captured Khorramshahr. Later that same year Iraq withdrew its forces and sought a peace agreement with Iran.

The war would have ended there if it were not for the Shia leader of Iran, Ruhollah Khomeini. He disliked Saddam (who was Sunni) and decided this was his chance to overthrow him. The Iraqi army gained confidence when they realized they were defending their territory. A static front was set up which was just inside and along Iraq's border.

The fighting continued for another eight years. Iran would send wave after wave of fighters, some of them untrained and unarmed, grabbed off the streets and conscripted into the army. It was an army of soldiers, young boys of 12 upwards, old men from the farms, anyone who could hold a rifle or not, even farm implements were carried. They wore green or white headbands with 'Allahu Akbar' written on them (God is great) or some other verses from the Koran.

Each evening during those years, at dinner time, we would watch **'photos from the front'** on TV. Those photos would never be allowed on Western television; they were raw, unedited clips showing horrendous, gory scenes of dead Iranian soldiers, many of them with their skin blackened by the chemicals used by Iraq. Of course, this was always denied by the government later, but we saw what we saw, the evidence was shown to us each evening.

Iran Child Soldier

There were many 'martyrs', the official figure of Iraq's dead was around 500,000, but it must have been more, much more.

Every day for the whole eight years streets all over Iraq would be decorated with banners for the dead. Sounds erupted with women wailing for those lost. Life was a nightmare. So many of my neighbours lost beloved members of their family - fathers, sons, cousins, nephews, uncles - not just as martyrs but as prisoners of war or missing in action.

Mahmoud's son, Haitham, was an officer in the Iraqi army. He was severely injured at the front, by shrapnel entering his stomach and causing damage internally. He was transferred to the army hospital in Baghdad. I could not bring myself to go and visit him. I knew that I would not be able to control my grief and did not want him to see me thus. I am glad that I did not see him in the state he was as it would be a memory I would carry with me forever. I wanted to remember him as that handsome, wonderful young man. We prayed that this beautiful young man would survive, and we were devastated when he died from his injuries a short while later.

Mahmoud, his father, blamed himself. When the call-up for his son had come, he could have paid money to certain 'officials' he knew to get his son's name taken off the list. The guilt stayed with him for the rest of his life.

One morning, early, we heard that dreadful wailing coming from the house opposite. It belonged to Subeha, a distant cousin of Ahmed. She was married to an officer in the army, a wonderful husband and father of three, an officer in the army who had, along with the majority of Iraqi men, been sent to the front. We knew when everyone in that house came out into the street, the women wailing and beating their breasts, that here was yet another victim of this war, I went out to see what I could do to help.

His wife had thrown herself onto the floor. She had torn her dishdasha and was pulling her hair out while her children held on to her. It was one of the saddest days in my life. These occurrences were common all over Iraq, there were thousands of funerals during those eight years. Orange and white taxis could be seen transporting the shaheed or martyrs' coffin on the roof rack. The instructions from those in government were not to open the coffins, the corpse may have shown signs of a chemical attack.

We just wanted the war to be over, it had gone on too long with such a loss of life.

I wrote a poem then about the suffering of a soldier in the front line of battle.

A Soldier's Cry

Mother, what am I doing here?
I'm cold, wet and scared
Shells smash into the ground
The sounds of death are all around
Our agony is shared

Mother, what did I do wrong?
To end up in this place
My friends are lying in the dirt
Many of them, bleeding and hurt
Tears running down their face

Mother, what are we fighting for?
The reasons have been lost
Thousands giving up their lives
They fill this place with awful cries
Then, who will count the cost?

Mother dearest, can I come home?
Just to see your face once more.
I'm so frightened being here
I know I mustn't show my fear
A brave soldier always, of this war

Mother, can you hear those screams
Of men in agony?
All day and night they moan aloud
Their leaders must be so proud
To see them martyred for their country

Mother, will you cry for me
If I do not return?
Who knows how long I must fight?
If it's wrong, or if it's right
You will be left alone.

Mother, my dearest aim
Would be to survive this war
Back home to your embrace once more
Freeing you from your pain.

At the first of many funerals I attended during the Iraq-Iran war, I wore my brand-new, unique and fancy slippers, brought from London. Leaving them at the door of the house, as was the custom, I entered and sat down wearing an abaya to cover myself. I sat for what seemed the appropriate length of time, listening to the mullah chanting the verses from the Qoran, but was not sure how to leave. Something must be said to the bereaved widow. I could not just turn my back and walk out, but what?

I tried to listen intently as others took their leave of the widow. When I thought I had got the wording right, I arose and made my way over to her. Bending down I kissed her on the cheeks and muttered the words *"Allah inteecom al tamor."* I got a funny look as I turned and left. At the door, I discovered some cow had stolen my slippers, leaving me a pair of old plastic ones.

At home I mentioned the words I had told the widow to my son, he collapsed in a fit of laughter. *"Mother, what you said to her was – May Allah give you dates! Tamour, (the fruit). The word you should have said was 'subour' which means 'patience'."*

The next day I returned to the funeral service. This time I made sure to sit near the door, keeping my eyes on the feet of the women as they entered, knowing that my slippers would appear sooner or later. When they did, I slipped them on and left, remembering to say the correct phrase this time and glad that I had managed to retrieve them.

One incident, which I remember, was on a day when I was having breakfast with the children, we heard that dreadful wailing coming from outside the house. Going out to see which house had lost yet another loved one, we were met with the sight of a sheep lying on the road, it had been hit by a car.

One of our neighbours stood over her sheep wailing and tearing at her clothes. Fortunately, the sheep was only dazed, it soon came round and was on its feet again. It was such a relief for the family. They made and sold cheese and yoghurt from the milk of their sheep. Also it would hopefully produce lambs for the future which the family could sell, providing them with an income. It was a precious member of the family.

Chapter 26

Sabra & Shatila Massacre (16th September, 1982)

When I switched on my radio this morning to the BBC World Service I was shocked to hear of the tragedy which was unfolding in Lebanon in the Palestinian refugee camps of Sabra & Shatila.

A massacre was taking place that night, carried out by Lebanese. Christian militiamen aided by 81 mm illumination flares dropped on the areas by Israeli aircraft. The Israeli army had surrounded the camp to prevent anyone from leaving while the massacre took place.

Many of those Lebanese Forces who had taken part in the massacre had been trained by the Israeli Army. Some of their weapons had been provided by Israel and it is well known that Israel supported them all the way. Their motive for taking part was said to be in revenge for the murder of Bachir Gemayel, the Lebanese Christian President.

The massacre went on for four days in which men, women and children were cut down. Some bodies were found scalped or castrated, pregnant women with their stomachs cut open, babies found beheaded or cut to pieces and thrown aside like so much garbage, even the elderly were butchered.

During this time, the perpetrators had felt hungry as later, wrappers from chocolate wafers printed in Hebrew were found littering the ground, along with remnants of C-rations from the United States army.

What had been going through the minds of those who carried out this act?

I felt at that time like the whole world had gone mad. It was just one atrocity after another, where would it all end, would it ever end? I wonder if, today, those who took part in the massacre ever have nightmares or feel remorse for what they did then?

A commission chaired by Sean MacBride, the assistant to the UN Secretary-General and President of United Nations General Assembly at that time, concluded that Israel was responsible for the violence. The massacre was deemed a genocide. In the same year, the Israeli Kahan Commission came to the same conclusion. They deemed that Ariel Sharon, who was the Defence Minister at that time, was personally responsible, forcing him to resign.

Iraqi Football (1984)

Saddam's son, Uday, took over the Iraqi Football Association and the Olympic committee. It was a mystery why he suddenly became interested in sports. He had never been much of an athlete despite his height and size. He did not know much about football, except that it was a very popular sport in Iraq, as was wrestling.

By taking control of the IFA and the Olympic Committee, he was able to exercise his sadistic tendencies at will and un-fettered.

The players who took part in sports, especially football or wrestling, were playing on borrowed time. If they dared to lose a match or get a low score, their fate would be imprisonment, usually, in al-Radwania prison, their eyebrows and hair shaved off, daily beatings, starvation and loud obscenities shouted during an interval by Uday over the loudspeaker.

During the season, teams would be summoned into Uday's office so he could lecture them on the folly of losing a match. He would spew out threats of cutting off their legs or some other punishment. To play a match after such brutal treatment, knowing that failure was not an option, must have taken a great deal of strength both physically and mentally.

Iraqi Footballers

Ahmed Radhi

Iraqis are mad about football. Over the years they had some great players and managers. The most famous one was Ahmed Radhi (1964-2020), he played as a striker. He scored the only Iraqi goal in the FIFA World Cup 1986. He was voted 1988 Asian Footballer of the Year. Ahmed Radhi played for the Iraqi national team 121 times and scored 64 goals for the Lions of Mesopotamia, as it is commonly known.

Uday Hussain was obsessed with him, refusing to allow him to play abroad. It is reported that at one time Uday had him imprisoned and tortured for refusing to join his newly formed team, al-Rasheeda, until Radhi conceded.

Radhi left Iraq to live in Amman, Jordan in 2006 with his wife and three children. In 2007 he decided to return and took up a career in politics. He was admitted to al-Nauman hospital, Adhamiya, with Covid-19 on 13th June 2020. After a few days he was discharged as fit. Unfortunately, he was re-admitted on 18th June when his condition deteriorated, passing away on 21st June in his 56th year. He died wearing his green football jersey.

Hussain Saeed (1958)

Hussain Saeed was born in our area, Adhamiya, in 1958. Like most youngsters, he learnt to play football in street games with his friends.

He moved to an area called al-Iskan, where he joined a youth club football team leading them on to win, with a 4-2 hat trick, an Iraqi Youth Centre Championship against al-Zawra. He was spotted by the manager of the Iraq national under 17 football team. Dawood al-Azzawi invited him to join the varsity team.

In his first match, Hussain won the gold medal in the 1975 Arab Schools Games in Egypt.

Ali Abbas Mshehed al-Hilfi

Played left-back, centre midfielder and left-winger.

Applied for asylum in Australia in November 2007 along with his fellow players Ali Mansour and Ali Khudhair.

This was after playing for the Iraqi under-23 side against Olyroos.

The Iraqi football team, for the only time, qualified for the FIFA World Cup in 1986. They ended up last in their group with 0 points.

Ahmed Radhi's header hit the back of the net while the referee blew the whistle for half-time; the goal was not allowed.

Mina Bird & Parrots

Ahmed liked birds. He had brought back a Mina bird from one of his trips one day. He wanted me to keep the bird in the house on a special stand. With all that was going on at home already, I was not happy at having this black creature sitting on his perch, screeching, pooing and throwing the soft fruits that it liked to eat all over the floor. Eventually, he was persuaded to take the bird away, we all breathed a sigh of relief.

Then, Ahmed turned up with two Amazon green parrots. Oh no, no way I said, one maybe but not two. So, one, named Jameela, was left with me and the other went to Amina.

One day, when I opened the parrot's cage to change the water, it escaped! It flew right out the open door and up into the sky. I managed to chase it down the road but could not catch it.

Ahmed was away on one of his trips abroad. Waiting for him to get back, knowing how much he doted on those birds, the children and I were terrified of telling him. We worked ourselves up into a frenzy, Faris pacing the floor, Mohammed coming up with different scenarios. They went around the neighbourhood each day knocking on doors, asking the neighbours if they had seen our parrot.

When Ahmed returned from his trip I told him that I needed to tell him something. Sitting down I looked at him with tears in my eyes, wringing my hands, I could not get the words out. I thought he would erupt into one of his rages. His beloved parrot had been lost, it was the end of the world.

Not understanding what had happened he looked at me.

"What is it, what's wrong, has somebody died, who?"

"No, erm, no it's not that, it's oh, how to say it?"

"Say what, for God's sake will you tell me what's wrong, is it one of the kids?"

Blurting it out I said, *"It's the parrot, the parrot got out of the cage and flew away. We could not catch it, it's gone, gone and I don't know where!"*

With this, I covered my face with my hands and burst into tears.

Ahmed sat and looked at me in amazement as I sat crying and shaking.

"Why are you in such a state? It happened, nothing to get upset about. I will go and see if any of the neighbours have seen it, for God's sake calm down."

This was the state of tension that we lived in, never knowing how he would react at any time.

He went around our neighbours asking if anyone had seen our parrot. One of the neighbours said he had heard a parrot squawking in his next-door neighbour's house, a house where my boys and Ahmed had already been. They had been told by the man living there that he had not seen a parrot.

Ahmed retraced his steps, knocking on the door he asked the man if he had our parrot, the man said he did not. He had *his* parrot which he bought from the market some time ago.

Ahmed asked to see his parrot. The man, knowing Ahmed's reputation in the area, let him in and, sitting inside a cage was Jameela. Ahmed recognized her straight away.

Ahmed was going to slap the man for lying, instead, he went over and picked up the cage with the parrot in it. Turning to the man he warned him to stay away from us and our parrot or he would regret ever being alive. Then he turned and brought the parrot back.

I refused to have it back in the house, the whole experience left me feeling that I should be in the loony bin. Fancy getting myself into such a state over a bloody bird! The children had been on tenterhooks as well, wondering and waiting for the proverbial axe to fall.

Completion of Babylon Restoration (1987)

This year Saddam completed one of his projects, the rebuilding of Babylon.

The 'Archaeological Restoration of Babylon Project' was begun in 1978 to restore the ancient city from its ruins. It was an ambitious project. The city consisted of a 30-metre entrance arch, 250 rooms and 5 courtyards. The plans also included restoring an amphitheatre built during the city's Hellenistic era (323BC-31BC). As the majority of the workforce was still away fighting in the Iraq-Iran war, Sudanese immigrants and Egyptian workmen were brought in to work on the project in three shifts, anxious to get the work completed on time for the Babylon International Arts Festival in September 1987.

We were treated to this gaudy festival on Iraqi television. Horse-drawn carriages carrying the Kings of Babylon, brightly coloured costumes of the era, singers and music made it quite an interesting evening.

The walls and arches were built high, nobody knew what height they had been before, but as the name, 'Babylon' meant 'Gateway of the Gods' every wall and arch should be high enough to live up to it.

Babylon was originally built by King Hammurabi 3000 years ago. Although an account of the thickness and height of the walls of Babylon was written about by the historian Herodotus of Halicarnassus, it is thought that this was hearsay and he had never visited the city.

Alexander the Great (Alexander III of Macedon) had planned to establish this great city as his capital. Unfortunately, after spending several days drinking wine as he entertained several important guests, Admiral Nearchus and later Medius of Larissa, he took ill of a fever which left him unable to speak. 14 days or so later, he died.

There are many theories of the circumstances surrounding his death. Poisoning was one, the length of time that it took him to die in agony might have ruled this out unless a certain plant was used, such as White Hellebore (Veratrum album), which was known in ancient times and can have a long period to act.

There is also malaria, typhoid or just the years of heavy drinking and many severe wounds suffered throughout might have done him in. We will never know for sure.

Nebuchadnezzar II (605BC-562BC), King of Babylon. He expanded and rebuilt his capital city extensively. The most impressive example was his restoration of the city's ceremonial entrance to the north, the famous Ishtar Gate, (the original had been looted by the Germans in 1914, hauled away brick by brick and reconstructed in the Pergamon Museum, Berlin).

Bricks from that era have his name inscribed on them, some, found on what is called Processional Street (the only street so far uncovered in Babylon), also had the name on the opposite side of Sennacherib (705-681BC) the King of Assyria.

Saddam wanted his restoration work to go down in history alongside these famous kings. He siphoned 500 million USD into the project. He wanted to make sure that not only every Iraqi but everyone in the world would know he rebuilt Babylon, even though the city is neither Arab nor Islamic.

Today, many bricks can be seen to carry the inscription: *'In the reign of the victorious Saddam Hussein, the president of the republic, may Allah keep him the guardian of the great Iraq and the renovator of its renaissance and the builder of its great civilization, the rebuilding of the great city of Babylon was done in 1987'.* He was under the illusion that perhaps he was the reincarnation of Nebuchadnezzar.

His plans to include the restoration of the Hanging Gardens of Babylon and the Ziggurat did not happen. I remember one evening the news programme requesting anyone, who had knowledge of engineering who could offer some sort of clue as to how the Hanging Gardens were watered, to get in touch with the studio.

Women & Business

Most of the businesses in Iraq were owned or run by men. Most women stayed in the home, looking after their families, bringing up their children. Few women could drive so it was ironic that, when the father or son of the family – if he was an officer, was martyred during the war, they would receive a compensation prize from Saddam Hussein which might be in the form of a brand-new car, an amount of money, or even in some cases, depending on how high up in rank the deceased was, land.

Widows had to cope with raising their family alone. Some were therefore forced to take over their husband's shop, with little business experience, to keep an income coming in.

Those who worked for the government during that time had to donate 1/3 of their salary towards the war effort.

Driving instructors, a rare sight before the war, were opening offices all over town, they were in high demand. It was considered unseemly for a woman to get into a car alone with a man but with no close male relative to stop her, as they were all in the army fighting, she was now free to take up driving lessons.

Women drivers became the norm. The widowed cousin who lived opposite, and her daughter, both learnt to drive. I was envious not knowing how to drive myself. I finally had driving lessons and passed my test, first time, at the age of 65 in the UK!

Due to the shortage of men, most able-bodied men had been conscripted into the army, Egypt became a vital source of migrant labour, the exact figure varies between 1.5 million and 5 million Egyptians.

Saddam had a fondness for Egypt and its people from the time he spent there in exile as a young man. The migrants worked as plumbers, bakers, vegetable sellers, any job that was needed. They sent money back to their families in Egypt to support them.

Egyptians also volunteered to fight with the Iraqi army against Iran. It is estimated that they made up about 50% of foreign fighters.

With so many thousands of widows, a decree was passed that any man who married a widow would receive an amount of money from the government. This was taken up by many Iraqis and Egyptians living and working in Iraq at the time.

Chapter 27

1988

After the 1988 cease-fire, the situation in Iraq became difficult due to Iraqi soldiers returning from the front. They resented the migrant workers who had settled into their jobs, married their women. Fights would often break out, spurious names would be called. Newspaper reports of 1989 showed that thousands of Egyptians were leaving Iraq to return to their home country partly due to the bad treatment they received by Iraqis.

Many Iraqi soldiers had become prisoners of war in Iran. There was sometimes news of them from other prisoners who had returned home having been released.

Mohammed's friend was one of the MIA soldiers, his family had not heard from him; he had been sent to the front during the war. His family would go and visit any returning soldier they heard about in the hope of finding someone who had news of their son. One day they sent us the wonderful news that he had returned home at last, thin and ill, but at least he was alive. Many others were not so lucky, for years their families yearned for news of them.

Halabja Massacre (1988)

Just before the war ended, we heard of another tragedy that took place in the Kurdish town of Halabja in the north of Iraq. I was listening to the radio, tuned in to the BBC World Service, as I did every day. The announcer was saying that news was just coming in of a massacre that had taken place on 16th March 1988.

As more information came in, we learned that Saddam Hussein had ordered a chemical attack on the town along with 40 other villages in the area, in the early hours of the morning. 5,000 Kurdish men, women and children were massacred and over 10,000 were maimed, blinded or suffered irreversible long-term nerve damage.

It was unbelievable. Running next door I informed my neighbours what I had heard. The local news would censor any hint of this occurrence, none of the populace would be aware unless they tuned into the foreign news channels. We did not have satellite TV at that time, just the good old BBC and Voice of America to provide us with the latest news bulletins.

The apparent reason for the attack, which we did not know at the time, was that Iranian forces had occupied Halabja 48 hours before, which was an important centre for the Kurdish resistance in their struggle for autonomy.

The full horror of the attack, known as 'Bloody Friday', unfolded over the next days and weeks. It was reported that about 20 planes had been seen flying over the area at 11.00 local time. They flew in groups of seven to eight planes per group and about 14 sorties, dropping a chemical cocktail of nerve gases which included mustard gas, sarin, tabun and VX. 75% of the dead were women and children. Horrific photos emerged of the Kurdish villagers lying in the streets where they had fallen, women holding their babies as they died, it was genocide.

Halabja was not the only place to be bombed by the Iraqi air force. There were about 40 other villages, Zardan, Saedasht, Marivan, Baneh & Saqqez to name a few, in the region, but it was the most heavily populated. 182,000 Kurdish from those villages had been killed by Saddam's vile attack on his people.

The attacks, part of the al-anfal campaign (Spoils of War), were supervised by a cousin of Saddam Hussein's called Ali Hassan al-Majid, his nickname became 'Chemical Ali'.

Ahmed came and told me that some of his friends in the airline had been taking in orphans from Kurdistan, those innocents who had lost their entire families in the chemical attacks and were only babies. He believed we should also take one or two perhaps.

I was against the idea; my children were enough of a handful, and I was sure that things in the country, which had not been stable for years, would eventually go from bad to worse, what would happen to such children if we had to return to the UK? I could not get their passports made to leave. According to Iraqi law, adoption is only for Iraqis and the adopted children may not be taken abroad.

It was a sad decision and I truly wished I could have helped, the event itself is something I will never forget. How Saddam got away with this murderous act without being brought to account by the West was unbelievable.

You can read more about this event here: *Iraq's Crime of Genocide*, Anfal Campaign Against the Kurds ISBN 0-300-06427-6

Cease-Fire (1988)

I was in the kitchen making lunch when I heard an almighty racket going on outside. Stepping out I found myself in the middle of what looked like the gunfight at the OK corral, pickups and cars were driving past the house with guns blazing. My neighbours were standing outside, some of them shouting out *'Alhamdullilah, Alhamdullilah ya rub'*, which meant *'thanks be to you oh Allah'*.

It was the 8th of August 1988, and we had just received the news that Iraq had accepted a cease-fire with Iran.

When Faris came home he took us all out to drive around the area. We saw youngsters filling up plastic bags with water and throwing them on the cars, something which would probably have got them shot by the irate drivers previously, but today everyone was happy. The long war was finally over and we could look forward to starting to live a somewhat normal life.

On 20th July 1988, a ceasefire was accepted by Iran and the long eight-year war finally ended.

The following year on the anniversary of the 'victory' Saddam opened a new monument in al-Zawra Gardens. This was a sculpture in the form of giant hands rising from the ground forming an arch each holding a 141-ft sword designed by Saddam himself.

The commission was won by Iraq's top sculptor Khaled al-Rahal. Sadly he died in 1987 before the monument was completed and his fellow sculptor, Mohammed Ghani al-Hikmat, completed the monument.

Plaster casts of Saddam's forearms and hands were used in the design. The sculptor took an impression of one of Saddam's thumbprints to use on one of the thumbs of the monument.

The Swords of Qadisiya is the official name of the monument. It forms a trio in Grand Festivities Square along with the Monument to the Unknown Soldier (1982) and the al-Shaheed Monument (1983).

The Swords of Qadisya, Baghdad, Iraq

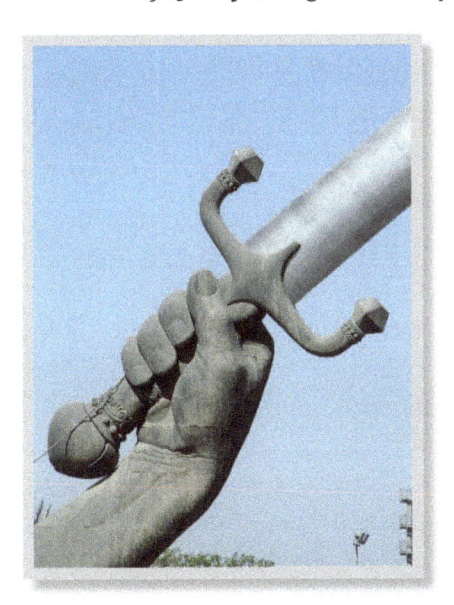

Close up of the hands of the Qadisya Monument modelled by Saddam Hussein

Chapter 28

Uday Hussain

It was in 1988 that Uday, Saddam Hussein's eldest and most volatile son, beat to death one of his father's bodyguards.

His name was Kamil Hanna Jajo, he was an Iraqi Christian of Assyrian heritage. Uday was upset because Jajo had been instrumental in introducing Saddam to Samira Shahabandar, who became his second wife.

At a party thrown for Suzanne Mubarak, the wife of the Egyptian president, Husni Mubarak, on 18th October, Uday picked up a club and used it to bludgeon Jajo, finally finishing him off by shooting him with his pistol in front of the horrified guests.

Mubarak of Egypt later described him as a psychopath.

Fedayeen Saddam (1995)

In 1995, Uday began to recruit young men from all regions in Iraq into his new Fedayeen Saddam organization. The 10,000-15,000 strong recruits were more of a paramilitary force, not part of the regular army. Uday used them for his many resources which included smuggling and suppressing his many opponents. They were well paid although never receiving an official salary, and well looked after with certain perks such as new cars, private hospital treatment. Their status meant they could coerce or apply force to remove property from the public, bully boys in uniform.

Disappointingly for them, government officials were off the table, dire warnings would be issued in case any of them got any ideas in that quarter.

Programmes on the TV showed them in their black uniforms singing about themselves. The programme would show them on training manoeuvres carrying the latest AK-47s, RPGs and AKM. They had black Darth Vader style helmets which, it is rumoured, were styled on Star Wars. Uday was quite a fan of that programme.

Youngsters from the age of 10-15 were recruited into the Ashbal (Saddam's Lion Cubs). Their training included infantry and small arms along with the usual brainwashing to keep them loyal to the Baathist cause.

We managed to avoid such recruitment, which was a great relief for us; sometimes it pays to know certain people and grease their palms.

Iraq Referendum (October 15th)

The girls and myself were taken by Mohammed to vote for Saddam in his referendum. There were no other parties on the ballot paper. We entered the building. My wish was to vote against him but that option was taken out of my hands when Mohammed took the papers, which had, "Do you approve of Saddam Hussein being President of the Republic?" from us and marked all of them yes! It was disappointing, he explained later that we were being watched, anything other than the 'yes' vote might get us into trouble. The country was run on fear, fear of reprisal, fear of punishments of the worst kind for petty misdemeanours.

I heard a rumour later that a dog had been seen running around town with '*La La Saddam*' (no, no Saddam), written on it in black paint.

The next day Izzat Ibrahim al-Douri announced on television that the President had won 99.6% of the vote. 8.4 million people are too terrified to say 'no'. I wonder who the other 0.4% were and what happened to them?

1990

It was just two years later, in August 1990, when we were just getting back to a normal life, such as it was, we heard the news announced on the radio that, in a surprise attack, early in the morning of August 2nd 1990 Iraq had invaded its neighbour, Kuwait.

Just a short time before, Saddam had shipped 100 brand new Mercedes 200 series cars to some of the top newspaper editors in Jordan and Egypt along with a 50-million-dollar payment to Egypt's Husni Mubarak for purchase of '*grain supplies*'.

Over 100,000 Iraqi troops had moved tanks, helicopters and trucks across the border. Within the next hour, the tanks were attacking Dasman palace, the royal residence.

The Amir had fled into the Saudi desert, but his private guard and his younger half-brother, Sheikh Fahad Ahmed al Sabah, had stayed behind to defend the royal residence. According to an Iraqi soldier who later deserted from the army, the brother was shot and killed, then his body was placed in front of a tank and run over.

It was the worst possible news. After eight years of a devastating war that had left the country heavily in debt, what could have been the thought in the head of Saddam to invade Kuwait?

Some people said it had been brought about through a Kuwaiti delegate at a recent meeting who had insulted the Iraqi delegate causing him to walk out. Others said that Iraq owed a great deal of money to Kuwait from loans procured during the war with Iran, and refused to pay it back. There was talk that Iraq accused Kuwait of siphoning off its oil using cross border slant drilling.

A few days after the invasion it was announced by Iraq that Kuwait had been declared the 19th province of Iraq.

The neighbours I spoke to, agreed with me; we had been through enough war and troubles for so long, here was yet another trial to go through.

By January 1991 the invasion of Kuwait had entered its 6th month. Iraq had complete control over all Kuwaiti institutions, such as hospitals, ministries, colleges and the media. The television station had ceased operations, the radio spewed out retransmitted Baghdad radio programming.

In the same month Saddam modified Flag Law No 6 where he added the Takbir, *Allah is the greatest* in Arabic script between the stars purported to be in his handwriting.

There was a growing threat after UN Resolution 678 in November 1990 which sanctioned allied forces attacking Iraq if it did not withdraw immediately.

There was an active Kuwaiti resistance that set off car bombs in public places such as the public square in Hasawi district which resulted in the deaths of four Iraqi soldiers.

Anyone suspected of being a member of the resistance was publicly executed, their bodies then being brought and thrown in front of their family home.

A well-known woman Kuwaiti resistance fighter was **Asrar al-Qabandi,** a thirty-three-year-old Bahraini. Her mutilated and newly executed body was dumped at her home two months after she had been detained by the Iraqi authorities on January 4th 1991.

Families were instructed not to remove the body for burial until two days later.

On January 21st Bob Simon, a CBS reporter along with three of his colleagues were captured by Iraqi army forces near the border of Saudi Arabia and Kuwait. They were detained in Baghdad until 2nd March then released after a high-level campaign internationally.

The UN Security Council issued 12 resolutions demanding immediate withdrawal of Iraqi forces from Kuwait, nobody took any notice.

The occupation took seven months, and the forces of Saddam Hussein looted the vast wealth of Kuwait. There were many reports of violations of human rights.

In August, Saddam decided to capture any foreigners who were in Kuwait and Iraq and hold them as human shields. It is believed that about five thousand hostages were rounded up. Many others managed to hide for the duration of the occupation.

On August 2nd 1990, a British Airways plane, BA Flight 149 en route to Kuala Lumpur, landed at Kuwait International Airport, as normal, for refuelling. The passengers and 18 crew members disembarked for the one hour stop-over. They ended up being escorted from the terminal by the Iraqi army and taken by bus to the airport hotel.

The captain, Richard Brunyate later escaped with the co-pilot. They hid, only going out at night for food, dressed as Arabs. Some of the other passengers and crew were also helped to escape by Kuwaiti resistance fighters.

There were British, American, Russian and Japanese among others working in Iraq who found themselves rounded up to be human shields, some with their families. Many of them were taken to the Al Mansour Melia hotel, on the banks of the River Tigris in Baghdad, others were taken to al-Nasiriya power station near Baghdad.

Saddam hoped his 'human shield' would deter the US from attacking Iraq so he placed many of them in the strategic military and industrial areas in Iraq. On August 23rd Saddam was shown on TV with some western women and children. He told them, "Your presence here and other places is meant to prevent war."

On September 27th Iraq threatened that any diplomats hiding Westerners in their embassy would be hung. Many influential people came to Iraq to request that Saddam release hostages. King Hussein of Jordan, Yasser Arafat, Sir Edward Heath, Mohammed Ali (boxer). It must have pleased him to get so much publicity.

On October 29th we heard that all French hostages had been allowed to leave Iraq.

In Baghdad, at that time when we went out in the car, we saw many people of different nationalities sitting on the street. They had travelled the long journey from Kuwait in a variety of vehicles, a distance of 670.0 kilometres. Most of them had brought as much of their belongings as they could carry. They sat on the floor trying to sell some of their furniture or other personal items to make enough money to feed themselves and their families before hopefully being repatriated back to their own countries.

Most of these wretched souls were camped out on the corniche along the river near the Indian Embassy, sleeping on the street, some with their families.

The Iraqis living in the houses nearby brought them food, water, blankets and let them use their facilities. People were so kind at that time and many helped with whatever they could. About half the population of Kuwait which included 400,000 Kuwaitis and several thousand foreign nationals fled from the country.

The Indian government arranged to evacuate over 170,000 Indians who had been working in the country, along with their families, over the next 59 days by flying almost 488 humanitarian flights out and back to India.

We did not support the invasion of Kuwait, therefore we did not want to purchase anything from these poor people even though it might have helped them financially, but we did help them by offering them some money and food whenever we could.

I thought it might be bad luck to have any of their items in my home. Some people took advantage of their plight. I watched one man bargaining with one of the families for some simple personal items that they were selling, he was trying to get a better price from the Indian father who was selling his wife's gold bracelets.

We began to see all sorts of goods from Kuwait stocked in the shops, items that we had rarely seen in Baghdad. Popular breakfast cereal, such as Kellogg's Cornflakes, Cadbury's chocolate, Nescafe coffee, magazines in English, like Woman's Own and Burda (which had once been available in Baghdad in the years before the war), such delights were much appreciated by us, ladies.

Shirley came over one day and we went to the local shops in the evening. Stopping by the confectioners she wanted to get a packet of cigarettes so I stood outside and waited for her. I noticed her pick up a bar of Cadbury's chocolate and leave the shop. Grabbing her arm, I walked her quickly away from the shop while saying, "*Don't look back, he might have seen you take it and come after us.*"

She stopped dead in her tracks, "*Hey, I paid for this chocolate along with my packet of cigarettes!*"

I was suitably put in my place.

Chapter 29

Food Rationing (1990)

The sanctions and a rationing system were imposed on Iraq in August 1990 after the passing of the U.N resolution 661.

The resolution declared that states should not deal with Iraq by importing or exporting any goods from Iraq or Kuwait. No weapons, no transfer of funds for dealing in such goods. Humanitarian aid was the only commodity allowed to enter Iraq.

Later, in September 1991 the Oil for Food Programme was initiated. Iraq was allowed to sell US$1.6 billion worth of oil to fund it. This took another five years to implement, a long time waiting for those families with little income.

The import of goods was heavily regulated by the U.N but of course, there is more than one way to skin a cat. Corruption amongst, not only Iraqi officials but U.N, was rife as always and it is well documented that bribes were known to be received.

I could not fathom the thinking involved in an embargo (although this has been denied) of essential items like detergents being banned in case they would be put to another use. Perhaps the powder could be used to make cleaner weapons of mass destruction.

The electricity was often cut off for hours in the day, but 193 *'electrical consultants'* each received a salary of $15,000 a month to make sure the supplies remained constant.

Oil-for-Food Programme - Wikipedia

We as a household were told to register each person belonging to the family, whatever the age. We were given rationing tickets which we used to collect the monthly rations from a nearby distribution centre, where we received a certain amount of food, provided by the government, from the local grocer, just near our home.

I remember the supplies contained 50 kilos sack of flour, 50 kilos sack of sugar, one large tin of ghee, washing liquid, a tray of 30 eggs (for a family of 8 of us for one month), bars of soap, packets of cigarettes (only Ahmed smoked), loose leafed black tea. In the beginning, we also got a couple of frozen chickens.

Due to the sanctions the prices of these items in the market were sky high so we did not often shop outside. If I wanted to make a cake for the children, five of the precious eggs would be sacrificed. My cakes were large, usually containing one kilo of flour, akin to a 'pound cake'. They were so tasty that they would not last long, getting gobbled up by the children. The two frozen chickens I received I cut into four pieces each and cooked, then froze the pieces to be used in meals later.

Ahmed was still able to get some supplies locally so we were not starving, it was just an inconvenience. I had to plan each meal carefully so there would be no waste. The poor cats did not get much to eat. They were therefore forced to fend for themselves.

Misha, the cat, became adept at climbing up the neighbour's wall to get to his pigeons. I even saw him one time in the garden eating a rabbit (not one of ours). Those cats would fight viciously over the small leftovers of rice and sauce that I could afford to give them.

Before this rationing, we would often socialise with our neighbours, going to sit and drink tea, eat cake and have a natter, putting the world to rights. When the rationing came in, neighbours did not have enough supplies to entertain visitors, so if we went to drink tea with them, we would take some tea, sugar with us. This was considered shameful as, according to Arabic culture, the typical visitor was traditionally welcomed warmly and served only the best the house could offer. We stopped visiting a lot, staying at home to avoid embarrassment.

According to news reports of the time, half a million children died in Iraq of malnutrition due to the sanctions imposed on the country.

Madeleine Albright, who was the UN Ambassador at that time, in an interview by Leslie Stahl in 1996 regarding the 500,000 children who it was reported had died of malnutrition during the embargo was asked, *"Was the price worth it?"* to which she replied, *"I think that is a very hard choice, but the price, we think, the price is worth it."* She came across as cold-blooded and hard as nails.

She had been brought up a Catholic but had Jewish roots, her parents had converted from Judaism in 1941. Albright declared that she had not known of her Jewish heritage. Is such a link ever forgotten?

The rationing is still in place at some level TODAY 2021 some 31 years later.

Samer Goes to School (1989)

Getting Samer to go to school, which he had just started at 4 years old, and which was just near the house, was a nightmare. He hated it, we would both stand at the gate to our house, him refusing to budge, me gradually moving from gentle imploring and offers of bribery to threats of dire consequences if he didn't go. It usually ended up with me almost dragging him across to the school opposite and pushing him inside.

In 1989 we had a trip to the UK. We stayed at Majid's house in Petts Wood for the summer school holidays. Three months is a long time to keep children entertained. Faris and Mohammed had stayed behind with their father so I enrolled the girls into a local school.

Once again, I decided to stay in the UK but chickened out when I noticed my eldest daughter, who was 13 at the time, making friends with a young lad at her school. Worrying that I might not be able to cope with the situation I reluctantly decided to return to Baghdad. There at least life was more under the eye of the family. Here in the UK I would be on my own, the last thing I wanted was for my beloved girls to succumb to the pitfalls of drugs, booze and peer pressure. Glue sniffing was all the rage that year, the television showed the most explicit adverts warning about it. Add to this the fact that my two sons in Baghdad were really upset when I mentioned that I was thinking of staying in the UK, so back we went.

Ramadan

Each year Muslims fast for a lunar month during Ramadan.

I first knew of this just after I had been married, in London. Ahmed explained the concept - no food or water to be consumed during the hours of sunrise to sunset, no lewd thoughts, no sex.

If a woman had her period she was not allowed to fast until it was over. The days lost could then be done throughout the year, once a week. Another way to make up for these days was to give alms to the poor.

I had been to Regent's Park mosque to say the Shahada to accept Islam and wanted to experience the period of fasting for myself. I was working on the switchboard in a ladies' college near Regent's Park, so I decided I would attempt the fasting and see how I got on. Ahmed did say that I was allowed to chew gum. (I discovered later that this was most definitely not allowed).

I was quite proud of my achievement in managing to fast for the entire month, happily chewing away at my gum, until the new crescent moon appeared and it was Eid. I was not so happy when I learned that my chewing of gum during this month wiped out my entire effort. I was consoled by the thought that I was innocent in my attempt and God would consider that, hopefully.

In Baghdad Ramadan was a social event. After the day-long fast, families would gather to have Fitur or 'breakfast' at dusk. Often visitors would be invited to partake in the 1st meal of the day, watching the clock as the minutes went by until it was time to eat.

All sorts of dishes would be prepared to start with water, juice, yoghourt drink (made with yoghourt, water, ice and salt) and dates. Soup would be next, usually lentil soup. Then some dishes of rice, different sauces of bamya (ladies' fingers with lamb in tomato sauce), spinach, chicken teshrib with chick-peas. There would be far too much to eat. After fasting all day the stomach was quickly full, so what remained would be kept for the early morning meal.

After the main meal, everyone would sit around relaxing, chatting about their day or watching the special entertainment programmes for Ramadan on the TV while drinking tea and eating some fruit or dessert, usually baklava in various forms.

Despite the lack of regular meals, not much weight was lost although the body went into a state of keto as most people had that awful keto breath. Partaking in lots of sweets curtailed it.

During the rationing phase, the meals were more frugal. It was a struggle to provide the selection of dishes that families had enjoyed before rationing. During that phase, it was known that people did lose weight.

Ramadan, being a lunar month, lasted for about 30 days and ended when the new crescent moon was sighted by Saudi Arabia. Sometimes this was a day over 30 or a day under 30, according to the lunar calendar.

By the end, everyone was just waiting for the sighting to be announced. Some countries even announced it early which made everyone around me moan at the thought of waiting for yet another day.

After the long fasting of Ramadan came the four-day long Eid holidays called Eid al Fitur, or Eid al Adha (sacrifice) which came after the annual Hajj to Mecca. New clothes would be worn, everything from the underwear to the sock and shoes. The children showed off theirs to their friends. Later that day or the next we would visit the family to show off ours.

Ahmed brought back clothing for the children from his trips and I would keep them, especially for Eid. Sometimes I would get a new outfit, rarely to my liking and mostly the size would be either too big or too small. One costume he brought back for me from Bangkok made me look like a fisherman's wife and was made of Lycra.

The holiday was mostly for the children; the adults were happy to see their offspring in their new attire.

One year I purchased some white cotton material from the local street vendor and made Faris a top and trousers, something like an Indian Kurta. He looked smashing in it and said it was the best thing he had ever had.

Off he went to the main house to greet his father for Eid. On the way some of his friends congratulated him on his new attire. Proudly he went up to his father, wished him a happy Eid and kissed his hand. Ahmed took one look at him and could not help but make one of his snide remarks about his clothing. Faris became very upset. When he came home he took off his new outfit and would not wear it again.

Each year the time for Ramadan changes, there is about a ten-day difference. So over the years I have lived in Iraq I have seen it move from winter to summer. Summers were the worst, enduring the long hot days without being able to quench a thirst made us all grumpy and tired. A good trick we found was to sit in the garden drenching ourselves with the cool river water from the garden hose.

Chapter 30

First Gulf War (1991)

The news we were hearing, was not good. Each day the situation seemed to get worse. Now we were hearing about a 'coalition of countries' getting ready to 'carpet bomb' Iraq after the United States made a move to enforce the U.N resolutions.

Some of my neighbours passed by and asked me what I thought of it all. *"Um Faris, what is going to happen?"* - as if I was the oracle of Baghdad. One lady stopped by as she was passing and asked me to get in touch with 'Mr Blair' to tell him, *"We don't want any more bombs."*

"He's not my uncle," I replied.

I advised those that could, to move out of the city and go stay with relatives in the provinces, nobody took me seriously. I heard remarks from many people that, *"the US will not bomb us; we haven't done anything to them or Britain. No, it's just threats,"* and they blithely went about their daily business.

In December, knowing what was coming, we arranged for Faris to fly to the UK on one of the last flights out of Baghdad. Hamid's eldest son, Majid Ridha, was living in Driffield, Yorkshire. He had a pizza shop and had offered Faris a job. Due to him being born in the UK, Faris had a British passport, there was no problem getting him out of the country. We did not want him drafted into the Iraqi army and ending up in a box on top of an orange and white taxi like many of the men of the family.

It was quite emotional saying goodbye to my eldest son, I did not know when or if I would see him again.

Ahmed took him to the airport, then he returned and got us all into the car so we could go and futilely wave to the plane as it was taking off, in the hope that Faris would see us.

Bakuba

Ahmed's brother, Hamid, had a farm outside the capital in Baqubah. It consisted of one farmhouse with two rooms, a kitchen and a bathroom. There was a separate room that was used for the seasonal workers who came to harvest the dates and other fruits.

After a meeting with the family, it was decided that we would all take our families and stay there before the start of the bombing. All thirty or so of us arrived at this small house. The men were given one room to sleep in and the women and children were given the second room.

There was electricity on the day that we arrived, water, plenty of dates from the thousands of date palms, plenty of oranges, tangerines, lemons and grapefruits from the trees on the farm. Chickens, ducks and geese were running here and there, their eggs would come in handy. Everyone brought their supplies with them, along with clothes, blankets, mattresses, cooking pots and anything else deemed necessary.

It was January 17th, 1991, two days before my birthday, I wondered what sort of birthday I would have. I did not have long to wait to find out.

That first day we sat and drank tea, ate sandwiches and chatted about the latest gossip and news like we were on holiday. The children enjoyed the freedom of running around chasing the animals, eating fruit straight from the trees. One of the geese kept chasing Samer around. It was the first time I realised that those birds have serrated beaks, just like rows of little teeth.

One of the young boys found a rifle in a hut which the guard of the farm used to sleep in. It was loaded and the boy came out and aimed it at some of the children. Thankfully his fingers did not reach the trigger mechanism and as soon as he was spotted with the weapon it was swiftly removed from his hands by one of the men. I shuddered to think what may have happened if it had gone off.

Uprisings

We heard about uprisings beginning in the South as returning soldiers rebelled against the government.

Hamid, the eldest of Ahmed's brothers had a son, Faris, who had been called up to fight in the invasion of Kuwait. We had not heard from him for some time and that news was worrying his parents.

Some of the women went off to use the shower room before bed on the first night, it was the only night that we had water. I decided I would have one the next day instead and was very disappointed when I went to the bathroom to find no water coming from the taps.

We settled down on our mattresses arranged on the floor and drifted off to sleep. It was at 2.38 am, that we were woken up by the almighty sounds of, what we thought were bombs dropping on us. The anti-aircraft batteries were firing at the jets screaming overhead. The sound was deafening. Most of the women began running around like headless chickens screaming and imploring Allah to save them.

This set the small children off and they started crying. I managed to calm some down but the din was something else, so I went and opened the door and windows on the pretext of relieving the pressure just in case.

Mahmoud's wife, Hamid's wife, Ali's wife all went and sat by the open door-opened, in case the glass windows shattered from the pressure of the 'bombs'. Hands up to heaven as they shouted out for Allah to save them and their children, I noticed the men were not included in their prayers.

Operation Desert Shield had begun.

Jets took off from Saudi Arabia and aircraft carriers in the Red Sea and the Persian Gulf to attack military targets in Iraq and Kuwait at 2.38am Baghdad time. 27 Hellfire missiles destroyed radar sites, 100 Hydra-70 rockets knocked out the anti-aircraft sites. This opened up the way for U.S Airforce F-15's and F-111 Ravens to enter Iraqi airspace.

The bombing went on for hours, it was recorded as the longest bombing raid in history.

We did not know at the time, not until we turned on the taps and no water came out, or the light and no electricity shone forth, that the first things the allies bombed were the utilities. The electric, water and telephone exchange, Iraq's Central Bank were destroyed.

When the night passed, and we were still in one piece, things on the farm began to calm down. One of the brothers had been informed that the noise we heard, and thought were bombs, was only the anti-aircraft, so not to worry, nobody was dropping anything on us. It was all on the poor souls in the capital, Baghdad.

The next day I watched as three U.S jets came along in unison, then they split up one going left and another going right, one straight ahead, to continue dropping their loads on and around areas of Baghdad.

I read an article years later that reported that propaganda leaflets in Arabic had been dropped hoping to sap the Iraqi's will to fight. Little did they know that the Iraqi army had already lost any will to fight. Those guys just wanted to get out of this war anyway they could. We all understood that the U.S was a force to be reckoned with. The Iraqi soldiers had a belly full of wars, enough to last a lifetime, they sure had no stomach for it anymore.

The following day the men went to the local market to purchase as much bottled water as they could find. They also bought sacks of rice, ghee, sugar, tea, tins of Nido milk powder and anything else that might be needed so we could stock up, who knew how long this would last?

They purchased large cooking pots for us women to cook in, flour for making bread, paraffin, matches and anything else that they could get their hands on.

One item we found embarrassing to ask for was sanitary towels. This was an awkward item to request, but Mohammed and Hussein were not fazed by it and were able to purchase some discreetly.

During the day we each managed to make ourselves useful by cooking various meals on top of four Aladdin kerosene heaters. It kept us busy and took our minds off the conflict raging elsewhere.

The men still got first dibs at the table. I found it most annoying to have to wait for my turn along with the rest of the females.

Mahmoud's wife, Nuryah, his second wife, (his first had died a year or so earlier), had just recently miscarried her baby. I got quite angry when some of the other wives began to make nasty remarks about her being lazy, saying she was not helping them cook or clean. I reminded them of her condition, that she needed rest and if they would like her to do a chore where she was sitting down like peeling potatoes or picking the stones out of the rice, then she could do that, but to back off and have some compassion. That seemed to work but the women were quite a handful, always finding something to moan about or find fault with.

Children, being young, were happy to just go and look for eggs from the free-range chickens. Some of them laid their eggs in the weirdest places like on top of a log, or under a bush. The older children were adept at collecting and hiding the eggs and secretly passing them on to their mothers to be cooked and eaten later. Samer had found a chicken that laid her eggs on an old tractor. Nobody else knew about her and he kept her precise location quiet. He would go each day to see if she had laid. She was reluctant to give up her eggs and would peck at him, so he found that if he peed on her she would move away and he could collect them up.

Eggs were important breakfast items. We were a large family, children were always hungry so the eggs came in handy as a quick meal. Sahar had managed to collect quite a few eggs which she hid in one of the cupboards. When she came to add some more to her collection she discovered they were gone. She later discovered that her stepbrother, Bassman, had watched her hide them, then sneaked in when no one was around and stole them. There was quite a row over that, but she never got them back. It caused yet another ruckus which almost came to blows between them both.

The kitchen was claimed by Amina as her domain. Nobody was allowed to go there without her permission, she designated herself as the Queen of cooking. One of the older cousins, Hussain, was not happy with her rules. He got up early one morning, got his eggs and began to cook them in the frying pan. Woken up by the smell of cooking, Amina jumped up, ran into the kitchen as if there was a fire, saw him at the stove and went crazy. Waving her hands in the air, she shouted at him about using the kitchen, etc. He, in turn, waved his fork at her with eggs on it, taunting her to do something about it. He was a big lad of about 20. Knowing she was no match for him, she turned her back and left.

Amina was a real troublemaker. She even let the wild dogs of the farm attack each other by throwing them bones.

The second night we found it easier. We were initially woken up by the barrage of sound from the anti-aircraft systems. Then we turned over and drifted off to sleep again. Subsequent noisy nights were calmer, things were just fine, no need to worry. It amazed me later that we could sleep through such chaotic nights with ease.

There were nights when I would dream, I still remember two of those dreams all these years after.

Dream 1

In this dream I was watching a circle of men. Inside the circle lying on the floor in a foetal position, naked, was an old crone. The men were throwing dice, the prize for the winner was the old crone.

When I woke up and thought about it, I interpreted the dream as meaning that the old crone was Iraq, the men betting on her were the nations currently bombarding us.

Dream 2

In this dream I was walking into a vast warehouse. As I looked I could see hundreds of large white plastic containers on the floor, the type that had once been filled with kilos of yoghourt, as far as the eye could see. Each container held a severed head.

It was some years later that I thought this dream was a sort of epiphany of what was to come when ISIS took over the country and beheaded many innocents.

Bathing was a problem, no water, no shower. I discovered a vertical water pipe outside the house which had a tap fixed to the top. Putting my thinking cap on I thought that the water would not be able to travel up, so why not bend the pipe horizontally, maybe then some water would flow, it was worth a try. I got one of the older boys to slowly push the pipe down to the ground, then we turned on the tap, yes there was a trickle of water!

We got a piece of flexible garden hose and attached it then dug out a hole in the ground where we could place a vessel. The water slowly dripped and filled up the vessel. It might take a while, but it was better than nothing, the water could be heated up and used for our ablutions and cooking. It was better than the nearby river water which was very muddy.

I managed to make some flatbread dough. As I did not have a recipe to hand I just threw all the ingredients that I thought would make up the dough-mainly flour, water and salt, to make a soft dough which I then rolled out thinly before cooking in a hot frying pan placed on the top of a paraffin heater.

We adapted to the situation we found ourselves in very well, it was like we were on holiday and having picnics each day.

I had brought one of my cats with me. He was quite happy to wander around the farm, wary of the vicious guard dogs that roamed there at night. Early one morning I was woken by Amina letting out a shriek, she had been woken up by an awful smell near her head. When she sat up and looked, she discovered the cat had shit on her blanket during the night. What a place for the cat to find to relieve itself!

She took the blanket out and managed to soak it thoroughly in whatever water she could manage. A little bleach was added which faded the lovely bright colours of the pattern. She hung it out to dry, then folded it up ready for the night. Now, we both had the same blanket which Ahmed had brought home from one of his trips. Mine still had the brightly coloured pattern but when I went to get it and spread it on my mattress, I saw that the colour was faded. She had switched the blankets when I was not looking. Marching over to her with it I asked for my blanket. "That is yours, Um Faris," she replied in all innocence. "No, it is not, mine has a SAFETY pin in one corner, this one does not, check the corners," I replied. Looking at the corners of the blanket she found the pin that I had placed there before I had arrived. Glaring at me she handed it over.

After years of experience, I was wise to her tricks. It was bad enough that when Ahmed came back from his trips abroad with the airline, he always went 'home' to the main house to let her unpack and take her pick of any goodies, even though I would write out a list for him to get, leaving me and my children with the leftovers. This time I was one step ahead of her.

Early one morning we were woken up by someone shouting and dogs barking madly at the large gates to the farm. These were kept locked at night-time in case thieves broke in and attacked us.

Getting up and running outside we saw Faris (Hamid's son who had been in Kuwait). He was at the gate, exhausted after travelling from Kuwait mostly on foot, then he was lucky enough to get a lift in a lorry. When we opened and let him in, he collapsed in a heap, the dogs had not recognized him and tried to attack him, but they were kept away.

When he had gotten some food and rest, he told us how his unit had been dug in outside Kuwait City. At first, they had rations which consisted of cans of broad beans, white beans, thick pasteurised cream, rock hard dark brown loaves of bread, cans of tuna and water. These items were to be shared out amongst the officers and the men, but these soon ran out and all they were left with was some dried mouldy bread and no water.

Their officers abandoned them one night. The men realising that there was no reason to stay and die for a lost cause, began to make their way back to their homes, walking along the 'highway of death' so named because the allies rained bombs down on the retreating Iraqi army killing scores of those souls who had given up the fight and just wanted to get back to their homes and families.

He had managed to reach his home in Baghdad. Finding it empty, he asked one of his neighbours, who informed him that they had left for Bakuba. He then continued on his way to the farm, sometimes walking, other times getting a lift from passing vehicles.

The poor young man was traumatised by the experience for many years later, suffering from severe migraine headaches and bouts of depression which I suspect was a form of PTSD.

During our stay at the farm, Sindus managed to twist her ankle. We took her to the local clinic. They had no x-ray available, so it was bandaged up tightly and she was given pain killers.

I noticed the fruit trees were slowly becoming devoid of fruit. Too many people helping themselves were depleting them. By the time we left, they were bare.

When the air bombardment stopped, I believe it went on for about 100 hours in total, the ground assault started. The road from Kuwait City and the border town of Safwan, Highway 80, continued to Basra in the South. It was later known as The Highway of Death. As the Iraqi army was retreating, in compliance with UN Resolution 660, the US strafed and pummelled the column for several hours using Bradley fighting vehicles, Apache attack helicopters and artillery units using DU weapons on the Iraqi forces who had Kuwaiti hostages and civilians with them.

Highway of Death – Wikipedia

We decided the time had come to return to Baghdad. The farm had become a hotbed of bickering women constantly arguing about mundane and petty things. *This one eats too much bread, that one has not helped with washing up* or similar. It was time to get back home. We prayed that there would not be any further bombardment.

Ahmed had received word that the airline was cutting its losses and he, along with many of his colleagues, was being made redundant; yet another nail in the coffin.

We did discuss travelling to Iran or Syria but soon gave that idea up. With our large family it would have been a nightmare and we had no friends or family in those countries.

So many people demonstrated against Operation Desert Storm throughout the world. It was amazing to hear about how much people cared - if only the British and US governments could be swayed by the people. In the UK millions marched in anti-war protests but Margaret Thatcher was unmoved. She played a powerful role in pressing the US President, "This is no time to go wobbly, George," during a telephone conversation on 26th August.

In Spain, 2 million Spanish workers downed tools and went out onto the street in protest for two hours. They were demanding a stop to the war and the recall of three Spanish warships that had been sent to take part.

An extensive account of the many battles that occurred during the Gulf war can be found on Wikipedia, here is a link:

Gulf War - Wikipedia

Chapter 31

Back from Baquba (February 1991)

Arriving back home we discovered that a rocket had fallen a couple of streets away from the house. Much of the glass in the windows of our home had been broken and the upstairs door to the balcony, made of steel, had buckled from the blast wave. We were so grateful we had not been home to experience that terror.

The house was full of dust, ants, cockroaches and of course, rat droppings. It took a major clean-up job to get things cleared up. Um Zainab came by and began to help us with the work. The broken glass of the windows were boarded up until we could get someone to come and replace them.

The girls and I went walkabout in the area to see how the rest of the neighbours had fared. Most of our neighbours had left the city when we had, but those who stayed said each minute of the bombing, they thought, was their last. It must have been horrendous for them, especially the babies and children who became traumatised in later years by loud noises or fireworks and guns being fired nearby.

As we walked along, we came into the street just behind us, which had taken a direct hit by one of the missiles. The sight before me was surreal. Trees lining the street and in gardens were all festooned with various articles of clothing, thrown out of wardrobes and cupboards and up into the air by the blast, to land on the branches of the trees, like early Christmas decorations. These items had come from houses destroyed in the attack. I stood looking at the scene in front of me, mesmerised.

Due to most people being out of the city there were few casualties but for these citizens returning to find their homes had been destroyed, it must have been devastating, losing everything in that instant.

We, along with the rest of the country, had no electricity, no gas for cooking, no petrol and very little water. What we did have were two

Aladdin heaters and some kerosene. The Aladdin heater was a round metal affair. It had a steel handle to carry it from one room to another. A circular wick made from fibreglass or cotton draws up kerosene from a tank in the bottom. When the wick is lit it heats up the kerosene turning it into a gas which is then burnt. This heats the air. The height of the flame is controlled by adjusting the exposed wick length. To turn it off is simply a matter of retracting the wick to snuff out the flame. The heater produces low levels of carbon monoxide and nitrogen dioxide, a deadly gas if confined within a room with no windows or doors open.

My neighbours, in the winter, could often be found huddled down near their Aladdin SOPA *(paraffin heater)* to get warm. Sometimes with their babies, doors and windows were shut to keep the cold out. It was no wonder children were often sick with chest problems, colds or viruses.

We had a large round metal tray with holes in it on one of our heaters. This tray fitted into the round space left by removing the cover. A kettle filled with water would usually be kept bubbling away on this tray most of the day, for making tea in the winter. There were often accidents in homes where someone, usually children, had run into the heater, knocking the kettle off and getting scalded.

Sindus herself had quite a shock when she had backed onto the metal tray as a toddler, just after having a bath and waiting to get dressed. Her back received quite a long circular burn mark which I applied the appropriate cream to.

Now I needed this Aladdin more than ever to make flatbread or place my cooking pot. It was a tedious process and took longer than usual to cook on, but it was better than nothing and many a meal was produced during that dark period.

Our house was lit by kerosene lamps. I did not like open flames with so many children around, so would not have lit candles except one, placed in a ceramic bowl in a safe area of the toilet at night so the children could see their way if they needed to pee. A bucket of precious water was kept inside the toilet for washing and flushing purposes as the cistern would take about two hours to slowly fill up from the trickle that was getting through. Our luxury of having daily baths became weekly, with just flannel washes in between. I wondered if this is what it had been like during WW1?

Due to the petrol and gas shortage, some enterprising soul discovered that, if a gas bottle was empty of gas, it still contained some liquid gas. The canister could be opened and this liquid propane could be poured into the petrol tank of a car, good for a few kilometres. What it did to the engine was anybody's guess. Our car did not seem to suffer any lasting damage from this procedure.

One thing I remember about those days after the bombing of Baghdad was the amazing sunsets we experienced. Instead of the usual yellow and orange sunsets, we were treated to purple and pink colours as the sun went down, it was quite a sight to see. This lasted for quite some time over the next few weeks.

Another sight I noticed was, the disposal of food waste in my area had become much less. There had previously been mounds of food left in various corners of the street for the local dogs or cats to eat or a man who used to come in his cart and horse and pick it up each morning.

Amiriya Shelter Bombing (13th February 1991)

Not long after we had returned from the farm, on February 13th 1991 we heard that an air raid shelter in Amiriyah had been hit by two GBU-27 Paveway III laser-guided 'smart bombs'.

After watching the news on TV which showed the severe damage caused, we learnt 408 people were reported to have been killed, unknown injured. Many of those who had managed to survive the attack were later interviewed on Iraqi TV. They mentioned that normally they would not go to the bomb shelter. They preferred to stay at home during an air raid but Saddam's police had come to their houses the day before the attack and told them there was going to be an attack and they must go to the shelter. They could not refuse to go. Many families took their belongings and left their homes for the shelter. They could not understand why, why would the Americans target a place where people were seeking refuge?

According to the Americans, the shelter was being used as a command post for the Iraqi military though no evidence was ever found of this. Herding people into the shelter was perhaps a way of trying to prevent it from being targeted.

I won't get into the 4th Geneva Convention of 1949, suffice to say that the US ignored all parts of it whenever it suited.

A mother who lost all eight of her children, Um Ghada, has made it her life's work to create a memorial for the shelter and serves as its principal guide. I could not even begin to imagine the pain and grief that a woman, or any mother for that matter, would go through losing all her children.

Not much is said these days about the attack and the dreadful loss of lives, no movies have been made about it, no books written (as far as I know). There was however, a play produced entitled *9 Parts of Desire,* written by Heather Raffo which has a character called Um Ghada and mentions the bomb shelter.

Nine Parts of Desire (Play) – Wikipedia

Soldiers who had managed to return from the front seemed broken in both mind and spirit. We heard things about the retreat that made our skin crawl such as the U.S ground troops using earthmovers and ploughs mounted on tanks to bury thousands of the Iraqi army alive in the trenches beneath tons of sand.

In the streets of Baghdad, a dreadful sight to be seen was soldiers who had nothing to eat, no place to stay, no money, sometimes not even shoes for their feet, sitting on the grounds with their hands out, begging passers-by for a few coins to buy food to survive.

Chapter 32

Mother Teresa (1991)

In June 1991 Pauline telephoned me at home, *"Mother Teresa is in town; shall we go and see her?"*

Mother Teresa had landed at the RAF airbase in Habbaniya, 89 kilometres from Baghdad. Arriving in a specially chartered U.N plane she was the first air traveller to arrive in Iraq after the Gulf War. Her mission was to establish an orphanage house in Baghdad.

News had quickly spread that she was to attend mass at a church in al-Za'franiyah district of Baghdad. Pauline and some of the other ladies were going, one of them gave me a lift and I accompanied them with my youngest son, Samer.

We went to the church and attended the mass, then waited in line for Mother Teresa to pass by. As I saw her coming along, I became quite emotional. She was such a tiny, frail-looking woman who had done so much for the poor in countries all over the world, her reputation preceded her.

As she passed us by, she reached out and placed her hand on Samer's head, blessing him, then moved on. Whenever he was naughty after that day, I would admonish him with, "Hey, behave yourself you have been blessed by Mother Teresa!". It was a special moment for us all and one that we will always remember.

Her orphanage is still there in Baghdad, it is called Sisters of Charity of Mother Teresa in Baghdad. I recently came across a story while researching for this book, about two of the orphans from that orphanage. Two baby boys were left outside the orphanage in Baghdad. They were both born with some level of underdevelopment in their anatomy. One had severely underdeveloped arms and legs due to chemical warfare. He was named Ahmed. The nuns took them in and raised them until an Australian humanitarian worker Moira Kelly took the boys back to Australia. She later adopted them both.

In Australia, she arranged for Ahmed to have surgery for his arms and legs. Prosthetic limbs were fitted which enabled him to take part in sports. After successfully playing Aussie rules football for his school, he then took up swimming. He broke a world record breaststroke event at the 2010 Australian National Championships. He broke another world record in 2011. At the 2019 World Para Swimming Championships in London, he won a silver medal in the Men's 150m Individual Medley SM3.

Birth Defects

The US used depleted uranium in their ordinance. If this enters the body, through open wounds or fragments of DU it can cause both radiological and chemical toxicity affecting kidneys and lungs. Many cancers - breast, lymphoma, bone cancer - can be linked to DU exposure.

Eight years after the war, DU was detected in urine samples taken from Gulf War veterans.

It was not only the US but the retreating Iraqi army that polluted the environment when they set fire to Kuwaiti oil fields. The soot raining down caused a toxic carcinogenic cloud covering the country.

There were 18 military US bases spread all over Iraq. From 2003 – 2010 instead of incinerating their waste, they burned it in massive open-air burn pits. Some of these were close to cities spreading the pollutant soot on the wind, contaminating the water in the rivers and fields. The air was thick with smoke, many people began to experience breathing problems like asthma and later COPD and lung cancer. This practice was declared illegal in 2010, but the damage had already been done.

Babies born in Fallujah exhibited high rates of mortality and birth defects. In September 2009, 170 children were born at Fallujah General Hospital, 24% of whom died within 7 days, 75% of those exhibited deformities including children born with two heads, no head, a single eye in their foreheads or missing limbs. The comparable data for August 2002 recorded 530 births of whom 6 died and only one of whom was deformed [54]. Environmental campaigners believed that either white phosphorus or DU, is a major if not only, cause of birth defects [71]. Birth defects in Iraq and the plausibility of environmental exposure: A review | Conflict and Health | Full Text (biomedcentral.com)

In Erbil a study conducted for the years 1990-1999 showed the rate of birth defects per 1000 live births, compared to western countries, to be 23.9 per cent.

A report from WHO stated that Iraq in 2004 had the highest rate of leukaemia than any other country.

Hawra

When Ahmed's brother, Salah's daughter was born in 1996 she was diagnosed with Downs Syndrome. Salah had been a soldier for a time during the Iraq-Iran war.

Other members of the family had children with birth defects. Aunt *Sohama* on his mother's side, had a son, *Baha,* born with spina bifida. After the Gulf War her eldest son, *Humam,* got married, his wife gave birth to a child with one eye in the middle of its face, like cyclops. The poor baby did not live longer than 48 hours.

Some of the news on TV at that time would show reports of babies born with two heads or without a body or a head, one even resembled a fish.

No sensibilities were spared, you got to see the whole thing, it was awful.

The south of Iraq, Falluja, Anbar and other provinces had a high rate of abnormalities. There is even a Facebook page where these unfortunate babies are displayed, some born as late as 2012, with the most horrific abnormalities which they do not survive. Knowing their foetus might be born abnormally, sometimes a blessing in disguise was when they suffered a miscarriage, as they were unable to have an abortion - it was against the law.

Iraqis accepted the birth defects as being a part of the ongoing environmental damage that affected their lives due to the wars.

There are high rates of certain cancers today, an ongoing legacy of the US bombs.

Here is a verse I wrote just before the Gulf War.

What's in a War?
April 1992

We're going to be zapped
So, I hope you've all packed
And reserved a seat on the bus
There isn't much hope
We've had plenty of rope
Put round our necks to hang us

"We've got lots of oil," hear poor Tarik* wail
"You can have as much as you need
We'll do what you say, though there will be some delay
Let's leave it until after the Eid!"

The Yanks are all drooling
At the thought of a bombing
A battleship is now on the way
I really can't moan
But I shall miss my phone
It's the only thing that brightens my day

Wait! There's been a reprieve
Go on – now you can breathe
America's looking elsewhere
Now its Libya's turn
To suffer and squirm
As the U.N try sanctions out there.
The U.N can be tough
But that's not good enough
When it's BUSH*pulling the strings

Why, we can't afford meat
Or shoes for our feet
Or those birds that lay eggs and have wings

I speak now of chickens
That cause finger licking
The leg is the part I like best
Some like the breast
Though I'd settle at best
For the livers, spread out on some toast.

- Tarik was Tarik Aziz, minister for oil in Iraq at that time.
- BUSH was George W Bush, USA president.

(Written during a time in Iraq where the USA had decided to bomb and impose sanctions)

Chapter 33

Radio

The radio was a lifeline to the outside world. I listened weekly to Alistair Cook's 'Letter from America', perhaps a music programme, sometimes a play-which was only possible if the children were at school, otherwise they made too much noise.

In December 1980 I heard the news from the BBC that John Lennon, of the Beatles, had been shot dead in New York, in 1981. A 35yr old lorry driver named Peter Sutcliff was arrested, his crimes were 13 women murdered during 1975-1981.

It was in 1992 that I heard Annie Lennox singing her new single 'Why'. It seemed to say everything I wanted to say to Ahmed, so I recorded it onto a tape along with some other songs that he liked and gave it to him. I thought I could somehow send him a message as I was unable to get through to him any other way.

Annie Lennox - Why Lyrics | AZLyrics.com

Although he did listen to the song several times when he played the tape, the meaning of her words did not get through to him. Our boat was not just sinking, it had sunk a long time ago and we were drowning each day.

Speaking English

Since their birth I had spoken to my children in English. I wanted them to have the asset of two languages and thought they would pick up Arabic soon enough.

So, listening to the radio, especially any children's programmes, entertained them. I would tell them stories before bed, making the tale up as I went along. I wish now that I had written these down. I cannot remember them at all, except one where the character was a princess who was very fat and wanted to lose weight. She heard of a local chef who cooked such wondrous dishes that his clients lost weight but stayed healthy. In the end, they fell in love and got married, after she had lost weight, of course, so she could fit into her wedding dress.

I had some children's books that I had brought from England, they had been well used through the years but when the children were little, they would ask me to read some of the stories about Cinderella and her Prince Charming, or Rumpelstiltskin, Toad of Toad Hall, Grimm's Fairy Tales and others.

I would place stickers on items around the home with the word written in English, 'FRIDGE, COOKER, DOOR, WINDOW, CHAIR, KITCHEN' to help them with their spelling.

The only drawback with speaking only English at home came at the time they started school. The two older boys did not have any problems as in their time the schools taught quite a lot of English subjects and the teachers were not so stressed with the state of the country.

Sindus had the most difficulty, not understanding what the teacher was saying to her when she started pre-school (rawtha). On her very first day she could not answer the teacher's question, she was slapped for being insubordinate.

To give him his due, when Ahmed heard about it later, he went to the school and threatened the teacher with violence if she ever laid a finger on any of his children again.

By the time the girls started school, the system was already failing. Not wanting the other children to have that problem in the future, I asked Ahmed to speak to them only in Arabic so they would learn more. This helped a lot when Suzanne and Betul started pre-school.

Miss Afifah

Miss Afifah was a teacher to all the children throughout their school years, she taught Art and Domestic Science. The classes were mixed in primary and the boys and girls sat together.

Miss Afifah treated the girls better than the boys. For some reason she did not like boys and would always lose her temper with them. On one occasion, in the 6th class primary, she became annoyed with one of the

11-year-old boys. He was from Palestine. Coming up close to him as he sat at his desk, she told him to stand up. Shouting at him she poked her finger at his chest with her face inches from his. This young boy lost his temper, grabbed hold of her fingers and twisted them hard, breaking two of them. Some of the nearby children intervened, pushing the boy back down into his seat before he could do any further damage.

Her cries had been heard by other teachers who came running to see what the fuss was, she was taken off to the hospital. The police were called along with the boy's parents and he left the school. Nobody saw him again after that.

She taught all my children, they still remember her and told me she was very old when she retired from teaching.

Pear Incident

One evening we were invited to Hamid's house for dinner. Ahmed took us in the car. After dinner, as it was a warm evening, we sat in the garden under the fruit trees.

Hamid had Seville oranges, as did most gardens in Iraq, apples and pears. His wife plucked a pear from the tree, put it on a plate and gave it to me. I took one bite, it was too hard to eat so I left it on the plate. When we left, my throat began to tickle. By the time we got home, the tickle was an itch. The hour was late and the children were in bed when I felt my throat closing up, suddenly I could hardly breathe.

I called Ahmed, when he saw me struggling for each breath, he took me in the car to the local hospital. I was seen by one of the doctors on duty who examined me. His diagnosis was a severe allergy to something. He prescribed an antihistamine. Unfortunately, due to the late hour, none of the pharmacies was open. We couldn't Google in those days. Ahmed said he would get the prescription in the morning, despite my distress.

At home, I found if I sat up straight my breathing was slightly better, but I could not lie down. I remembered that I had a bottle of antihistamine liquid in the fridge for the children whenever they got bitten by mosquitos and the area swelled up. Going to the fridge I grabbed the bottle and swallowed the entire contents. Slowly I felt the swelling of my esophagus recede, within 30 minutes I was almost back to normal.

I remembered that pear. For years after that I blamed it for my reaction, refusing to eat pears believing I was allergic to them. It was only later, when I thought about it, that I remembered Hamid had his fruit trees sprayed with pesticide each year, the pear had not been washed before I ate it.

Iraq Television

Television programmes in Iraq throughout those years, unless it was Ramadan, were not very entertaining. There were few foreign programmes.

The children would settle down to watch the regular cartoons in the afternoon which were all dubbed into the Arabic language. I used to sit with them as I liked to learn more words in Arabic. I could follow quite a lot of the plot now as my Arabic language had improved, except when it was classical Arabic, which I found difficult.

Cartoons

Throughout my years in Iraq, I have watched many cartoons, movies, series on TV. Our lives were very simple - no nightclubs, no social clubbing like the Alwiyah Club, Sports Club, Engineers Club etc. We stayed at home so the TV was our censored window to the rest of the world.

Bashar was a popular cartoon about a little bee who had lost his mother. In each episode he had such adventures flying around meeting other insects to make inquiries, searching for his mother. I believe he eventually did find her.

The Blue Submarine, originally called **Space Carrier Blue Noah**, which was my favourite - each week the captain would take the sub here and there. In the end, he died, which was so sad for us all, both the children and I got upset. I thought it was a bit weird having a death in a children's cartoon, even weirder that I, a grown woman, looked forward to watching it. It was better than nothing.

Adnan and Lina which was popular was a prophetic Japanese anime cartoon dubbed into Arabic. The original name was **Future Boy Conan**. It was based on **The Original Tide** by Alexander Key and had its premiere in 1978.

The series prophesied the end of mankind. The hero Adnan had supernatural abilities, Lina had a mysterious grandfather. There were no more humans on earth and the sea was full of shipwrecks from a devastating world war. They were the only survivors of that war.

Lady Oscar was another anime cartoon shown on TV. This was very popular with my girls. Lady Oscar was a strong, beautiful and quite obviously gay. Woman, she dressed like a man and she fought like a man for her rights in each episode.

Grendizer, a Japanese super robot anime series and manga. The opening chorus in the Arabic version was sung by a popular Lebanese singer called Sami Clarke.

Sindbad – Sazoki – Sally – Georgie -Sally -Sandybell – Majid (Pinocchio).

Most of the cartoons were Japanese anime manga.

We loved the cartoons more than the movies, and still find them interesting to watch today on YouTube.

Fridays we would usually have an Indian movie with subtitles so I got to know quite a lot of actors in Bollywood like Raj, Shashi, Shammi of the Kapoor family, in their escapades.

Most of the women singers had the voice of the popular voiceover singer of the time, Lata Mangeshkar or her sister Asha Bhosle, the male voices would be of Kishore Kumar. They all sounded the same no matter which actor was starring in the movie.

Some weeks we would have Egyptian movies with those wonderful actors and actresses - Omar Sharif, Faten Hamama, Yusef Fahmi, Ahmed Zeki (he was one of my favorites), Ahmed Ramsi, Adel Eman, a comedian with many funny movies, born in 1940, still alive today, I believe. Most of the others are long gone. Some of my favorite Egyptian movies -

A Dinner Date (1981), with Suad Husni and Ahmed Zeki-very dramatic plot.

al-Haram with Faten Hamama (1965) black and white, very dark plot.

Cairo Station (1956) Farid Shawky, Hind Rostom, black and white serial killer plot.

I learnt how to recognize the Egyptian, Syrian and UAE accents from those movies on TV.

Foreign movies would be heavily censored, kisses or nudity of any kind would be cut. Sometimes I would wonder what was happening. At the hint of a pucker the actors would suddenly be transported elsewhere, it became hard to follow the plot and I would be left wondering what had happened.

One evening a movie was shown on Iraqi TV which broke all the protocols - it had everything, sex, kissing nudity. As soon as I saw something was happening I got into a panic, jumped up and stuck my bum into the TV to block the view from the children. Unfortunately, I had not turned down the sound so lots of moaning and gasping could be heard before I realized what was happening and turned the TV off.

The next day we saw a news bulletin, many people had called in to complain about the movie. One man said his children had been watching it (at 11 pm) and he was shocked at the content. The producer responsible for airing the programme came on TV to apologize saying it had "slipped through their censors." Many of us thought that it was an experiment to see if they could get away with showing such a naughty movie and what the public would say about it.

In 1987, at 7 pm the streets would be emptied and silent, no phone calls made, no visits. It was time for the latest US fantasy-drama series on television, *Beauty & The Beast,* starring Ron Perlman as Vincent and Linda Hamilton as Catherine (with Arabic subtitles). I learnt later that one of the writers and producers of the show was George R.R Martin (Game of Thrones).

All my neighbors were hooked on to it, the latest episode would be excitedly discussed the next day over glasses of chai. Tote bags and various other items carrying the photos of 'Bincent' appeared for sale in the market, probably made in China.

Spanish telenovelas were a new thing. They were shown in 1992 and onwards, safe as houses to watch. Iraqis loved dramas and love stories so these were very popular and the talk of the town. They were of course dubbed into the Arabic language.

Marielena (1992) Spanish. Starring Lucia Mendez as Marielena and Eduardo Yanez as Luis Felipe. The plot was about Marielena, a humble girl who comes to work in the house of Luise Felipe and his wife. He is a handsome guy and so the inevitable happens, she falls for him and gets pregnant. It ran for three years and 226 episodes.

Guadalupe (1992) Spanish. Starring Adela Noriega and Eduardo Yanez.

Plot summary: Guadalupe is the illegitimate daughter of a rich man who refused to recognize her until he died. Feeling sorry for her he left her all his money but cut off the rest of his family. She moves into her new estate (where the relatives are living) and meets Alfredo. She cannot decide if she is in love with him or hates him.

Both dramas were filmed in Miami, Florida by Television Espanola (TVE).

VHS Tapes

Ahmed's nephew, Majid, was studying in England. He recorded programmes for us onto VHS tapes. Ahmed brought them back from his trips to London. Of course, these would not be censored.

We never knew what was recorded. When the tape was played, I would sit with the children and we would watch together. We did not have a remote control for the TV, so I would be jumping up, like a Jack-in-the-Box to block the screen at any hint of naughtiness. It became easier when we changed the TV for one with remote control.

In one movie the actor and actress began disrobing, anxious that no nudity would be seen by the (still young) children, I moved the tape on hopefully to a safer spot and not land in the middle of a humping session. One of my children asked me why they were taking their clothes off to which I replied, "Time to do the laundry, dear." They were still small enough to accept my remark as the truth in the innocence of youth.

Sometimes the TV adverts would be left on the tape. Being for products in the UK, it was a novelty for us, we enjoyed them. I am sure nobody in the UK did.

In one comedy programme, the comedian did a spoof about an alcoholic drink called 'Disarono' where he was at a party. He and a woman were having the drink, he turned to the woman and said, "Fancy a shag?"

My children did not understand that word, so they asked me what it meant. *"He asked her if she wanted a biscuit,"* I said, smooth as silk. I only hope in later years they did not ask any of their English friends if they fancied a 'shag' while passing them a packet of biscuits.

We looked forward to those movies and comedies which we would watch as a family. Ahmed was not a fan of movies or television unless it was a documentary about wild animals. His favourite ones were Crocodile Hunter with the late Steve Irwin, Jacques Cousteau with his wonderful films about the sea and the creatures therein, and many other series about wildlife.

Sometimes in the afternoon when the children were at school, I would invite my neighbours, Haibet and Ilham, to come and watch a VHS taped movie. Closing the curtains to block out the bright sunlight we settled down with our 'chai' and cake.

The ladies preferred the horror movies best. *Texas Chain Saw Massacre (1974)*, had us all laughing at the antics of someone chasing screaming people around the forest with a chainsaw and eventually cutting them up, it was ludicrous.

Our afternoons were precious times for us and we enjoyed each other's company without the raucous children.

Chapter 34

New Neighbours

One day I noticed a pick-up parked opposite my house, new neighbours! They were from India and the husband worked for the Indian Embassy which was fairly close to us, on the river.

Once they had settled in, I took a cake that I had made and went across to introduce myself. The family consisted of four - two girls, mother and father. We became friends over the next few years and my daughters would often spend time with their girls, one was called, Sweety. I cannot remember where they came from in India but I do remember that they were Sikhs, the father wore a turban.

Our other neighbours were friendly towards the family, although they were considered idol worshipers.

On one occasion as I was passing by their house, I noticed a man sitting in the front garden. He had a long grey beard so I assumed that he was their grandfather coming to visit. I waved hello as I passed and went on my way. Later on, that evening, when I saw the mother I asked her how long their grandfather was staying. She looked puzzled,

"We have nobody staying, Sandra."

"Oh but I saw an elderly man sitting in your garden this morning, he had a long grey beard," said I.

She started laughing, "Oh dear Sandra, that was my husband, he had unrolled his beard!"

I was embarrassed, to say the least.

When they had to return to India they left their address with me. I did write for a while until the postman was drafted into the army so we no longer received posts. I lost their address in the following years but I would love to be able to contact them again.

Saddam's Birthdays

Each day we would have news reports on TV of Saddam Hussein going about his daily chores, sometimes part of a meeting with foreign dignitaries. In his early days he felt safe enough to travel outside the country.

Ahmed went as a flight engineer on a flight out of Baghdad to take Saddam to Russia. He returned with a massive Russian made television. It must have weighed all of 15 kilos and had a mahogany case. It was all valves and knobs, there was a diagram of the various parts. We watched it for years until it eventually died. Nobody we asked thought they could repair it even though we showed them the diagram (which was in Russian). So, under the stairs, it sat for a couple of years until Ahmed was able to get someone local to repair it, no easy feat with the Russian language signs on it. That was the last time we had it fixed. When it broke down again it got stored away and replaced by a more up to date model.

Saddam had declared that 28th April was his birthday, I seriously doubted that he even knew when he was born but nobody would dare to argue with him about that. The celebrations were always televised for his loyal subjects to watch. Each year his birthday cakes would be larger than the year before, various groups of school children came to his palace to sing his praises - he was always shown with children of various ages- they would appear more and more frantic as they tried to impress him. The tiny tots would always get my sympathy as they stood and spewed out a poem written just for him which must have taken their parents weeks to drill into them.

Saddam would always be impeccably dressed in his bespoke suits flown in from Europe. He liked to wear white. There is no doubt that he appeared as a handsome man, Satan in a suit, a despot who would turn on anyone he felt was about to betray him or already had. The cake would be cut, sometimes with a sword, but I never saw him eat any of it, in case it was poisoned. His enemies were everywhere.

There were often political programmes shown on TV, one programme recorded in July 1979 showed Saddam at one of the first meetings he had called of the Baath Party. Having just taken over the presidency of Iraq from Ahmed Hassan al-Bakr, who had been given an ultimatum, resign or face the consequences. Knowing that he had no choice al-Bakr complied.

He was forced out so that his deputy, Saddam, could take over. Saddam quickly convened an assembly of leaders of the Ba'ath Party on July 22nd.

The RCC secretary, Muhyi Abdel Hussein, had at the time, objected to handing the reins to Saddam. For this he had been taken, tortured and his family threatened; he 'confessed' to taking part in a plot, he was coerced with the promise that he would come to no harm, into giving details of a Syrian-based plot against the Iraqi regime, naming 68 co-conspirators. Nobody knew if there was any evidence to support this.

As I watched the programme later I saw Saddam, no emotion, no heart, no empathy, no soul, sitting calmly smoking one of the fat Cuban cigars gifted to him by Fidel Castro, who had given up smoking and was once quoted as saying, *"The best thing you can do with this box of cigars, is give them to your enemy."*

As each name was read out during the meeting, guards moved forward and began to hustle those named out of the hall. Ten names at a time were announced. Looks of horror began to appear on the sweating faces of those party members sitting in the meeting, as they realized that, soon, perhaps, their name would be the next one called out. Some of those being roughly removed called out praises to Saddam as loud as they could in the hope of being spared. They all knew their end was near. Their families would face the fact that their loved one would not ever return alive, perhaps they would never know where their bodies lay.

By the following month, hundreds of members of the Ba'ath Party, anyone who had ever muttered a word against Saddam at any time, were executed - this was a purge.

After that dreadful day, those who were wise kept their mouths shut, even at home, in case their remarks were leaked, sealing their fate.

Rumours flew around of swimming pools filled with acid in one of Saddam's palaces where unfortunates ended up or members of the Baath Party disappearing without a trace along with their families. The air was heavy with suspicion of neighbours who may be spies for the government.

Everyone had to become a member of the Baath Party, my two sons did when they were older, Samer was too young at the time.

Improving Baghdad

In the early days of his presidency, to improve his status with the Iraqi people, Saddam improved the infrastructure of the country's roads, building highways to replace the dirt roads, started up health clinics with doctors and dentists, paediatricians, baby clinics for vaccinations, hospitals and improving many areas of the capital.

1979 saw the launch of his anti-literacy campaign. Many Iraqis, especially those farmers and peasants living outside the capital with little or no schooling, could not read or write. The legislation called 'law number 92 for a national comprehensive compulsory literacy campaign' was passed for all 15-45 years old to attend classes for literacy. A fine of $30 or jail terms for one week was announced for any person who refused to attend the classes, which took place in the evenings at schools all over the country. Iraqis who claimed they could read but were then found to be illiterate would be fined the equivalent of $90 or jailed for one month. There were programmes on the TV each day for those who were unable to leave the home. I found them especially useful, settling down with my exercise book and pen to learn the language.

The United Nations Educational. Scientific and Cultural Organization awarded Iraq its annual prize that year for the most effective literacy campaign in the world.

To this day I can still remember some of the sentences such as '*Rashid Y'azrah, Zeinab tamal*', (Rashid plants, Zeinab works), and can read some Arabic after a fashion although I have forgotten much of it. I also found it useful when the children began 1st class at school and I could look through their Arabic reader books. I learnt some of the Alphabets and simple words such as Nar, Noor, Dar, Door (fire, light, house, houses).

Arabic is written from right to left, although the numbers are written from left to right. To start reading a book or magazine you started from the back and worked your way forward. Even today I tend to forget when I pick up an English magazine and start reading from the end.

Ahmed often swore at the TV when his president appeared. I worried that the children would at some time convey this to their peers or teachers. The results of that would not bear thinking about. Although I warned him so many times, he continued.

When the children were little and Ahmed was absent if Saddam came on the box, I would appear to be enthralled, calling the children over (they were little and did not understand) to, "Come and see Amo (Uncle) Saddam, he is on TV, my how handsome he looks!" He would be Uncle and at other times Baba (father) Saddam.

Although this charade made me feel sick at times, knowing of all the truly dreadful acts he had committed and how many people's lives he had destroyed, I knew that those were dangerous times, so I played the game.

Talking to anyone about events which we all knew about, even on the telephone, which we suspected was bugged, was a dangerous business. When I spoke to my friends regarding any current affairs we referred to anything to do with Saddam as 'Mickey Mouse' cartoon episodes in code.

Ahmed had no qualms about discussing current affairs with all and sundry, especially when he was sitting in a taxi, the driver would become his sounding board. If anyone had reported him to the secret police, then he would have been in some serious trouble. It was a good thing that he had many friends in high places. If there was ever any trouble they would drop him a warning beforehand.

Chapter 35

Yasmin and the Television Incident (1983)

Amina's TV got broken, the wheel attached to the leg of the table had become loose rendering the table unstable.

Yasmin was sitting watching a cartoon with her half-brother, Basman. She started laughing at something in the cartoon. Basman must have thought she was laughing at him. Getting up, he pushed the TV, knocking it over and breaking the screen. At that moment Ahmed came in from shopping carrying a watermelon. When he saw the broken TV he threw the watermelon onto the floor and started shouting. Basman blamed Yasmina, her father grabbed her and threw her down the hard, stone stairs.

She was 4 years old. It was a miracle that she did not get broken bones or worse. Sindus, hearing her screams, ran to her and quickly managed to grab her and drag her out around the back of the house, away from her father's rage. She was afraid he would come and hurt her more.

Ladies of Baghdad (1987+)

One day in 1987, while Ahmed was away on one of his flights, I received a telephone call from one of his friends, also a pilot in Iraqi Airways. He noticed my Arabic was not good and asked me if perhaps I was the maid (many of the Iraqi Airways personnel had maids usually from the Philippines or other Asian countries).

I informed him, somewhat irritably, that I was Ahmed's wife, and was English. Then he switched to English, he was unaware that Ahmed had two wives, he was quite surprised, *"I have someone here who is also English,"* he said, *"would you like to talk to her? It is my wife, Pauline?"* From that moment my time of being without any English-speaking friends in Iraq ended.

Pauline was, and still is, a wonderful, outgoing, funny person. She invited me to one of her 'gatherings' at her home, where I was introduced to many other English-speaking ladies. They would meet up in homes once a week, taking turns as hosts when they could. During those invitations, I met Helen A, Linda, Pat J, Diana al-S, Moira, Christina and Christine J, Ann G and Shirley, Carol, Camilla, Eileen, Mary x2, Janet B. The ladies came from all areas of the UK.

Each week at a meeting they would bring a homemade dish for the table and we were often delighted with the sight of various delicious home-baked cakes, pies and savouries. We exchanged gossip, both from back home and various local titbits, magazines for various knitting/sewing patterns etc.

One Christmas, as we were sitting together one of the ladies said, "Let's sing a Christmas Carol!" We all looked at each other because suddenly nobody seemed to be able to remember one. I piped up with, *"There is a green hill far away, without a city wall."* Everyone started laughing and one of the ladies reminded me that it was a song of the crucifixion of Jesus and not his birth, oops!

I was given my very first set of Agatha Christie books by one of the ladies who was returning to England for a while. They proved useful later when Shirley and myself would mark out passages on various ways to kill our husbands, all good fun at the time.

The children gradually got to know one another and would sit together chatting or playing outside in the garden. My youngest, Sam, was about two years old at the time I first met the ladies and I was still breastfeeding him, so the ladies were amazed when they saw me feeding him. Pauline nicknamed me 'earth mother' as I had more children of younger ages than anyone else.

Some of the ladies, Helen and Diana, if I remember correctly, worked in the Baghdad International School. Most of the other ladies stayed at home with the children. On some weeks we have been invited to other groups that one or more of the ladies attended. Tuesday, there was what we called the 'German' group of ladies, on another day there was an American group.

Those gatherings were what we looked forward to each week, a change in our housebound lives, a chance to speak in our language, listen to jokes and anecdotes. They were a lifeline for many of us.

Shirley was from Tottenham, London. We liked each other from the start. She had five sons (lucky lady) and lived with them and her husband in Yarmouk.

When Faris learnt how to drive, no test pass was needed, just a bribe to the office that issued licenses, he was able to take me to see these friends (only with quite a lot of persuasion).

Shirley's son would also bring her to mine sometimes for the evening, although the back doors to his car sometimes got stuck and if he brought us home in it, I would have to climb into the front seat to get out, this usually ended up with us in stitches.

One evening, I invited her to dinner, the dessert was homemade apple pie and custard. Not having a small enough pot to make the custard in, I improvised and made it in a metal jug on the gas cooker.

Just as I had served her the piece of apple pie, and she had the jug of custard in her hand, I heard one of the children outside say, "Hi papa". Ahmed had turned up! He had a habit of making 'remarks' and I knew if he saw that metal jug with custard in it there would be one of the 'remarks'.

I grabbed the jug out of Shirley's hand and rushed into the kitchen with it, hiding it away. She, poor thing, did not have a clue what was going on and sat there with her apple pie plate still in mid-air. I later apologized for grabbing the custard out of her hand and explained the reason after he had gone.

Her husband, was just as difficult, for want of a better word, as mine. She had lots of anecdotes about him, one being the time when she was cooking a meal. Usually, she would cook rice with tomato, known as 'red rice' with this particular dish, but he wanted white, plain rice. Unfortunately, he neglected to tell her. As she was not psychic, she cooked the usual red rice. When he came to the table and saw the colour of the rice, he picked the platter up and threw it on the floor in a fit of pique. Later I wrote a poem about it for her.

On occasion, to amuse ourselves, we would get out one of the children's large map of Iraq and plotted out a route of how we would run away with all (13) of our children, which roads we would take, through Iran or Turkey, by bus or by train. Looking back now on those times it seems hilarious.

Quite a few of the ladies had similar problems at home with their men - arrogant, overbearing, controlling. I am sure they had similar thoughts at some point in their marriages. Some of the ladies even managed to escape from their spouses and back to the UK.

One lady told her husband that their washing machine was not working properly, so each week she would take a bag of 'laundry' over to one of her English friends until she had enough clothes to pack up and leave.

After friends had mentioned certain incidents to me, I would often write them a little verse about it to cheer them up.

When we moved over to the main house we had a larger home with parking space and their cars could be parked out front on a Saturday. Ahmed told me that a man he knew in the local police had come and asked him why I was having these meetings with 'foreigners' each week, it was being noticed and he should warn me to be careful. I had visions of myself and my friends being tortured then strung up in Tahrir Square accused of spying for the British - it was quite worrying.

Ahmed arranged to go and see the local head of the Emin (secret police). He told him that we were all mothers from the UK meeting up with our children each week, passing out knitting patterns and recipes, all very innocent. We missed our families back home and he assured them that he popped in on us from time to time, so we were given the green light, phew!!

At Pauline's house one weekend we decided to try the Ouija board and call up spirits. The children cut out letters of the alphabet, which we arranged as per instructions (one of the ladies had a vague idea of the procedure) with an upturned tumbler placed in the middle. None of us had a clue at what we were doing, we had seen it in movies so followed that plan. The lights were dimmed and a candle was lit, then we sat around the table and one of us, I think it was Pauline, said the magic words, "Is anybody there?". After a few moments of nothing happening she repeated the message, "Is anybody there? Speak, we are waiting." Nothing happened even though we all concentrated very hard, the spirits were not biting tonight. As we looked at each other someone said, "The spirits don't seem to be around, they must have gone to the pub!" Laughing, we gave up our only foray into dabbling with the Ouija, turned the lights back on, blew out the candle and got back to chatting.

One of our friends, Janet, was married to a Sabean Mandaean. They lived near the local mosque with their family. Sometimes on a Saturday, the topic of religion would be brought up.

One week I happened to mention to Janet the Prophet Mohammed (PBUH) was mentioned in the Bible. I had a bible and got it out to show her the verses;

Isaiah 29:12 *And when they give the book to one who cannot read, saying, "Read this," he says, "I cannot read."*

John 16:12-15 *"I still have many things to say to you, but you cannot bear them now. When the Spirit of truth comes, he will guide you into all the truth, for he will not speak on his own authority, but whatever he hears he will speak, and he will declare to you the things that are to come. He will glorify Me, for he will take what is mine and declare it to you. All that the Father has is mine; therefore I said that he will take what is mine and declare it to you."*

Janet promised that she would look these verses up in her Bible when she got home. When we next met she confirmed the verses were the same. Shirley and I then decided it might be useful to research the Holy Bible and the Holy Koran to do comparisons. See what similarities we could find in each book. This took us some months but we both felt that the time spent on it was educational, to say the least, and we learnt quite a bit about both religions. It made a change to plotting escape routes!

Note: Our children grew up together, they still keep in touch with each other today. Many are now married with families of their own so we still get news of them all. I have started a group on WhatsApp for us to chat with each other, also a Zoom call most Wednesday afternoons, it is called Ladies of Baghdad.

School Holidays

The school holidays were the worst times, for the long hot summer holidays of three months, the heat of above 50 degrees C would be unbearable. We only had ceiling fans in the mushtamil which were kept on night and day. They did not help much. It was a relief when the water cooler was eventually brought and attached to one of the windows upstairs. That however was not without a tale in itself.

When Sindus was a year-old, Ahmed arranged for us to go on a trip to the North of Iraq along with his newlywed brother, Saidi, and his wife. We were going to travel by car. It was a long journey of about six hours along uneven and pot-marked roads. Although I requested that we leave early in the morning to escape the heat of the summer this fell on deaf ears. I was worried about taking a one-year-old on such a journey, we had no air conditioning in the car and she might become overheated.

We set off in the afternoon, the heat was intense. After about an hour my prayers were answered in the shape of a stone hitting our windshield and shattering it causing us to turn around and go back home while we got it fixed.

We stopped halfway and had something to eat in a café. I was not feeling too well with nausea. I was not aware then that I was carrying my twin girls.

Saidi's wife spoke little English and my Arabic was not so good. Coupled with my intense shyness with strangers I kept quiet most of the time. This caused her to believe I did not like her. She complained to her husband that I was aloof and unfriendly which in turn made Ahmed take me to one side while he admonished my 'bad behaviour'.

Sindus took up most of my time. When we were in a shop one day she spied a soft toy in the shape of a rat of all things. It was grey, dressed in red trousers and a waistcoat. She grabbed it off a shelf as we were passing and would not let go. Ahmed bought it for her, it was her comfort for some years until she put it inside the cooker at home. When I put the oven on to cook something it got a bit scorched.

Back to our visit to the north of Iraq. The food was wonderful, there was so much fruit of all kinds. Peaches, apricots, grapes, I saw walnuts growing on trees-who would have thought it!

All too soon our visit was over and we returned to Baghdad. After a while Saidi's wife and I became friends, I explained how shy I was, I think she understood.

Air Cooler Incident

Ahmed decided to put an air cooler on the upstairs balcony. He had purchased a large one from the market. When it arrived at the house, somebody had not done their measurements properly, it would not go through the front door. There was a large palm tree right outside the front door and his brilliant idea was to get a pulley and rope to heave the air cooler up to the level of the balcony. The pulley was a metal one and not very big, the air cooler was extremely heavy.

I watched him banging a nail high up on the tree and through the pulley. The children were all standing around the base of the tree, curious as to what was happening. I knew what was going to happen, any fool could see it, turning to him I said, *"Ahmed, that pulley will not hold the weight of the cooler, it's not strong enough."* "What are you talking about woman?" he replied. *"Don't you know, I am an engineer?"*

Gathering up the children, I ushered them inside the house, closed the door and we sat watching the scene unfolding through the large window, while the *'engineer'* tied a rope around the cooler, threaded it through the small pulley, hauling it up, (a feat of pure engineering there), resulting in the cooler crashing back down as the nail holding the pulley became dislodged from the tree. He was lucky that the very heavy cooler did not fall on his head.

The damage to the cooler was not too bad, just slightly buckled on one side. It was later hoisted up by workmen men using a ladder and ropes.

Sindus managed to trap her fingers in the fan blade of that cooler one year when she was little. She was lucky they were not chopped off. Thank goodness, the fan stopped and she only got the backs of her fingers scraped.

Sindus was always getting into mischief, climbing up onto the stone bannister and falling face down onto the hard, stone stairs on one occasion, to split her forehead open. I was going to give her a slap for scaring me but when I picked her up she had blood pouring down her face. She needed four stitches at the local hospital.

We had a fish, in a plastic barrel half full of water outside the door which one of the boys had caught in the river. It was Sindus who decided (at 4 years old) to climb over the barrel to see, look at the fish. She fell headfirst into the water, only managing to hang on to the sides by her hands. If I had not heard her gurgled screeching she would have drowned.

Another time, when she was three years old, she put her soft toy rat into the bottom of the oven where the plate warmer was. When I turned on the oven the poor thing caught fire and I only just managed to save it by grabbing it and dumping it in the sink. There was a singe mark on the back but otherwise, it was fine but she would not play with it after.

Chapter 36

Non-Communicado Incident

There would be occasions when Ahmed and I would stop communicating with each other. This would usually be after one of his outbursts. They upset everyone, there was no reason for them, just some slight would set him off. He would stop talking to me, so we both got some peace for a while and a calmer house.

One incident that I remember quite clearly was when I had just come home from the hospital after giving birth to my youngest daughter, Yasmina in 1979. I was resting in bed with the newborn.

Ahmed came and asked me where a Philips screwdriver was. I had no clue, where it was. After he searched for it for a while he had one of his outbursts, shouting and screaming about 'people' moving 'his' stuff. For someone who had just gone through the trauma of birth, the incident sent me into a depression that took me some weeks to get over.

Two years later I discovered that I was pregnant again. This time Ahmed decided that I should have a termination. My protests resulted in threats of divorce and being sent back to the UK without my children. As it was illegal to terminate a pregnancy unless there was a specific medical reason, he contacted a friend who was in the medical profession and he produced a report stating I was not medically fit to have the baby. It was then arranged for me to be admitted to the hospital for the procedure.

I felt lost, broken and helpless. My depression after the termination led me into a deep, dark place where I functioned like a robot. I grieved for my baby, alone and in silence. I am not sure if my children understood what had happened, perhaps the elder boys did, but the younger ones did not. It took me many years to overcome the trauma of that time, even today it affects me.

My twin daughters remember one time, it was their birthday. We had been invited to Mahmoud's house, he wanted to do them a birthday party.

I had to call Ahmed at his brother's shop and ask him if we could go. He refused. When I reminded him that it was his twin daughters' birthday and they were looking forward to seeing their cousins and having a nice time, he completely lost it, shouting at me down the phone about doing as I was told.

Well, for once, I lost my temper, and-oh dear oh dear-I shouted back. I think I even called him something not very nice. He screamed down the phone that he was coming home immediately and I would be sorry, before he slammed the telephone down.

I shakily replaced the received, the children had heard everything, they looked terrified. We sat and looked at each other for a few moments. Jumping up, I quickly told them to get their things ready, going out to the nearby main road, we got a taxi to Mahmoud's house. When we arrived there, they rushed in ahead of me and burst into tears. My sister-in-law took them into the kitchen to calm them down and Mahmoud asked me what had happened. I informed him of Ahmed's outburst, he could see how upset we all were. I believe I reminded him of an Iraqi saying which quite shocked him, which goes *'the tail of a dog will never be straight'.*

It was not long before we heard a car pull up outside with screeching brakes. We all ran into the back bedroom and locked the door, sat on the bed holding each other tight while we listened to all the shouting outside.

Mahmoud was fully aware of his brother's temper and knew what to expect, Ahmed stormed into the house shouting out, *"Where is she? I am going to kill her."* Mahmoud was finally able to calm him down and get him to leave, it was no easy feat.

We felt terrified when Mahmoud took us home later, the poor girls kept waiting for their father to rush in and start arguing. It was a relief when he stayed away, probably on advice from Mahmoud, and we were able to relax only when it was past the time for him to have come. My daughters suffered trauma during that time. Each birthday of theirs, for some years after, would be a reminder of that day.

Chapter 37

Khairya (1984)

My mother-in-law had been taken to hospital. She had fallen and fractured her arm. Ahmed and I took the children to see her. She had difficulty feeding herself so I took her some food and fed her. I asked her when she could come out.

She was very upset and began to cry, she told me that none of her children wanted her to stay with them. Their wives did not want to have to take care of her. Even her beloved and very spoilt married daughter made the excuse that she would love to take her, but her husband had objected.

I felt sorry for her, she had so many children and only one daughter, none of them offered to take their mother. I told her she could come and stay with me for as long as she liked, we would love to have her. I put a single bed for her in the lounge near the large window so that she could look outside at the palm tree or the sky. She had always called me Saan, not as bad as some neighbours who called me Cinderella or Ajnabya (foreigner).

She needed injections each day for an underlying blood condition, I never did find out what it was but her skin was always very dry and needed to have cream applied regularly. It may have been Thalassemia, which is found in the Iraqi population, but I cannot be sure, it was described to me at the time but all these years later I have forgotten. The doctor came to see her now and again to check on her health and how the arm was healing. It was very difficult to get her into the car each day to take her for her injection. (One time her knickers fell down as she struggled to get in). The doctor suggested I could give her the injections, showing me how to fill the syringe and which area on her buttocks (upper out quadrant) to inject. The first few times I found it hard to give her the injection for fear I would hurt her, but she always told me 'edich khafeefa' (you have light hands). After a few times I found it easier.

Giving Injections in Baghdad

In Iraq people preferred to have an injection to taking capsules. The injection worked faster and did not upset their stomach, doctors readily prescribed them. Mostly amoxicillin or erythromycin was prescribed for infections of the throat or chest, a regular occurrence in a country with such contaminated water.

One of my neighbours, hearing from Khairya that I was so 'light handed' came to ask me if I could give his elderly grandmother injections. I was nervous about injecting someone other than Khairya but he said she was bed-bound and he would find it too difficult to take her to the hospital.

Going to his home nearby I looked at the ampules the doctor had left, they were simply vitamin E, I assumed not harmful. According to her son, the doctor had visited recently to check on the old lady and told the family that she was nearing the end of her life. Preparing the syringe carefully, I went to inject her. It was then that I discovered how tough her skin was, like an elephant's; it was difficult to push the needle in. Over the next three days, I went each morning to inject her, she was mostly asleep and calm. Each time I made sure that she was breathing before I administered the shot and stayed for a few moments after to check again. On the fourth day, early in the morning, I heard the familiar sound of wailing, signalling a death, coming from close by.

When I asked Faris to find out what had happened, he went out. Returning shortly he told me that the old lady had passed away, and then he said the police would be coming to question me about the injections I had been giving her!

"Oh shit, oh Christ, don't tell me that, they were only vitamins, nothing that could have killed her, what am I going to do now? She was on her way out anyway, it's not my fault!"

I promptly burst into tears, the look on my face when I began to imagine being arrested and ending up in prison, possible tortured or raped, was quite a picture.

Eventually, when he saw my distress, he started laughing,

"*Calm down Mum, I'm joking*". That almost got him a slap, but the joke was on me.

Over the years other neighbours would come to me with their injections, I got quite a reputation in the area. One of the ladies had been married very young at 14. After a year she had still not been able to get pregnant, her husband had taken her to a gynaecologist. After some tests, the doctor declared that she was perfectly healthy but prescribed some hormone injections for her.

She came to me one morning with the injection which was preloaded, the needle was quite thick so I was rather wary that, even with my reputation as a 'light touch, she would feel it. I asked her if she was sure she wanted to have this injection. She was only 15 after all, having hormone treatment to get pregnant at such a young age would surely not be recommended treatment. She assured me that she was willing to go ahead. Her husband and his family wanted to make sure she was fertile, like a prize heifer; if she did not produce offspring she would be replaced.

Removing the cover of the needle, I swabbed her buttock, saying a silent prayer as I plunged it into her. When I said, "Ok all done," she looked at me in amazement. She had not felt it except for a bit of pressure. My reputation was secure, at least for now. She went on to have many children without any further hormone injections.

A law passed in 1987 called Personal Status Law and Amendments decreed that a person may not marry until they were 18, a judge would marry the couple under this age if the parents give their consent.

Daughters were considered a liability among many traditional families, they needed to be watched constantly in case they disgraced the family by exhibiting *loose* behaviour. It was easier to pass on the responsibility of their daughters to a husband. Many girls were married off at 12, in the provinces, if they showed any signs of maturity. The husbands were often a lot older at 25+ years. Sometimes elderly, richer men would take a fancy to a young girl, the family would agree to the marriage. After a few months or years the old man would tire of his young growing bride and divorce her. Her family would have to take her back, it was rare for a 2nd groom to come along. I thought it was wrong at so many levels, but this practice had been going on for centuries

Hamid

Hamid came one day and asked me if I would come to give his wife a course of injections, she had become quite ill with flu-like symptoms. My son, Faris, was driving by now and took me twice a day at 6 am and 6 pm, every twelve hours to administer her shots until she recovered.

She had a lady who would come each day to clean for her. This lady had a small child whom she brought with her, a son. When I asked her how old her son was, I was surprised when she told me he was six, he looked far too small to be that age. When I mentioned this to her she said that he did not grow very fast. Thinking there must be a medical reason for this I suggested that she take the child to a doctor to find out the reason for his stunted growth.

I later discovered, when I saw her again, that she had taken my advice. The doctor had diagnosed her son with malnutrition, advised her on the appropriate diet and prescribed vitamins. Since then he had been growing normally and she would always remember me as being the only person to have noticed.

Our Cat Named 'Furtooshi'

Our lovely cat Furtooshi became ill. I found him one day just lying in his place with a streaming nose and mouth. He could not eat or drink and barely looked at me, I suspected feline flu. There was no money to take him to a vet but I did have some amoxicillin ampoules leftover from Hamid's wife. I was not sure the exact amount I could give him or even where I could jab him but thought it was worth a try. I did not want him to die.

Getting the ampoule ready I drew up a small amount into the syringe, gingerly reached down to him, lifted a hind leg and gently injected an area. He was so far gone that he did not even flinch. Twice a day for the next two days I repeated the injection. On the third day he lifted his head and licked my hand. I felt there was hope.

Each day after that he responded more. Taking some water and a little food, he gradually regained his strength. He still allowed me to inject him. It was as if he knew that I was helping him. He made a full recovery. The children were so happy, he had been with us since he was a tiny kitten and they were very fond of their 'Furtooshi'.

It was very sad that, a few years later, he was attacked outside the house one night by wild dogs. His injuries were fatal and he died a short time later. We buried him in the garden, the children laying some flowers on his grave.

Khairya

Khairya had now recovered the use of her arm and was almost back to normal. It always amazed me how she could devour a sandwich. This was not made with soft sliced bread but the diamond-shaped samoon. She had not one tooth but her gums were as hard as a rock. Despite being fed several times a day, she would often forget that she had eaten and ask for her meal. When I reminded her that she had just eaten, usually five minutes or so before, she would get quite annoyed.

"She is trying to starve me to death, look how skinny I am, she does not feed me, I'm starving!"

Complaining loudly that I was trying to starve her to death when any visitors came, she would tell them that she had not eaten a thing all day.

Always, when she ate something, she sneezed quite loudly, spraying a mouthful of food everywhere. The children and I would wait for this explosion and make sure we were well out of range of spraying crumbs and debris when it happened.

One of her favourite treats was the Iraqi *Dondurma*, a special type of delicious ice cream made with mastic, milk, cream, corn starch and sugar along with different flavourings. Ahmed or one of the boys would bring it for us in a large 1-kilo tub, as a special treat.

The children asked me one day when her birthday was, so that we could do her a party. I confessed that I had no idea, neither did anyone else in the family, especially Khairya. In her time births were not registered in any official way, she could only remember her mother telling her that she was born during Eid, which one (there are two each year and it varies according to the month), she did not know. The children and I decided to pick a day, I made a cake and we told her it was her birthday. She was so happy, nobody had ever celebrated her birthday in all her life. We wrapped up a few simple presents for her, a shawl, brush, new nighty and the children sang 'happy birthday' in Arabic.

Word had reached Mahmoud that we were doing a little party for his mother. He turned up with her '*birthday*' present, a coil of copper tubing from his shop which he placed around her neck telling her it was gold. He also had quite a weird sense of humour.

Sabiha, the cousin who lived opposite, was a regular visitor to the house, often sitting and chatting with her. On the days she did not come, Khairya would sit in her chair and shout out, "*Sabiha, Sabiha.*" Of course, Sabiha could not hear her, being across the road inside her house, and I would say this to Khairya each time to no avail. She insisted on calling out loudly for her until I sent one of the children over to ask her to come and have tea with us.

I had soaked her black abaya (a long black cloak affair worn over the body from the head to the floor, very useful if you wanted to pop out quickly without changing your clothes), in a bucket in the bathroom to get the dust out before I hung it up in the garden to dry.

On that day she decided that she wanted it. "*My abaya, where is it?*" she asked me.

"It's soaking, I will hang it soon, then when it is dry you can have it," I told her.

"*I want my abaya*"! she repeated over and over.

Despite explaining several times where the item was, she did not seem to understand. She began to get quite upset about it, so I went and got the bucket, plonking it down in front of her so she could see her abaya in it. Only then was she calmer.

Being a light sleeper I heard an almighty crash one night. Jumping up I rushed out of my room and over to her. The heavy wooden pelmet along the window above her bed was now lying across her. She had wet the bed, and being next to the window she was able to reach out and grab hold of one of the long curtains to dry herself, pulling the whole heavy wooden pelmet down. It was a miracle that it had not landed on her head and injured or kill her.

I had to move her bed farther away from the window after that, just in case. I didn't want the police coming to question me about murdering my mother-in-law!

When I was in my ninth month and close to my due date, I was no longer able to lift her to get her to the toilet. She was quite frail and unable to walk unaided. It was arranged by Ahmed that she should be moved temporarily to the main house, where Amina could take over, and Khairya's son, Ali's, wife would help.

A bed was set up for her in the main lounge area against the wall where she could sit and receive visitors. As I accompanied her I explained that it would only be for a short while until my baby was born, then she could come back and stay with me again if she so wished.

The children and I were sad to see her go, she had become such a welcome part of the family. The children enjoyed her antics and looked forward to sitting beside her while she told them tales of her childhood. She once told them of the time when she was a small child and the British soldiers had come into Baghdad, she said she had learnt some English from them, as the crowds of children had followed the soldiers who were marching along.

"What English was that, BeeBee?"

"*Gone ya fuckers, gone ya fuckers,*" was her reply.

Chapter 38

Samer's Birth (1985)

Faris took me to the hospital when I went into labour with Samer. I was well used to the procedure by now, so I took a novel with me that I had been saving up, especially for this occasion and settled down in the labour ward to read it until I felt that the time had come for the baby to be born.

I called the nurse to inform her that I was sure the time had come, but she did not believe me.

"*Not yet, not yet, you are reading your book, not a peep out of you, how can it be time?*" she said.

She soon changed her mind when she heard me starting to push!

It was an easy birth. I knew all along that I was carrying a boy this time, it just turned out that I was right.

Faris was waiting outside the delivery room with one of his friends. He was 17 years old. When the baby was born the nurse mentioned to me I had a son with "*quite large testicles*" before he was wrapped up and she took him out to Faris, placing him in his arms with the words, "*Congratulations, you have a son.*" "*Oh no, this is my brother,*" he replied. He still remembers that incident today, and how a smiling baby Samer was put into his arms.

I recall Faris's friend went and bought me a kebab sandwich from the shop nearby, which I thoroughly enjoyed as I was hungry.

I had mentioned previously to one of the ladies in the family that, even if I did have another girl, I would say it was a boy, so no more remarks would be made by Salah. When Ahmed came to the hospital, he picked up his son, undoing the baby's clothes to check that it was indeed a male child.

Dad Dies (1986)

"Mum, there is a postman outside with a special letter for you."

I went to the door, the postman stood there with a registered envelope, it had been forwarded by Interpol. When I opened the letter I discovered that my father Bernhard had died in London of heart failure. It was so unexpected, I knew that he had problems with stomach ulcers but did not imagine that he had heart problems as well.

Ahmed was away on a trip when he returned I asked him if I could go to the UK to bury my father. He said he would see what he could do, but I knew it would not be easy. Samer was only 9 months old, the twins were 8 years old and Yasmin was 7. It would be difficult to take them and even more difficult to leave them.

I was now an Iraqi citizen. To leave the country I needed an exit visa, this was not something easily obtained. Although Ahmed had frequent trips to London, he would not have the time nor the knowledge to arrange a funeral.

I did not go, instead, I got in touch with my friend, Rita, who promised to arrange for the cremation. I did not have any money but she said she would cover the expenses until I could send her the money through Ahmed.

I was eternally grateful to her for her help at a time when I needed it the most.

Although Ahmed had many more trips to London after that, he always refused to send Rita any money. This I could not understand. He was responsible for me, I had no income so, surely, he should also help me when I needed it? A death in his own family would see him doing all he could to support family members both practically and financially, but not for me; yet another brick had been placed in the wall between us.

When we finally got to go to England some years later, I sold whatever gold we had, the children's small bracelets, earrings, and mine, so I could finally repay Rita the money I owed her. She never asked me for it, not once, she understood my position and knew that I would repay her one day.

Khairyah Passes Away (1986)

I would go and see Khairyah (my mother-in-law) each day to make sure that she was being turned and washed regularly. I could see though that this was not the case.

She developed bedsores through being left in one position for too long, or soaked with urine. She was often left alone in the evenings for hours while the women went off visiting family. There were times that she fell out of the bed, a single bed with no guard rail, which had been set up in the lounge for her.

Her incontinence seemed to be a problem for the family members who were tasked to care for her. They complained bitterly about how much she smelt, especially when she defecated. If it was Amina's turn to change her soiled clothes, she retched continuously. The others complained the smell was keeping visitors away.

I offered to have her brought back to stay with me but, because I now had a new baby as well as the other small children to care for. Ahmed and his brothers did not think that this was a good idea. Despite my best efforts to get her some comfort, she slowly began to decline.

One morning the telephone rang, it was my sister-in-law. "*Please come to the house, Um Faris. It is my mother, she does not look well.*" Putting on my abaya, I made my way to the main house at the end of the road. When I entered and I saw her state, I knew she was on her deathbed.

She was pale and clammy, her breath was rasping, and she was in and out of consciousness. I sat beside her, wiping her face with a damp cloth and holding her hand, talking to her softly, telling her not to be afraid.

I insisted a doctor be called to check on her, when he came he agreed that she did not have long to live. Not quite knowing what to do, I recited the Muslim prayer of the Shahada for her.

Other relatives and neighbours had been informed. They slowly began to arrive, sitting around the room, at first quiet, reverent. As the time passed, looking bored by now at how long it was taking the old lady to pass out of this world, they began to chat amongst themselves. They discussed the latest gossip, what they had cooked for dinner, how to cook this dish or that dish, their voices at first low then became as usual very loud. When one of the women started giving her recipe for how to cook okra to another, it was too much for me to bear. Turning around to face them I told them all to leave, go to another room, "*This woman is dying and all you are doing is making her dying hours a joke!*" Or words to that effect.

Their faces expressed shock, maybe because I had not pronounced the sentence correctly in Arabic. Perhaps I had said something different as

I was prone to do, but they quietened down, some moved off to one of the other rooms. It pays sometimes to be a foreigner. If any of the Iraqi women had asked them to leave, there would probably have been a fight.

A short while later her breathing stopped for good, she was gone. I kissed her cheek, I did not tell anyone for a while, just sat next to her still holding her still warm hand, only realizing her passing was a fact when she began to slowly grow cooler, then I covered her face with the sheet.

This woman, who had given birth to more than 6 children, five of them boys, had been mostly ignored and left to die in her last days on earth. None of them wanted to be responsible for her in her later years. It was so sad and quite an unusual occurrence amongst Iraqi families, they normally revered their elderly.

Only one of her sons had taken his mother out for the day when she was staying with me. He took her home with him in the morning and brought her back in the evening; it was a lovely outing for her.

As soon as those in the room saw me pulling the sheet over her head they realized that now she was at last, deceased. All hell broke loose, it was as if nobody had realized that she was indeed going to die. The house began filling with the sound of deafening lament, keening, wailing, hand thumping, beating breasts. I wondered what people back home in Britain would have thought of it all.

The rest of the family, having been informed by telephone, began to arrive. Abdul Hamid's wife, Um Rayath arrived by car, getting out of the vehicle she entered the house, starting her wailing at the door.

By this time my mother-in-law's body had been wrapped in her sheets and placed in the middle of the floor. I sat close to the body covered in my Abaya, a long black cloak that was customary for the women to wear when out. I had pulled it over my head and was sitting quietly with one of my hands placed on Khairyah's slowly cooling body, when Um Rayath suddenly stopped mid-wailing and coughed. For some unknown reason, as I heard her, I started laughing hysterically, the tears rolling down my face, I pulled the cloak more over my head and rocked back and forward with mirth. They thought I was overtaken with grief, no one suspected it was the opposite.

Looking back on it now, I suppose it was a form of grief, and probably a release of my pent-up emotions at that time. I was so fond of Khairya, the way that she had been neglected by her children was shameful. One day they would be old, what goes around comes around.

The funeral was quickly arranged. In Islam, the body must be buried as soon as possible. A woman came to the house to wash and prepare the body. Khairya must be washed three times, according to Islamic ritual, while certain verses from the Koran are recited over her body. Olive oil soap is used to wash every part of the body. This is rinsed off each time with water containing berries. Camphor powder is placed on the seven areas of her body that touched the ground when praying - the forehead, the palms of her hands, her knees and her elbows - her hair combed. Sometimes dust is placed on the eyelids to remind us that dust we are and dust we shall become.

White cloths are placed on the head and the torso before the entire body is wrapped in a white shroud. Khairyah had brought her shroud years earlier from Mecca when she had done her obligatory visit there along with her sisters.

All this procedure took over one hour. She was then placed into a wooden coffin, which was loaded onto the roof of Hamid's car, to begin her last journey to the family vault in An-Najaf al-Ashraf, about 160 kilometres south of Baghdad.

I have a phobia of being buried alive. The very thought of it makes me panic. These thoughts slip into my mind whenever I see a coffin or grave. Was that person dead when they were placed inside that earthen tomb? Stories have appeared in the newspapers of occasions where the person who has been declared deceased, has suddenly sat up wondering what was going on. Once the body has been buried, who would think of checking afterwards if that person had not been trying to get out of their coffin? I suppose the embalming process would ensure that the person would *not* wake up again, but in some countries, like Africa or other 3rd world places, many cannot afford to have their loved ones embalmed.

The funeral itself was a seven-day affair held in a large tent placed in front of the house for the men. A separate area was provided inside the house for women. Many people attended from both tribes of the family. She came from the al-Zubaidi tribe and her husband had come from the al-Khafaji tribe. They did not come empty-handed, some brought 50-kilo sacks of rice or sugar, live sheep, cigarettes, tea, ghee, in fact, anything that might be needed for the guests at the funeral service.

A loudspeaker was set up on the upstairs balcony for the mullah to say the various prayers throughout the day and into the night.

The kitchen was full of women cooking various dishes which would be served to the guests, with rice, dates, lots of strong black, bitter Turkish coffee served in small cups. One of the dishes was *Torshana*, a stew made of dried apricots, lamb, almonds, dried plums and a few sweet onions. The origin of the dish is believed to be Persian. It is one of my favourite dishes. It is expensive to make so it is mostly made at funerals. Whenever I heard of a funeral nearby, I would be off like a shot in the hope of getting a taste.

At Khairyah's funeral, when this dish was made, I asked for a portion to be saved for me in the kitchen until later. One of the ladies hid it in the cupboard for me. I was most disappointed when, later, I came to partake of my dish and found some low life had eaten it!

It was the custom each year during the Eid holiday, for members of the family to travel to An Najaf and visit the grave. They could then undertake any repairs necessary to the vault which may have got damaged by the rain over time, or vandalized.

As the years passed, fewer and fewer family members were willing to make the long and arduous journey to Najaf. I never did, I wanted my memories of her to be mostly good ones.

MEK in Iraq

In 1986 Saddam gave permission for the construction of a massive complex for the MEK (People's Mujahideen of Iran) in, al-Khalis, Dyala Province, which is about 65 kilometres north of Baghdad.

Covering six square kilometres of bare land with no roads or buildings, it was developed into a city by the MEK members (with financial help from Saddam) consisting of a garrison, barracks, farms, lakes and a broadcasting station. There was even a university.

The area was named Camp Ashraf, in commemoration of the first wife of Massoud Rajavi, Ashraf Rabiei. She was an Iranian guerrilla and had been killed in 1982 when Revolutionary Guards had raided her safe house in Northern Tehran. Massoud Rajavi was the leader of the MEK along with his second wife Maryam Rajavi whom he married in 1985. Maryam Rajavi became a member of the MEK when she was twenty-two, just after her sister Nargis was killed by SAVAK (Iranian secret police under the Shah 1957-1979).

The MEK transmitted anti-Iranian broadcasts which we could pick up on our TV at home.

There were about 2000-3000 living in al-Ashraf camp, men and women who were training as fighters. Saddam wanted them to take part in his war with Iran, which they did. Following the acceptance of the cease-fire by Iran in 1988, worried that Saddam would desert them and hand them over to Iran, MEK's army attacked Iran from the West. This campaign was a complete failure for MKO/MEK, thousands of their army perished in the assault by Iran named Forough Javidan Operation.

Chapter 39

Dust Storms

"Look at this dust, it's all over the place again."

"Mother, it's your glasses, they need cleaning."

I had spent much of the day, with the help of the children, cleaning the house after a dust storm. Every nook and cranny and surface was covered in the fine desert sand which had been blown in on the wind. It happened regularly, especially in the hot summer months; the house had to be cleaned each day from top to bottom.

Sand and dust storms rage for 20 to 50 days each year in Iraq, mostly during the summer months. The war with Iran, where much of the desert was churned up by tanks, contributed to the dust blown in. The average height of a dust storm would be from 3,000 – 6,000 feet high.

Sandstorms, which mostly occurred in the vast desert of Iraq, can reach heights of 50 feet (15 meters).

The vacuum cleaner that we had was old and temperamental. It would spew out more dust than it collected and this dust had covered my glasses. Other than that we used a small hand brush made from woven palm fronds, quite efficient but also a dust spreader.

The marble floor tiles were wiped over in the morning and in the afternoon, the patio outside the house would be hosed down each day with the river water which was piped into a separate tap in the garden and contained many nutrients but also mud when the river was high after the seasonal rains.

Our flat roof was not washed every day. Only if it was summer and we had decided to get away from the oppressive heat by taking our mattresses upstairs and sleeping under the stars on metal beds. During this time it was vital to rise early in the morning before your face became covered in nipping flies.

Washing Rugs

At the end of winter, we would have the large Iranian Kashan wool rugs in the rooms removed and cleaned by some men who passed by like clockwork each year.

There were usually three of them. They would lift the rugs and take them out into the long patio. They would each grab a part of the rug on one long side. Lifting it in unison they would shake it, releasing clouds of dust before laying it back down onto the floor and soaking it with water from the garden hose. Adding a little bit of washing-up liquid they would then scrub the rug all over using wooden blocks, then rinse it several times in clean water. When they had finished, they rolled the rug up, stood it on its end to drain while they repeated the procedure for the other rugs.

After completion, the rugs would be taken up to the roof to be spread out in the sun to dry. This would usually take a day. When they returned the next day, the rugs would be sprinkled with Naphthalene, to prevent moth attacks, rolled up again and placed into storage until next year.

Night Sky

The sky at night was full of stars when it was clear enough to see them. When we slept on the roof we would lie on our bedding looking up. What I knew of the constellations I would point out to the children, the ones I knew, *"Look, that is Orion's Belt, over there are the Seven Sisters, that is Mars, Jupiter."*

On some nights we could see shooting stars. It was on one of these nights Sindus pointed out a star that was moving across the night sky.

"Look, Mum, what is that?" As I looked at it, and before I could dismiss it as a satellite, it suddenly shot off to the right, then up in a straight line, then off at speed and disappeared. No satellite then, no shooting star either, too fast for a rocket, maybe it was Captain Kirk on one of his missions.

One night we spotted a weird shape on the moon, we did not know what it was, but it looked out of place.

Truffles

A delicacy in Iraq are truffles, (terfeziaceae). Known as 'the meat of the poor man', these are seasonal desert truffles found only in the spring after the rains, in the desert areas near Anbar Province and the North of Iraq. They are of different sizes, small like tangerines, pomegranate, or if you are lucky enough to find them, rare and large like melon depending on the area and the amount of rainfall.

They appear in the market covered in a fine layer of sand, sold for a lower price than their richer cousins in the West. Once the prized truffles are brought home, they needed to be washed thoroughly and scraped on a brick to remove any stubborn sand particles from the gnarled surface. They are then dried, chopped and placed in plastic bags for the freezer.

Added to different dishes they have a creamy, delicate mushroom taste and are simply delicious. Although I enjoyed eating them, I did not look forward to preparing them and cleaning the sink of mud afterwards.

Dates

Placed between two rivers, the Tigris and Euphrates, Iraq has amazingly fertile soil. It is famous for the quality and abundance of dates. There are date palm trees everywhere, we had several growing in the garden.

It is estimated that 30 million palm trees produced 100 million tons of dates yearly mostly for export. They dominated the world's market for dates in 1980.

Before I went to Iraq, the only dates I had ever seen were those little boxes with plastic forks around Christmas time.

In Iraq, I tasted real dates, big soft brown dates with a certain kind of sweet taste. Many varieties, which are still available today range from brown to light yellow colours. The most common types are Amir Hajji, Dayri and Khastawi.

Each year a man would come and shin up our date palms in his bare feet using a rope slung around the fat palm trunk, to pollinate the flowers at the top. Then later, when the fruit was ripe, he would be back with his basket, shin up again and cut down the big bunches of dates for us. Because of their high sugar content, they can be stored and kept for ages.

There were other fruit trees in our garden. Seville oranges aplenty (these we used a lot in any cooking that required lemon to be added), I also made marmalade. A mulberry tree was nearby (Tuwt in Arabic), it had white fruit and the children would throw their slippers up into the branches to knock down the small berries. Dark red fruits could be found on other trees in the area.

Popular fruits amongst the children were also crab apples and greengages. The latter was very sour so salt was sprinkled on them before eating, limes and lemons received the same treatment. I often wondered in later years if all that salt would cause any health problems, so far, the children seem to be healthy enough.

Khairyah made date vinegar, soaking the dates in a large barrel of water in the garden, leaving it until maggots formed, which meant the vinegar was ready to be used, it was extremely acidic. She strained the liquid to get rid of the maggots, bottled and distributed some of the vinegar to the family or neighbours. She made yummy pickles by soaking cucumbers, turnips and beetroot in the vinegar. I always thought she made the best pickles in the whole country.

Bulbul Chicks

One year our 'tree man' dislodged a nest of chicks belonging to bulbul, a bird common to Iraq. Instead of shinning up the tree and replacing them, he dumped them outside my door along with the dates he had collected from the tree. I was not inclined to attempt climbing the 12-foot palm tree myself. With so many cats around I was worried they would end up as cat snacks, so I picked the nest up and took it inside. It contained five tiny chicks, only a few days old, with no feathers, their eyes still closed.

I sat with the children looking at them while we tried to figure out what to do. With the cats around, their tiny lives were in danger. We looked outside to see if the parent birds were hovering around looking for their offspring, no sign of them.

I sent the children off with instructions to find some food for the chicks. Shortly they returned with various worms and small insects as sacrifices. These we impaled on a toothpick which I tapped on the side of the birds' little beaks, amazingly *open sesame* - in the offering went and down the hatch.

The children and I took turns feeding those little creatures, watching them get their feathers, opening their eyes. They had lovely colours consisting of white near the head, yellow under the tail, grey and black feathers elsewhere.

We kept the cats away as best we could and not one chick found itself being chewed up. They grew strong and big. It was wonderful especially when they started flying, one after another they took off from the backs of chairs or the pelmet above the window. We only lost one chick when I sat on it at dinner one day not realizing it was on the chair.

The time came when I told the children the birds must be released outside so they could go and find their way in the world, get married and have more baby chicks, but hopefully not in our palm trees.

We took them out and watched them. Hesitant at first, they turned heads this way and that before flying off into the blue yonder. I don't think they ever came back to see us, like in a fairy story, but could not be sure, there were so many of them flying around outside.

It was a lesson for the children in how to care for small things gently with love and compassion. If I found any small creatures in the garden I would call the children to show them the tiny bat, pink baby snake, hedgehog, etc.

Scorpion

I taught them the dangers too, scorpions, big spiders, snakes, insects that could sting them like the big yellow hornets. If one of those stung you, you certainly knew it.

I was visiting the widow opposite one day for a cup of chai when one of the children came, *"Faris has found a 'spider' under a chair in the lounge and the cat keeps trying to play with it. Come quickly, Mum!"*

When I entered the house and went to look, the *spider* was a very large, very black scorpion. Mohammed stood with a large piece of wood in his hand ready to flatten it, Faris stood with a can of insect repellent ready to spray it. *"Faris, please do not, whatever you do, spray that thing, we have no idea what it will do if it gets zapped."* Not having ever seen a live scorpion before I imagined it jumping up and stinging one of us.

Going into the kitchen I returned with a clear plastic container. Removing the lid I quickly bent down and placed the open end on top of the scorpion, which stopped it from harming anyone. Getting a piece of stiff cardboard, I slipped it underneath. Shaking like a leaf, lifting the container I righted it and then managed to get the lid on slowly as I removed the cardboard. We had caught ourselves a live scorpion. It looked deadly but at the same time magnificent.

"Wow, Mum look how big it is!"

The children, knowing it was well caged and unable to reach them, sat around the container which I had placed on the table. Their faces were in awe, they understood how deadly it was but found it mesmerizing.

Throughout the day various friends of the children came to see our captive which I had placed on the dining table. Some neighbours' wives heard about it and came too, marvelling at the shape and size of it. I thought of selling tickets to view our spectacle!

In the evening, Ahmed came. He decided to take it away to show his friends. I asked him to release it someplace away from people, but he told me later that, after his friends had seen it, he threw it on the fire and burnt it alive.

Rats

Rats and mice were a big problem in Baghdad. In the bathroom, we had a large drain hole in the floor for the water to run down. I had it covered with a heavy brick to stop rats from pushing their way up into the house. This was removed when anyone had a shower.

One day, after their shower, one of the children forgot to replace the brick on the drain. During the night as we were sleeping, I felt something moving above my head as I lay in bed. I had baby Samer in his cot next to me. I was not alarmed, thinking it was one of the cats which often climbed up on the bed to sleep. Then I felt it again so I reached out my hand to switch the bedside light on and got the fright of my life when I saw a very large rat who had just walked across my pillow, sitting above the baby's cot looking at me brazenly with its beady eyes. Immediately picking up the baby I left my bedroom and went upstairs to the children's room and slept there for the night hoping that the rat or rats would not climb up the stairs and follow me.

The next morning when I came down again there was not one rat to be found, they had gone back down the drain. I covered it again with the brick reminding the children to be careful about replacing it.

Once when I came out of the kitchen, I saw a rat sitting on the stairs. It did not move at all. It just sat there. I think it must have eaten rat poison because it didn't run away nor look afraid of me. Not quite knowing what I should do, I went next door to my neighbour who had a little shop - part of his front room - where he sold sweets, drinks and various other items out of his window to the locals, and asked him if he would come and get rid of the rat for me.

He refused, he said he was afraid of rats. I think he was more afraid of coming into my house while Ahmed was not there though, so I returned home. The rat was still sitting on the stairs. I went and got a hammer, walked up to it and hit it on the head caving in its skull. It died instantly. I was quite shocked at the ease in which I had killed it, I had carried out my first rat murder. Picking it up by the tail, I put it in the bin outside.

After that there was no stopping me. Faris had a pellet rifle, there were times when I would take it and shoot at any rats I saw near the house, picking up the dead animal and putting it in the bin outside. I have seen rats climb up a vertical wall to get to the flat rooftop above. They are very adept with their sharp little claws at hanging onto brickwork. I never felt afraid of them, rats, mice - they were all the same to me.

Samer had a rat jump out of the toilet while he was sitting on it one day, which made him afraid to go to the toilet for a long time after that unless I stood outside the door.

Sabiha, my neighbour called me each time she spied one so that I could go over to her house and bring my pellet rifle, by shooting any she had, to add to my tally of dead rats.

Lizards were abundant around us, they often came into the house and would run along the walls. Amina was afraid of them, so I used to get satisfaction from wiping them off the wall in her direction whenever I could. It was a delight to hear her screeching.

Cockroaches

Cockroaches are an insect that creeps me out and there were many of them in Iraq. They lived a life of luxury in the drains, gardens and other areas of the homes.

I kept all foodstuffs in containers with tightly fitting lids and made sure to wipe up any spills on the floor or counter as I knew they would pick up the scent of any debris and come running to get their fix. They would still wander around the walls and other places in the house.

One day I obtained a large bottle of insecticide from the pharmacy. When I got home, I poured copious amounts down all the drains and sinkholes in the house, even flushing some down the toilet. Then I sat down to read a novel. After only a few minutes I noticed a cockroach scuttle along the floor, then more, and more, until the whole walls and floor seemed covered in the little brown buggers who had rushed up out of the drains to avoid annihilation.

Running out of the house with the kids, we stood in the garden. I noticed that the creatures were slowly turning their 'toes' up. We waited patiently for them to make their way out of this world.

The vacuum cleaner came in very handy for getting rid of the hundreds of corpses.

Chapter 40

Iraqi Citizenship

The time had come when I must take out Iraqi citizenship in 1980. So far, with Ahmed's various 'connections' we had managed to avoid it. Now Saddam Hussein was insisting on all foreigners who had been residents in the country for over a certain number of years to register as Iraqi citizens.

I was supposed to hand over my British passport to the authorities in exchange for an Iraqi one, along with an identity card and Iraqi 'birth certificate'. I would thus become bound by travel restrictions imposed on me as an Iraqi citizen. I was not about to concede to any handing over of my precious British passport. When the time came I announced that it had been left at the British embassy for safe despatch back to Britain, nothing could be done about that.

My new passport was green in colour. Inside it stated that my eyes were 'blew'. My identity card, an addition to the passport, stated that my father's name was Dorothea, which I am sure he would have been puzzled to know. I was now a fully-fledged Iraqi, I still have those documents today and take them out from time to time to look at.

Aathamiyah – King Faizal

The area we lived in was near to Makbarra al-Malaki, or The Royal Mausoleum in A'athamyah, Baghdad.

Here lies King Faisal II (1935-1958).

He became king at the age of three upon the death of his father King Ghazi. His uncle was Regent until Ghazi became of age.

As a teenager, he attended Harrow School in England along with his cousin, King Hussein of Jordan. In 1953 he fully took over the kingship duties of Iraq. In 1958 he was brutally murdered, along with most of his family in a coup.

After Sindus started school, when she was in the 2nd or 3rd year she would always come home late. Her habit was to wander around the King's Grave, sitting in the gardens there, while I was at home wondering where she was. On occasion, she would take her younger sister with her. They both went to the same school. I attempted to frighten her out of going. *"Sindus, you must stop going to that place! There is a monster living inside, he comes out when he is hungry, to grab little children and eat them! One little girl disappeared and only her finger was found."* Looking at me her bright blue eyes went wide, and her mouth formed into an O shape. For a while it worked, she avoided the area. The fact that the monster might get her one day did not deter her for long, she was back there after a while, searching for gruesome remains.

"Sindus, are you not afraid of that monster getting you?"

"No Mum, I want to see what it looks like."

The area is not far from Abu Hanifa Mosque, a prominent landmark of Baghdad, and is one of the oldest areas of Baghdad, dating back to the Abbasid era.

Um Zainab

One of my dearest neighbours lived only a short walk from me. Her name was Um Zainab. She was married to a distant cousin of Ahmed's (many of the neighbours in the district were related to Ahmed's family either through his mother or father). She was short in stature with fair skin, light brown hair and hazel eyes.

Her children, five girls but no boys, much to her dismay, were the same ages as my daughters. I would often visit and sit drinking tea in the small lounge area of her two-bedroom brick house in the morning or afternoon.

We became very close friends, although she spoke no English. She would often help me with my Arabic and I taught her some sentences in English. She had been educated up to a certain level but left school when she married young.

She had a clay oven in her small garden where she made the flat khubz bread each morning. The dough, made with wholemeal flour, was made quite wet. When it had been left to rise for long enough she would shape a handful into large balls, placing these onto a large metal tray covered lightly with flour to stop them sticking. Filling the clay oven with tree branches cut into smaller more manageable pieces, some kerosene was thrown over them which she lit with a match. When she was satisfied that the oven was at the correct temperature a wet cloth would be swirled around the inside walls to clean off any previous soot debris. Wetting her hands first, one of the balls of dough would be taken up and swiftly passed from one hand to another until it became flat, like a pizza base before being slapped firmly against the inside wall of the oven.

Sometimes she would let me place the dough. It was very hot work indeed and I noticed that she would have a couple of old sleeves cut from items of clothing on her right arm to protect it from the heat of the oven. When the bread looked ready, she would lift it off from the oven wall with a large pair of tongs and throw the round bread into wicker basket placed nearby.

We would have that delicious hot bread later with some cheese and tea.

When she became pregnant for the fifth time, she longed for a boy. Unfortunately, another girl was born. This was such a tragic occurrence for her that she rejected the baby. When I went to see her and congratulate her, I found her distraught, unable to look at her daughter. Her face was red from crying and she had been slapping herself, calling herself an idiot. She refused to feed the baby girl or even look at her. The tiny baby had been placed in a crib since she had been born and left to cry, in the hope that she would soon starve to death.

I had only just given birth to my youngest son, Samer, and my maternal instincts were very strong. Seeing the baby hungry and wet I was mortified. It was a shocking fact that the poorer families, would sometimes leave the unwanted girl child to starve to death. I went over to the crib. Lifting her I changed her wet clothes and put the tiny girl to my breast to feed her, while I did so I spoke softly to my friend, explaining that she must accept her child. *"I have four girls, Um Faris, what will my husband say now that he has yet another daughter?"* *"Please, Um Zainab, it is a sin for you to abandon this innocent, what has she done to deserve this, but be born?"* *"Take her then, you bring her up, she is yours now!"*

Afraid for the baby if I left her I gathered up her daughter. Turning to her mother I said, *"Listen to me carefully, Um Zainab. I am taking your daughter home with me. I don't know you, and you don't know me until you agree to accept your child."*

Leaving the house, I took the baby to my home. I hoped that my plan would work. She would not be able to leave her baby for long, I knew that she loved all her daughters and was a good mother, she was just in shock at having yet another girl.

It took only a short time for her to come to her senses. She came to my home in tears, apologising for her behaviour and hugging me. I put her daughter into her arms with the words, "She is so beautiful, just like her mother, a true gift from God." She named her daughter Jinan; she was indeed beautiful and loved by both parents.

According to Islam, that baby girl and my son Samer were deemed siblings as they had both been breastfed by the same mother.

It was sad when, two years later, when she was about 7 months pregnant again, as she was returning from an ante-natal appointment at the local hospital, she tripped and fell heavily in the street. Getting up she continued home not realising that she should have gone back to the hospital and got checked.

A few days later she miscarried her son, the boy that she had always longed for.

Helping the Midwife

Next door to Um Zainab lived yet another cousin of Ahmed's. His name was Mahmoud al-Bakr. His wife Fathyla was a lot younger than him, she was his second wife.

During her pregnancy, she would often come and sit with Um Zainab and me, having tea and nattering. She would ask me to place my hand on her stomach. She wanted her child to be born with blonde hair and blue eyes, just like me (both her husband and she were brown-eyed).

When she went into labour, one of her children was sent to ask me if I could be with her for the birth. The local midwife was already there with her. She was an old woman who had birthed Ahmed and most of his siblings.

It was the first time that I had been present at live birth. What shocked me at the time was the absence of any gloves or other PPE being worn by the midwife.

The procedure was very primitive. The birth, itself, went smoothly. She produced a fine little boy, but there was a problem with the placenta. The midwife tied a piece of string she produced from her bag around the cord and then cut it with an old pair of scissors she had also dragged out of her bag. She quickly wrapped the baby boy in swaddling and placed him in a bassinet. This took only a few moments. Turning back to the mother she then wound the cord coming from the placenta around her hand and started to tug it to remove the placenta.

Aghast at this I placed my hand on her shoulder and said,

"La, La, mayseer heechi!" (No, no, not like that).

I was sure that what she was doing could end in disaster. Once again, my foreignness let me intervene and she stopped. I was able to explain that she should wait for a few minutes, then press on the mother's stomach, this action would help the mother push to expel the placenta.

I had given birth to seven children by then so knew what the procedure was. Even though she had brought many babies into the world, who knew how many of them or their mothers had survived her practices? If a mother caught sepsis and died, bled to death or the baby died, who would blame the midwife? It was deemed Allah's will after all.

It seemed that my advice worked. After a short while the placenta was duly expelled and a bonus was that the baby boy had light green eyes and fair hair, so mother got her wish after all.

Faris Incident 1

Faris failed in his 2nd year of high school. Ever inventive, he changed his results to show us that he had passed. We all thought he was in the third year until one of his friends came to the house needing some help with his homework. "You are in the year below him, how can he help you with your work, unless it is English you need help with?" I said.

"Oh no, Aunty, he is in the second year with me, he failed his exams, sorry, I thought you knew!"

He had let the cat out of the bag by telling us!

Chapter 41

1981 – Osirak Attack

One Sunday, June 7th, we heard the most almighty bangs from a distance. Soon we discovered that a nuclear components factory (Osirak) still under construction in the Za'franiyah area had been attacked by Israeli jets.

Iraq's nuclear reactor purchased from France in 1976, Osiraq was situated in Tuwaitha, 17 kilometres southeast of Baghdad.

The operation was called *Operation Opera.*

Fourteen Israeli jets crossed over Jordan. When they were contacted by the Jordanian ATC they spoke with Saudi accents explaining that they were Saudis on a patrol and had veered off course. As they passed over Saudi airspace, they switched to Jordanian accents with the same excuse for being in the area.

The raid had been ordered by the Prime Minister of Israel, Menachem Begin. According to some reports, the Saudis were angry and felt insulted that its territory had been used by Israeli pilots, who had signalled falsely that they were Jordanian.

The reactor, which was still being built by French and Italian engineers, so was not operational, was destroyed in the raid. It was reported that the raid had been carried out on a Sunday to reduce the loss of life of foreign workers and consultants, this being their day off, but ten Iraqi soldiers and one French civilian were killed in the raid.

Almost one year earlier to the day, an Egyptian scientist, Yahya El-Mashhad, who headed the Osirak nuclear programme and lectured at the Engineering Faculty at the University of Baghdad, was found murdered in his hotel room at the Meridian Hotel in Paris. Mossad was suspected of carrying out the assassination but there was no firm proof. El-Mashhad joined a list of scientists from the Middle East whom Mossad had a long tradition of wiping out over the years.

1992

There is going to be a wedding! A cousin of Ahmed was getting married, we were excited. The bride was quite young at 16 and the groom was barely 22, this is quite normal in Iraq.

The bride was brought to the main house and taken upstairs. I was asked to come along and meet her. She was a pretty girl with long black hair and hazel eyes, quite slim and of average height. She had a wonderful personality, always smiling and so happy that she was getting married.

The groom had seen her from afar each day as she went to school and instantly fallen in love. This was though, an arranged marriage. He was a handsome chap, tall and slim with handsome features and brown eyes. When he had asked his family to go and ask for the girl they had done so. Her family had also asked after the boy and his family from the local Mukhtar (mayor). The information given out was satisfying and the deal was done.

When I arrived at the house I was taken up to one of the bedrooms upstairs. The scene that greeted me made me stop dead in my tracks.

There the bride lay on her back, quite bare while one of the ladies was working away at her bikini line with a cloth spread with a sticky concoction to remove the genital hair.

This concoction was called sheera. It was made from citric acid or lemon juice and sugar, heated up on the stove in a pan until it became thick and sticky, a cheaper homemade alternative to waxing. The warm mass was spread on pieces of cotton cloth, applied to the hairy bit then after a few minutes, yanked off. Her arms, underarms and legs had already been worked on and they were now smooth as silk, albeit red and mottled from the trauma.

I was directed to sit in a corner and a drink of homemade lemon juice was pressed into my hand. My eyes were fixed on the scene and I could hardly breathe, never in my life had I seen such a thing!

As soon as the process was completed the rest of the women there had a good look to make sure of the smoothness. Unfortunately, the young lady had, after such an assault of her delicate area, developed a rash, quite a lot of small red spots sprang up. The whole area looked quite a mess. When she was shown this in the mirror she burst into tears. *"How can my husband see this, what will he say?" she cried.* The women made soothing reassurances, olive oil was applied to the area," tomorrow all would be gone by the time of the wedding," they reassured her.

The next day, early in the morning, the bride was relieved to find that her genital area was now clear. She was taken by her mother and sisters to the local hairdresser to have her hair and her make-up done before going back home to get dressed in her wedding finery. I had been invited along on her journey and must say she looked like a beautiful bride indeed.

As we waited in her home we soon began to hear the sound of the wedding procession coming along the street, a band playing the traditional wedding tunes and cars full of the groom's family all leaning on their horns, blaring aloud as the groom was brought through the streets.

His car had been festooned in white ribbons and bows. He was dressed in a traditional thawb and gown. When he stepped out of his vehicle and walked into the house, he looked like Lawrence of Arabia in his headdress and long gown (minus the blue eyes of Peter O'Toole of course).

His bride was nervously waiting for him to approach her. She stood up for him to kiss both her cheeks and the top of her head, then she followed him out of the house with her mother and sisters in tow. They climbed into cars waiting for them. They made their noisy way to his house where the party was about to begin (the actual marriage had already taken place earlier when the imam had come to her house).

The bride sat next to her husband and the party began. Loud music, the louder the better, the families danced to familiar beats of the national Chobe dance, always found at weddings. The males were all dancing in their traditional way, round in a circle with the lead dancer twirling a string of prayer beads a lot of Arab males (and females) carry, and they bent down in unison then jumped up to the beats.

During a lull in the festivities, the groom's mother came up to the bride with her gifts - of a set of gold, (usually 22 carat). She placed the earrings, bracelets and necklace on the bride before kissing her on both cheeks.

It was then the turn of the groom's mother to place her gifts, also of gold (the earrings were kept in their box seeing as the bride only had two holes in her ears for earrings). Other members of the family brought their offerings, mostly money in envelopes. Further gifts would be brought to the newlyweds later during the seven-day period following the wedding.

As this was a traditional wedding, there would be no honeymoon trip for the couple.

I had brought my envelope with some money and placed these in her hands before kissing her on both cheeks. Soon it was time for the wedding couple to make their way to a room that had been prepared for them. The room had been freshly painted in bright colours, the bed had been covered in a gold spread adorned with pearls, there were curtains to match, a bowl of fresh fruit had been placed on the side.

The bride and groom entered and the door was shut while the ladies began to undulate in loudly. Many of the guests spent the next 20 minutes dancing and clapping, making as much noise as they could.

After 20 minutes had passed, the groom's brother went up to thud on the door, *"Hey brother, come on hurry up, if you cannot do it then I will come in and do it for you!"*

Roars of laughter from the guests greeted this announcement. After a few minutes more, the door suddenly opened. The groom stood triumphant on the threshold holding up a white cloth spotted with fresh blood that proved his bride's virginity, the deed had been done.

I was so relieved that I had got married in the UK as I don't think I could have survived the embarrassment of that custom.

Chapter 42

Oliver Reed – Film – Al-Mas'ala Al-Kubra

Oliver Reed, at 42 years old and rumoured to be drinking two bottles of whisky a day, had been invited to come to Baghdad to star in a propaganda movie for Saddam.

He stayed at the Mansour Melia hotel along with his burly French bodyguard, his teenage girlfriend, Ken Buckle, the head stuntman the rest of the cast including Marc Sinden, son of well-known actor Donald Sinden, who was cast as Captain Dawson – this was Sinden's first movie, he had mostly played in the theatre.

The Mansour Melia was one of the grandest and most popular hotels in the Middle East, it had swimming pools arranged in the pattern of the Olympic Rings.

The English title of the movie was *The Big Question*, it was to be a war movie. It was shot in Kut, 170 kilometers outside Baghdad. The location chosen was in the desert and the heat at that time of the year was intense at 50 degs. The movie was directed by Iraqi director Mohammed Shukri Jameel, who had a reputation of being one of the finest directors.

The plot of the movie was like a modern-day Lawrence of Arabia complete with an Arab uprising against invading British forces during the late 19th and 20th centuries. A massive cavalry charge involving over 40 horses took place. Unfortunately for the horses, many of them did not survive the brutal tactics used in the movie to drag them down at the right time. It was the last movie to use a stunt technique called *The Running W*.

During the filming, Saddam invited Oliver Reed and Marc Sinden to dinner at one of his many palaces. Present at the dinner was Saddam's eldest son Uday, his foreign minister, Tarek Aziz, and a bevy of generals in their finery.

Saddam spoke Arabic throughout the evening which was interpreted into English for his guests, during one particularly long ramble Oliver Reed said to Marc Sinden, thinking nobody would understand English, "What a c***." At the end of the evening, as Saddam was leaving he passed by Oliver Reed and said in English "Mr. Reed, I hope I did not bore you too much."

(Esquire Middle East Image).

Diary Excerpt (1993)

Here are some excerpts from a diary I kept in the year 1993.

There has been trouble up in the North too as American planes patrol the Safe Haven area for the Kurds. They are under threat from Iraqi jets.

At 6.30 pm we have just heard the air raid sirens again; we saw tracers in the distant sky and heard sounds of bombing from afar. The BBC reported in Baghdad there was no sign of any aircraft or missiles.

One of Mohammed friends came with the news that in the South around 70 jets were used in a daylight raid by American, British and French air forces and 21 people are now reported killed.

Martin Fitzwater, White House spokesman announced, "Continued defiance of U.N security council resolutions will not be tolerated."

Samarra Trip

The children asked Ahmed if he would take them on a trip. It was a Friday which is a holiday in Iraq like Sunday is in the UK. It was decided that we would go to Samarra, 125 kilometres north of Baghdad, a trip of about 1h 30m, or by the Ahmed way, which was as fast as he could drive, about one hour.

The girls helped me pack up some food and drink for the journey. We set off. I remember Ahmed had been very argumentative on that day. He had brought some chocolate along, a bar of Cadbury's Fruit & Nut, during the journey offered me some. I declined, this set him off and he lost his temper, all over a bar of chocolate.

I asked him to stop the car, when he did I got out. I refused to go any further telling him to leave me there by the side of the road, out in the middle of nowhere in the desert. I was not able to continue listening to his raging. He seemed to realise that everyone was upset, quickly calmed down and persuaded me to get back into the car. To everyone's relief, the rest of the trip went without any further outbursts.

Samarra is one of the largest archaeological ruins in the world. In ancient times it was the Abbasid capital the traces of which run almost 40 kilometres along the river Tigris.

The children wanted to attempt the climb up the famous spiral tower otherwise known as Malwiya, erected in the year 847.

There was no handrail, the further up you went the dizzier it looked. I watched them from below clenching my hands, my heart in my mouth imagining one or all of them falling off and landing headfirst in front of me, until they finally turned and came safely back down to terra firma.

We visited the palace ruins with the sunken bath complex containing lovely mosaics.

As the children wandered all over the site they found many small clay tablets with cuneiform writing on them. Later, I asked an archaeologist who was the father of one of my daughter's friends, to look at them. He told me they were lessons from school in the time of around 75 AD. We kept them safe in a shoebox at home in Baghdad where I hope they are today.

I wish I had a camera in those days, I am sure the photos would be a delight to look at today.

Al-Rasheed Palace Hotel Attack (17ᵗʰ January)

Mohammed came out of his room at 10 pm to tell me that he could hear air raid sirens. At first, I laughed, I followed him into his room and listened, just faintly in the distance I could hear the rising/falling wail of the sirens.

"It is probably being tested, in case there is an attack," I said.

"This is the 2ⁿᵈ anniversary of the Allied air attack, I expect that this is just to remind us about it all."

I was astonished therefore to hear a new sound, anti-aircraft. Looking outside I could see the tracer bullets lighting up the night sky.

We even went completely daft, running around the house switching off all the lights and lighting up candles, a habit left over from the previous bombings even though the surrounding houses were all lit up and the streetlights were still on.

We had no idea what was going on, we could not see or hear any planes, but a whooshing sound overhead alerted us to the fact that a missile had just passed over. Whose it was and where it was going, we could not tell.

I turned the radio on, tuned in to the BBC hoping to get some information. It was silent about any attacks. It was only in the next few hours that the story began to unfold.

A missile had landed in the front entrance to the Rasheed Palace Hotel, destroying the reception area and lobby. This was what we had heard whooshing over our heads at home, we were close to that area. Over 700 delegates were staying in the hotel to attend an International Islamic Conference, ninety or so of them foreign journalists, one of whom was quite badly injured in his head by glass shards from a shattered window.

Peter Brinkmann was a reporter for Germany's Bild newspaper. We later saw pictures on TV of him being visited by Saddam that night.

Two of the Iraqi receptionists were not so lucky, they lost their lives, the body of one of them was shown on TV. It was said she was struck down and killed instantly. We were horrified to see on the television the pictures of the injured as Saddam visited the hospital. Wishing them well he told the German journalist-through an interpreter- *"I wish that it had been me who had sustained these injuries to my body instead of you-our guest."* He stopped on his rounds to pat a small girl on the head, then sat opposite her on a bed while he asked the doctors about the extent of her injuries.

She had received some injuries to her back and slight wounds to her eyelids and lip. She was about 3 or 4 years old, crying from the trauma and pain. Saddam promised to send her a gift. I noticed on a later news report that he had kept his promise. She was shown resting her tiny hand on a large blue box placed by her side, a present from Baba Saddam.

We finally went to bed at about 2.30 am, the girls took the mattresses off their beds and placed them in my room on the floor, in case further missiles were sent over.

The next morning, I tuned into the news again to hear more of the story. VOA reported that it was not clear if the missile that hit the hotel had been an American cruise missile, it could have been an Iraqi surface to air missile. I seriously doubted it.

The report also said that parts of the missile recovered from the hotel were from an American cruise missile, which had been deflected by Iraqi anti-aircraft missiles. It was just a 'coincidence' that a second missile fell on the home of Layla al-Attar, the Iraqi artist who had made the mosaic of George H. W Bush situated in the entranceway to the hotel lobby and which was walked on by everyone who entered that area, killing her, her husband and housekeeper. Her daughter, Reem, was blinded during this attack.

The two receptionists were given a state funeral this morning and many people are angry at this attack as the intended target was at least 15 miles away from the hotel and the USA was always saying how precise their aim was that they could target the head of a pin.

January 20th

As of 8 am this morning, Baghdad time, the Iraqi government has declared a ceasefire in respect of the inauguration of the 42nd President of the USA-Mr William Jefferson Clinton. The ceremony took place in Washington DC at 8 pm (local time).

June 27th

The rumour was that while the former U.S. President George W.H. Bush had been scheduled to visit Kuwait in April 1993, there had been an attempt to assassinate him with a Toyota Landcruiser car bomb. The vehicle, which was recovered by the Kuwaitis, contained around 90 kilos of plastic explosives.

The U.S President, then Clinton, suspected Iraqis after 17 of them, who had been arrested in Kuwait, confessed to the plot. They later retracted their confessions saying they had been beaten and tortured by the Kuwaitis.

It was reported that 23 Tomahawk Cruise Missiles had been launched from U.S Navy warships-USS Peterson in the Red Sea, and cruiser USS Chancellorsville in the Persian Gulf, into Baghdad's downtown area. Their aim was supposed to be the Iraqi Intelligence Building in Mansour.

Rations

We had been given a raise in rations from this month which included more flour.

Local meat (lamb) is now 100 dinars a kilo. Imported lamb (New Zealand, Saudi Arabia) is 55 dinars a kilo. We have also been able to get some Irish boneless beef (Tara) for 40 dinars a kilo.

A tray of 30 eggs is 72 dinars, life is very hard for those with low income.

Iraqi Dinar

Before the Gulf war, the Iraqi dinar was printed by De La Rue in the U.K. They were known as Swiss notes. After the war the notes were printed in China. It is rumoured they were badly printed on printers that were formerlyused to print newspapers. The paper was of poor quality, the ink often ran and the notes were easily torn. They were often counterfeited; the value was so low that large bundles of notes would need to be taken in a plastic bag to go shopping for simple foodstuffs. We were getting as bad as Nigeria.

Witchcraft

Many Iraqis believe in sorcery or witchcraft. It was believed that certain spells could be performed to change the course of someone's life.

It was rumoured that Amina was a dab hand at spellbinding. The children and I would often find rather strange looking little rag bundles containing various items such as bird bones or bits of rancid fat with unidentifiable herbs which had been thrown into our garden.

I was advised to let the young Samer pee near the threshold of the house to stop any unwanted hexes from entering. Needless to say, I did not bother with that, once he started he might like the habit and never stop.

One story I remember was when Ahmed's brother, Ali, had a large amount of money stolen from his house. He went to a local sheikh who was famous for finding out things using a mirror and a young child-for a fee of course. When Ali explained the situation, the props were prepared. The child seemed to go into a trance in front of the mirror and, after a few minutes, produced a name.

Lo and behold, it seemed to work. Ali knew the person and immediately went to find him. The outcome was successful as that person named had indeed taken the money. Ali was able to recover much if not all of it.

I have no idea how this worked, it is not logical nor feasible, but there you are, some things are beyond our comprehension.

Most houses had a blue eye symbol on the wall to protect them from the evil eye. Many women and children wore jewellery with this icon for the same reason. The eye comes in different colours, the most popular colours in Islamic countries are light and dark blue. The dark blue offers protection from fate or karma, the light blue overall safety and health.

There are white, black red and pink ones. White offers the wearer wealth, black offers power, red is for courage and pink is for love and friendship.

I have two blue ones purchased from Amman and Cyprus which are hanging around the house, so I consider myself safe, for now.

I was amused one Eid holiday when I found out that Ahmed had gone to a local mosque to purchase a sheep to distribute to the poor. The man selling the sheep had taken the money from him, then also taken money from the next person and so on, so he had 'sold' the same sheep umpteen times!

Pressure Cooker Incident

Just behind our mushtamil was an alleyway. There were small houses there that were occupied by families on the lower end of the economic spectrum. One morning around 11.30 am there was an almighty bang, it was as if a bomb had gone off. Running out of the house I found several of my neighbours standing in the street wondering what had happened. There was some screaming coming from the alleyway. We made our way there and discovered one of the houses had its window broken.

The lady of the house was standing outside shouting, covered in blood (this turned out to be tomato sauce). She explained that her pressure cooker had exploded, her small kitchen walls were covered in tomato sauce and so was she. She was shaking from the shock so we got her a chair to sit on, gave her some water and the ladies went to see if they could help clean up the mess. It did not help that armed guards came running from Saddam's palace (which was just up the road) as they thought a bomb had exploded. When they saw the situation they left, satisfied.

Thankfully her small baby had been asleep in another room, although the noise had made him cry, he was unharmed.

Soon things were in better order and she had calmed down enough that we could leave her. It was a miracle the metal from the pressure cooker had not hit her, only the window and that could be replaced. They were a family on a lower income. We got some money together and paid for someone to go and replace her window and paint her kitchen.

Chapter 43

Moving to the Main House

The children were growing, our mushtamil was now deemed too small for all seven of them so Ahmed did a deal with his brothers regarding transferring the ownership of the main house into his name and giving one of his brothers the mushtamil and the land it was on.

Amina already lived in the main house with her children. Ahmed decided to split the house into two large flats, she would live upstairs and I would have the downstairs. The space was much bigger than we had been used to. We had the use of the front garden while she would have the back garden. He also arranged for two kitchens to be built on the back patio.

When I discovered that there would be a window overlooking our front entrance, I objected bitterly. She would be able to see every movement we made, who was coming and who was going. I knew in my heart that it had been her request. My words fell on deaf ears, the window was placed. Sometimes though I wondered whether it had been her decision or his.

We moved into the house and gave up our independence. The children at least had their bigger rooms. We had a large area in the front with a patio containing an ancient garden swing (this was requested by upstairs' family to be moved into her garden but we stood firm on our wish for it to remain in the same place it had been for many years).

I got my first microwave oven, it was something of a novelty for the neighbours who came for tea. They always asked me what it was. Trying to explain to them how it worked was difficult so I used to get a frozen bread out of the freezer and pop it into the microwave to show them the defrost procedure, it was magical.

My freezer was an upright one with eight drawers. I froze lots of vegetables like okra, eggplant, broad beans, desert truffles and of course the Iraqi khubz and samoon bread. That was in the days when we still had a regular supply of electricity to rely on.

Samer Spectre

"Samer, Samer! Get one of the girls to dress you, we are going to Uncle Mahmoud's house."

I was standing at the entrance to the kitchen and had just noticed Samer running into his sister's room. Going into the room I asked them where he was.

"He's outside Mum, playing with his friends."

*"No, he's here, I just saw him, where is h*e hiding?"

The girls looked at me puzzled, he was nowhere to be found in their room. I went outside to see. Amazingly he was there, playing. He had not come into the house at all, so who had I seen running past me? It was a mystery then and it still is today.

On another occasion, all the clocks in the house stopped at the same time, I told the children, "It's the end of the world!"

Should I contact Beyond Belief, Fact or Fiction?

Rabbits

One of the English ladies in our group, Carol, who lived in Dora, asked me if I would like some rabbits as pets. Samer was eager to have them so I agreed to have two males. The children and I made a large cage for them out of old chicken wire and a metal cooler frame in the garden.

Carol brought them the following week, they were two fluffy little bunnies and the children were so excited. The bunnies settled in, running around the house playing. We had some cats that were allowed inside at times when Ahmed was away and all the animals got on so well with each other, even eating from the same bowl.

What I did not realise at the time was that, instead of two males, I had a male and a female. With all the humping going on this soon became obvious. Although I separated them immediately, the damage had already been done and within a short time, we had baby bunnies. The cage outside became their home.

One day I noticed that one of the babies, a new-born white one with a grey face, had been rejected by its mother. I sat near the cage for a while watching, each time the little one wanted to feed she nipped it and ran to the other side of the cage.

Sindus had the bright idea of taking the mother into the kitchen, turning her on her back and letting the baby feed on her teats. It worked like a charm, we did this several times a day, each of the children taking a turn. The mother rabbit must have wondered what was happening. The little bunny started growing strong enough to eat on his own, then his mother was left alone.

We decided to keep him in the house, he copied the cats in the use of the litter tray. When the weather became cold he curled up with them in the warmth of the paraffin heater.

The children named him Zargor, after a chewing gum sold in Iraq at that time. In a few months he got too big to stay in the house. I noticed that he had a habit of nibbling at the electric wires and may get electrocuted. We decided to put him back outside in the cage with the other rabbits but they attacked him after a short time. We heard him scream and brought him back into the house. Unfortunately, he went stiff with shock and died of fright.

The children were upset, as they always were at the loss of a beloved pet. They were not happy that I had decided to replace him with the other rabbits and blamed me for his death.

I tried to make up for it by having a funeral and burying him in the garden. Sorry kids, I did not realise what would happen.

Sindus and the Dog Attack

Ahmed kept a guard dog outside, his name was Rocky, he was a big, brown and black mixed breed. During the day he was kept tied up, and released at night to wander around the garden.

Anyone who thought about climbing into our garden would not last very long. He was a vicious mutt, he had attacked Ahmed more than once.

He was fed mostly on scraps from our kitchen and sometimes Ahmed would pick up a nice bone from the butcher for him to chew at.

One evening Ahmed had come downstairs and was sitting talking to the girls. Sindus had just had a shower, she was in her dressing gown with a towel wrapped around her head. Her father asked her to go outside and up the stairs to get his blood pressure tablets from Amina.

As she stepped out into the garden Rocky launched an attack at her, aiming for her throat. Screaming out to us, she raised her arm to protect her face and throat. When we heard her screams we rushed outside. Seeing the scene before us, I ran straight over to her. Picking up a nearby brick I brought it down as hard as I could on Rocky's head. For a moment he was stunned, he stopped his attack, enough for Yasmin and her sisters to drag her back inside into the house.

As I examined her, I found she had injuries to her arms, there were teeth marks where that mad mutt had sunk his canines into her flesh, the scars are there today. I insisted she was taken to the hospital to get them treated and a tetanus injection given.

Although I was mad as hell that my child had been almost killed by that crazy, vicious dog, her father refused to have it put down, saying it was just doing its job. I swear if I had a gun in my possession at that time, I would not have hesitated to despatch that crazy animal, adding it to my tally of rat murders.

Chapter 44

1994

On June 4th 1994 a new decree was announced by the Iraqi Government.

Decree Number 59 stated that those who were found guilty of robbery or theft would have a limb or limbs amputated. For first offenders, it would be a hand, second offenders the left foot.

This started a trend for amputations which had not previously been known as punishment for any crimes in Iraq.

Presidential Decree 115 – Amputations

Yes, you read that right, no mistake.

Saddam issued a further decree, Decree Number 115 for anyone who failed to report for military duty or defected from the army to have one of their ears *surgically removed.* I say surgically but that would have involved an operation. The Decree did not specify how much of the ear should be removed so mostly the entire ear was just lopped off.

Deserters from the army would be branded with a X cross on the forehead between the eyebrows to distinguish them from other types of criminals. A most barbaric act.

One evening, as we were sitting outside in the patio, we heard a noise in the garden. Putting on the outside light Ahmed got his gun, went out and let the mad mutt loose. He found a terrified young man in military uniform, thin as a rake, hiding in our back garden. The mad dog went for him immediately but thankfully Ahmed was able to pull him off.

The lad was cowering down, shaking like a leaf. Upon questioning he said he was being hunted by the military police. He had escaped from their pick-up truck which was taking him to the local hospital to have his ear removed as this was the second time he had absconded.

We all knew the consequences of his actions, we had heard the news and understood what would happen to him. Ahmed did not hesitate, he told him to climb over our back wall and into the neighbour's garden. From there he would be able to make his way along an alley and to the river. We wished him luck and hoped that he would not be caught.

A short time later, the military police came knocking. We permitted them to search the garden knowing the young man had made his escape and we hoped he would be able to make his way back home to his family.

The mutilation of deserters was a barbaric act. Doctors and specialists were aghast at the order, but this was Iraq, there was little they could do about it. If it came to their turn to operate they had no choice but to comply, their life was on the line if they refused.

No anaesthetic was used. The patient would often pass out from the shock and be carried out of the hospital on a stretcher, back to languish in a prison cell.

Most of the wounds were not treated again. The wound became septic. Nobody but the victim was bothered if he lived or died, here was one less *traitor* to bother about. If the victim was unfortunate to be caught a second time, the other ear or, horrifically, a hand was lopped off.

One of Faris' doctor friends discovered that he would be asked to perform this gruesome procedure. To refuse meant he would be imprisoned or at worse, executed. He took the drastic step of injecting his arm with paraffin. This caused sepsis and he eventually lost his arm. He told Faris later that he would rather lose his limb than cause pain and suffering to any individual, it was against his Hippocratic oath. He is well known in the area we lived in, A'athamyah, Haibet Khatoon, Baghdad.

One evening as I was sitting watching TV during those times, I could not believe what I was seeing - a documentary was being shown about a new procedure to make and attach prosthetic ears!

It was illegal for doctors to perform any surgery to re-attach the ears of victims (Decree 117).

Someone in broadcasting had a macabre sense of humour.

During this year Saddam ordered the closure of all nightclubs and bars, no more bar girls to come and sit with you plying you with drinks that were ten times more than normal, be prepared for a huge bill on leaving.

The death penalty in Iraq was not just for murder. Various other crimes had been added over the years such as, car theft, currency changing, money laundering, desertion from the army for three periods (the other times would result in losing your ears), joining a separate organisation which was not the Ba'ath Party, corruption and so on and so on. The phrase 'off with their heads' comes to mind. Perhaps guillotines would soon be imported to be set up in Tahrir Square!

Radio Gaga

Ahmed brought a new telephone for Amina. It was one of those digital handsets that she could carry around and talk on. This was a novelty in those days. She was a proper phone freak and spent many hours on the instrument talking to her family and friends. I was the same, many were the times that I had spent an hour on the phone chatting to one of my English friends and Ahmed going crazy trying to get through to me. Sometimes he would call Amina and ask her to send one of the kids along to ask me to put the phone down.

On this particular day, I was, as usual, trying to tune my radio into BBC World Service, when I picked up a voice speaking in Arabic that sounded familiar, it was Amina talking on the phone! What were the chances of that?

"Girls, come here quick, Amina is on the radio," I said.

"What, Mum what are you talking about?"

"Listen", I said, "That is her, isn't it, talking on my radio?"

It seemed that the wavelength I had stumbled across was the same one as her new digital telephone.

We sat down around the radio and listened to her conversation. It proved very enlightening to hear what she thought of us as well as what she thought of her husband.

We were able to spend regular sessions sitting listening to her long telephone gossiping, which we called *'listen with Mary Fisher'*. For quite some time in the weeks that followed, she slagged off each one of us regularly.

One of my sons, who also enjoyed listening in on her conversations, decided one day that he had a conscience. Frowning he announced that "*It was not the right thing to do.*"

He informed his father, who at first thought my son was joking. When he discovered this was true the new digital telephone was disconnected and our almost daily entertainment was too. We had heard enough, what she thought of us had become quite clear, every one of us had not escaped her tongue.

Attempted Assassination of Uday Hussein (1996)

The word on the street was that Uday had been shot at as he drove in downtown Baghdad. We did not know if he was alive or dead. The boys had been out and about trying to discreetly find out more about the incident, and there was very little coverage locally.

There were several versions of the story and more than one group which later claimed it had carried out the attack. Here are some of those versions:

Uday had been cruising along on his way to one of his *parties with ladies*, a polite way to say personal orgy and rape affair. His car was one of three white Mercedes, all of the same model and with the same number plates on to confuse any possible attacker. It stopped at traffic lights in al-Mansur district, just outside Karkh Sports Club at the crossroads with International Street.

One man stepped out in front of Uday's car to throw a grenade while quickly moving to the left of the car, firing a Kalashnikov machine gun into the interior, concentrating on the driver. That was the only mistake they made, as Uday was not driving the vehicle as they thought but was sitting in the back passenger seat.

Once this was realised, three other shooters came forward, all firing into both Uday's car and the following two containing his bodyguards. Uday had been hit by eight bullets, one of which had entered his spine.

The men who carried out the attack belonged to a resistance group called *al-Nahada* (The Awakening), founded by an electrical engineer called Hamoud Ali, who had been captured and tortured to death by Iraqi security forces. They had been planning the assassination for two years. An earlier attempt to get at Uday at one of his farms outside Baghdad, in an area called Salman Pak, had not been successful because on that day Uday had decided not to go.

Another group calling themselves 15 Shaaban Movement claimed responsibility some years later. Led by one Sharif Salman a 27-year-old from Shatra, Iraq, his story as told to The Christian Science Monitor in 2003, stated that Uday was driving his gold-coloured Porche alone along the street in Mansour trawling for girls when the attack happened. Sharif said that over 50 rounds were fired at Uday, and 17 bullets hit him but he still survived.

Another theory was that the attack was by tribe members from Tikrit in retaliation for the shooting of Uday's half-brother.

Uday was driven to Ibn Sina hospital in Baghdad, by an Iraqi singer named Ali al-Sahir, an acquaintance of the renowned Iraqi singer, Kathem al-Sahir.

Uday's left leg was shattered. He was seen after a few months walking with a limp and using a cane. One of the bullets was reported to be lodged too close to the spine to be removed, he suffered from multiple seizures.

Two surgeons were brought over from France on December 16th to treat him, Patrick Philipe and Dominique Thana, the same doctors who had treated Wathban al-Tikrity, the half-brother that Uday had shot on August 7th 1995.

Despite extensive investigations and hundreds of people being detained by the Iraqi authorities and tortured, nobody was ever found and charged with the crime.

The people living around me seemed happy and sad at the same time, happy because someone had taken the initiative despite the risks, to rid the world of this debaucher, sad because the attempt had not been successful.

It was later rumoured that he had acquired a body double. We would pass the time when Uday appeared on television, peering intently at the screen at his features, did his eyebrows look different? Was he a bit shorter than normal, what about the cleft chin? Was his voice any different?

Chapter 45

Diary Excerpts (1997)

I received a diary this year as a gift from a friend, it is about the only place I recorded what was going on around me. Much of it was about the children.

Madeline Albright was made the first female Secretary of President Bill Clinton she held this post until 2001.

There was an earthquake on 21st Jan in China measuring 6.4 then a following quake 6.3. in Jiashi County, NW China beneath the Tarim Basin. 12 people were killed and 40 injured.

We installed an illicit satellite dish up on the roof, very cloak and dagger. It was marvellous for watching international TV programmes or news from around the world instead of the constant re-runs of Arabic movies or propaganda on Iraqi TV. It was however against the law, we had to keep quiet about it, the punishment for owning one at the time was reported to be six months in jail or a fine of $100.

A rumour circulated that the person who sold and installed the illicit dishes was the same person that then reported the owner to the authorities, earning himself a reward-if he was asked to remove the dish by the authorities, then he would get to sell it all over again. Quite a lucrative business.

Our neighbours watched various Arabic series on the normal TV. We were lucky, with the dish and receiver, we could watch the same series only more up to date than them. Sometimes we had to bite our tongue not to tell what the next plot was!

When the then Pope, John Paul II became ill we watched a news report about him. The news about his health had also been reported on Iraqi television but no images of him were shown.

In a conversation one day with one of my neighbours she mentioned this. *"The news yesterday was that the Pope in Rome is very ill,"* she said.

"Oh yes I know, he does look quite ill." (I had seen a news item about him on the satellite).

"Oh, how did you know he looked ill, where did you see that?"

"Why on the TV, it was on late, a very short clip, you must have missed it," said I, with my heart in my mouth.

She may be a neighbour, but it was difficult to know whom to trust in this country; it was best to keep things quiet.

We covered the receiver with a pretty cloth and hoped nobody would notice. If any visitors came unannounced the illegal item was quickly switched off and covered up. This became quite stressful at times. Helicopters could be heard passing overhead on occasion, searching for dishes on the rooftops, our one was camouflaged with a sand coloured cloth and some old chairs.

The children came up with novel ways of disguising the receiver.

"Put it in a wooden box, one of those decorated ones," said one.

"We can hide it around the back of the television, nobody will see it there," said another.

Although we had full possession of the receiver, Ahmed attached a splitter wire leading from it and stretched outside the window to the upstairs window so that Amina and her family could watch it.

This caused quite a few problems. We wanted to watch all the English language programmes, they wanted to watch all the Arabic series. In the evening, if it was time for one of the popular Arabic dramas to be on, the upstairs family would start banging their feet on the floor for us to change the channel. It was too much for any one of them to make the short journey downstairs to ask us politely.

Sometimes, just to be annoying, I would switch the channel to one of the nature programmes instead. It was especially gleeful if it contained fornicating monkeys or other animals, when they complained to Ahmed I feigned ignorance.

We watched the live broadcast of Prince Naseem Hamid's World Featherweight fight with Tom Johnson at the London Arena, Millwall.

What a fight that was, there were some moments when Tom Johnson had the upper hand or fist. Naz came through by flooring his opponent in the eighth round. Iraqis liked him, he was a Muslim with Yemeni heritage (Naseem was featured on a Yemeni postage stamp in 1995), and they liked his various antics before entering the ring. On one occasion, in his fight with Vuyani Bungu, he entered on a 'magic carpet'.

Blood Koran

"Sandra, have you heard, Mickey (Saddam) has commissioned a copy of the Koran to be written in his blood?"

*(*We referred to Saddam as Mickey Mouse, his wife was Minnie and his son Uday was Pluto. We never knew if the telephone was bugged and certain keywords might trigger a recording of our conversation*)*.

I was on the telephone with one of the ladies from my group when this news was doing the rounds. She told me that it would take two years to complete and use up 27 litres of his blood.

"27 litres! He will be anaemic after all that blood loss. He is using his blood to write, surely that is haram? Isn't blood considered negus (dirty) after it has left the body? It's crazy!!"

The Holy Koran was commissioned on a whim by Saddam when he was visiting his son Uday in Ibn Sina (Avicenna) hospital, Baghdad in 1997 on his 60th birthday.

It was produced by Abbas Shakir Joudi, it contained 6,000 verses and 336,000 words. It was ceremoniously handed over to Saddam in September 2000.

Upon the news of the book, countries in the Islamic world were aghast at his heretical act, as I have said above, blood is impure, to write the words of God in it is seen as an act of blasphemy.

After Saddam's death, another dilemma faced by those in whose care the book was placed - they could not destroy it as it contained the word of God, they could not display it, someone might break in and steal it. So, it has been hidden away in a secret place, never to see the light of day.

Saddam said the book was a tribute to God for his murdering, chip off the old block, son, Uday, surviving the attempt to assassinate him in 1996.

The Jews of Baghdad

The Jewish population in Baghdad can trace their lineage back almost 2,600 years to the time when Nebuchadnezzar conquered Judah in 586 BCE and brought them to Iraq – then known as Mesopotamia – as slaves. This is mentioned in Psalm 137 of the Bible.

By 1921, the British installed a Hashemite kingdom in Iraq by installing King Faisal 1 who was a man tolerant to all religions and sects including the Jewish community. Under his reign, they flourished and enjoyed life without fear for the next 37 years.

In the Jewish Quarter of Baghdad, That al-Takia, in the area known as Shorja, there were approximately 150,000 Jews, the 2nd largest community in Baghdad. The Great Synagogue of Baghdad contained over seventy silver and gold-encrusted Torah scrolls and was purported to have been large enough to hold twenty thousand people.

Properties along the area on the Corniche known as Abu Nawas were mostly owned by Jews, the cafes and coffee shops were alive each evening with the sounds of chai (tea) being served and the clacking of domino tiles as men enjoyed passing their time playing the game.

The mood in Iraq began to change with the rise of Naziz. The Iraqi Government supported the German Naziz. In 1943 Mein Kampf was translated into the Arabic language and became available in Iraq. Almost overnight anti-Semitism began to creep in amongst the Arabs. Nazi propaganda began to spread into schools and in the media.

Jewish families, sensing the winds of change around them with the rise of Arab nationalism, began to bury the religious symbols of their faith. They changed their dialect to appear more 'Arab' as their assets were frozen. The Grand Mufti of Jerusalem, Haji Amin al-Husseini met with Hitler in Berlin where he declared to the Fuhrer that they both had the same enemies 'The English, the Jews and the Communists'.

On June 1st-2nd 1941 there was an anti-Jewish riot that resulted in the death of approximately 180 Jews. The British did little to curb the rioting masses at the time. Between 1949-1951 there began a mass exodus of Jews from Baghdad. 120,000 Jews left Baghdad during this time. Some of their houses were marked out with red handprints known as 'hamsa'. They closed up their homes with all their belongings inside, ceramics, crystal furniture were all just left, even their shops were just closed up with the goods inside. These were eventually looted by the Arabs.

After the 6-Day War in June 1967 further restrictions were placed upon the remaining 2000 or so Jews in Baghdad. Their telephone wires were ripped out by the authorities in case the family supplied information to Israel. There was a stream of disappearances and hangings, over 90 Jewish men were never seen by their families again, very little information was known about their fates.

By 1970-1971 Jews were not allowed passports, they had to be smuggled out of Iraq through Basra to Iran or Erbil in the north of the country.

It was the end of an era, from the crowning of a Jewish Miss Baghdad- Renee Dangoor in 1947, having to carry yellow identity cards in 1963, the public hanging of Jews in 1969, the outcry of this spectacle by other governments resulted in secret executions of Jews being carried out in the years 1970, 1972, and 1973.

My brother-in-law, Ahmed's brother, had many friends and acquaintances during those years some of whom were Jewish. One family came to see him just before they left for Israel. Forbidden to take any of their belongings except some clothes and personal items (5lbs weight) they placed into his safekeeping an amount of gold jewellery. The plan was for them to eventually return to Baghdad, he promised to keep these items safe until they did. He told me about the gold when we were sitting one day having a meal at home, that the Jewish family never returned to Iraq to claim their jewellery and he kept his promise to them throughout his life up until his death many years later when the gold was sold and the money used for charitable purposes as he wished.

Praying

Just before Ramadan in 1972, I decided I would like to learn to pray properly. I had not bothered before, the house and the children kept me on my toes most of the day so I did not think I would be able to spend time five times a day to pray. Now, was the time. Going to my next-door neighbour, I asked her if she would take the time to teach me. *"Of course, Um Faris, it would be my duty and my pleasure,"* she replied.

I spent many weeks learning the procedure, words to the various prayers, timings etc. She was puzzled that I kept my eyes shut during the prayers and I had not realised I was doing it, so I was advised to keep them open. Ahmed's family were Shia, so the prayers and the way to pray were slightly different.

Sunnis place their hands down by their sides while praying, Shia places theirs over their abdomen.

One thing I was not sure about was the morning prayer, Salat al Fajr at dawn, before sunrise. I was not too happy about having to get up at 3 am, but my neighbour told me I could merge the early morning with the 2nd one, the noon prayer, Salat al Zuhr.

The 3rd one is Salat al Asr, the latter part of the afternoon, just after sunset is the 4th prayer, Salat al Maghrib, and finally the 5th prayer or Salat al Isha between sunset and midnight.

I enjoyed doing my duty, it became a routine. Sometimes the cats would jump on my back when I was bending down in prayer. To break off and brush them away would mean that I had to start all over again so normally if there was anyone within hearing distance I just said my prayers louder to alert them of my problem.

These days, if I tried to get down on the floor it would take at least three people to get me up again, but the chair sometimes comes in handy.

Mohammed aged about 9 years old, came running into the house (mushtamil) from the garden saying there was *part of a man in the garden*. Confused, I went outside with him. There was nothing to be seen. When I asked him what he had seen he said that he had seen a man with his hair in a ponytail, he was fair and had a little moustache and a beard. He was very friendly and they talked for a while, about what though he could not remember. Now he was gone, but Mohammed remembered his legs were not there; it was just space where they should have been.

Faris, when he was much older, mentioned that he had seen a woman in the house, but she was not there, so what was going on in that area I don't know.

I do know that the land and house next door to us belonged to our family. The tenants paid a minuscule amount of rent, just a few IDs a month and they had lived there for years. When I moved into the main house, these tenants were asked to leave, the family wanted to build more houses on the land. There was quite an uproar at the time, after which they eventually left and more houses were built and rented out. Anyone who rented those places had someone die after a short time. It was believed the land is cursed.

Chapter 46

Diary Excerpts (1997)

February 5th

Ann and her husband Mustafa are leaving for England. Mustafa and their son Leith left in the afternoon today, there was a bit of worry over Leith's passport having the wrong date in it. The officer in the passport office had written 2nd January (2/1) instead of 1st February (1/2) It was feared this might cause some problem when they reach the border. They would have twelve hours to worry about that on their journey to Trebil. As it happened, it was not noticed and they passed over and into Jordan without incident.

The news from the USA today was about the basketball player O.J. Simpson. He has been found guilty in a civil trial and must pay his dead wife's family and her boyfriend's family over 8.5 million dollars in compensation.

Pauline is in England. Today I received a letter from her without any stamps on. Maybe because it's been so very cold in Carlisle and she forgot.

February 6th

Ann left for London today, we shall miss her a lot. Many of the group have decided to pack up and leave, it is a big decision. After living so many years here, you get used to living a different type of life.

February 8th

Ramadan is finally over and today is the first day of the Eid holiday. This year will be the same as last year, with no money to spare so we will be wearing the same clothes.

Ahmed has invited all his brothers and their families to a meal at his place upstairs, plenty of money for that. The children and I stayed at our home, plenty of nice programmes to watch on TV.

February 10th

Ahmed took us all to see the area where Uday had been shot in Mansour district, then we went on to Karada, Mesbah and Hindyah.

In the afternoon he took Samer and Maysoon to the Riding Club and Samer rode a horse. He told me that the horse was so large and he had been terrified of falling off.

Each year during the holidays there is a talk by Ahmed or Faris that we can join one of the clubs, either Sports Club (Nadi Rayatha) or Hunting Club (Nadi al-Saed), Alwiyah Club.

There were many clubs and they had various programmes throughout the year. Swimming pool, outdoor cinema, restaurants and bars but the problem was the expense. Just the Sports Club charged 60k dinars to join, most of the other clubs were in the same region. It was a lot of money.

I think there was another reason behind the fact that we never joined or went. Our daughters were now teenagers and pretty ones at that. Uday frequented these places often. If his eye fell on a suitable female there would be no stopping him from taking her back to his place to do anything he liked before she was discarded like trash or murdered and disposed of. So, we understood the dangers of attending any of these clubs and the need to protect our girls.

February 15th

Today we had the first group gathering before the Ramadan month. The ladies are getting fewer and fewer, many have travelled. We were a large group in 1988 when we first started meeting at my house on a Saturday at 6:00 PM.

Those who have left are Diana al-Saadi, who worked at the International School, she was the Dean and left in 1996. Linda al-Obeidi (Scots) left with her four kids in 1996. Pauline al- Tikriti left with her three children and husband at the same time. Wendy al-Chalabi, left in 1994 with her daughter, Janice al-Ghailani left about 1995, Mary Karukchi left with her husband and kids in 1994. May Khoury and her daughter Moira left 1995 and 1996.

We took the satellite down today, too much of a worry about having to pay the massive fine of 200K Iraqi dinars, plus losing the satellite and not forgetting the piece de resistance of spending six months in prison, probably Abu Ghraib where torture is carried out before lunch.

February 24th

News today on the radio was about Elizabeth Taylor the renowned actor, she has had a 4-hour operation to remove a tumour from her brain and is recovering well in hospital.

Judy

One of Ahmed's relatives, who lived opposite us had a German Shepherd dog that had just given birth. She asked us if we would like one of the puppies when they were old enough. Normally I would not have agreed. After the incident with Sindus, I never wanted another dog anywhere near us, especially an Alsatian. The children pleaded, promising the usual promises that they would take care of it until I gave in and agreed. Excitedly, they eagerly awaited the day until the puppies would be old enough.

After a few weeks, the puppies were brought over for the children to make their choice, a small black bitch pup which the girls named Judy. After a couple of months, she was brought over to us. Sahar volunteered to sit up with her some nights, the little pup missed her mother and siblings so would spend the night crying. After a few days, she settled in and became one of the family.

Ahmed took an immediate dislike to her. While she was little he would always kick her as he passed by until she grew older and one day she bit him on the ankle. After that he left her alone.

Buying a Baby in Baghdad (February)

One morning a neighbour came to me, they had a visitor from UAE, a German lady. He asked me to come, as her Arabic was not very good, and translate for her.

Entering the home of my neighbour, I introduced myself to the lady. She told me her name was C. She was a slim lady with fair hair and green eyes. Happy to finally have someone to talk to, she told me that she had come to Iraq to adopt a child. She was married to an elder son of my neighbour, they lived in UAE, her husband would be joining her later.

At that time, I was unaware of the true reason for her visit, so I informed her that, as far as I knew, under Iraqi law, foreigners could not adopt any children in Iraq. Children who were adopted by Iraqis could not leave Iraq under any circumstances. This fact did not seem to worry her at the time.

C was staying in a hotel in Baghdad. After a few days, to save money, she left the hotel and moved into the small house of my neighbour, Um Jasim. It seemed such a tight squeeze, the family already had many children, but they managed to make room for her.

One day, one of their small daughters came to ask me if I would go once again to the house, when I arrived, lo and behold, she sat on the sofa with a baby in her arms!

This baby belonged to a distant cousin of Ahmed's. The family lived nearby and the child had been born three days previously.

The family was poor, especially with the current rationing situation in Iraq, food prices were high, the dinar had been devalued, life was tough for families with little work available and many mouths to feed.

It seemed that, all along, the plan for C to come to Iraq supposedly pregnant, then claim to have given birth prematurely, had been hatched before she arrived.

This led the way to her registering the baby at the German Embassy in her name, getting a birth certificate and a passport for the baby to enable her to take him back to the UAE when her husband arrived.

The family received an amount of money from the couple, I think it was in the region of 3 million Iraqi Dinars, approximately US $1500, to help them get through the next few months until the rations were distributed.

Everyone seemed happy, they believed their son would be well looked after, away from the constant wars and poverty of this country.

The following week I took C shopping for baby clothes and various other essentials. She was getting anxious as her husband had still not contacted her with the details of his arrival and she was feeling cramped living in the family home with the baby. I invited her to come and meet with my Ladies of Baghdad group on Saturday.

She enjoyed meeting all my friends, they delighted in the baby and congratulated her on her new addition. I had not mentioned any of the incidents to my friends, I did not think it was appropriate. When they read this, the penny will surely drop!

C's husband came, at last, they came to see me and he informed me that he had been told he would have to do six months of army service before he left Iraq, despite having paid 12,000 Iraqi Dinars before he left the country previously. After negotiating with authorities, informing them that he was working in UAE, he was required to pay one month for each year he had been out of the country. The exact amount I did not know.

After a few days touring Baghdad, they finally left. Before they left, they both came and had some tea. She left me some novels in German which I passed on to one of my ladies who attended a German group.

I have recently heard that, after the death of Sabah in UAE, his wife left with the child to return to her native Germany.

May 28th

This morning one of the *Emin* (security police) turned up at Saidi's shop in central Baghdad and asked him to come to the police station for questioning. Saidi, terrified, promptly fainted. The scam was for these policemen to go to each shop in turn with threatening behaviour. He would then suggest to the shop owner that a trip to the police station could be avoided by paying a 'fee' in cash.

Everybody knew about it but most people just paid up for a bit of peace. Saidi had blood pressure problems, terrified of any consequences, he passed out before the guy could ask him for the money.

Ahmed's was the neighbouring shop. When the officer walked into his shop and started his spiel, Ahmed (who had noticed his brother fall) became incensed and immediately jumped upon the officer. They both rolled around the floor and out into the street punching each other. The officer managed to pull out his weapon but Ahmed gave him such a clip round the ear and the other shop owners had come out in support that he decided it would be safer for him to run off. He did not come to that area again and no more was heard about the incident.

Chapter 47

Taxi Incident

On May 28th, Sindus, Summar and Um Zainab's daughter Wasan Saduck decided to get a taxi home from college. Normally the three girls would sit in the back of a taxi cab, never would one of them sit next to the (male) driver. Sindus decided that she would break this tradition and therefore climbed into the front. The other two girls tried to insist that she get into the back with them, but she refused.

As they entered the house after their journey, Sindus was completely hysterical and the other two girls were both crying. Sindus started to bang her head against the wall and scream, it was as if the world had come to an end and I did not have any idea what was going on. I got hold of Sindus to stop her from hurting herself on the wall and begged the girls to tell me what had happened. The paedo taxi driver had exposed himself to her just before dropping the girls off at home.

They were all in a state of shock. It took a long time for me to calm them down. I did not want anyone from upstairs to hear the commotion because, if her father had heard about it, he would probably have beaten them both up and forbidden them from going to college again.

Getting into a taxi cab and sitting in the front seat next to the male driver, it was just asking for trouble. It was bad enough getting on the bus to go to and from college. The lads would always try to touch the girls inappropriately. Most of the time the girls would hold their hard folders over their bottoms as protection, but that left their chest open to an elbow or arm being accidentally on purpose pressed into it. The buses were always full during rush hour, the passengers were squeezed in, sometimes the lads would hang onto the outside as the bus drove along.

After a while, Sindus calmed down and began to get angry at the way the driver had treated them. I explained how he probably saw an opportunity to get some excitement, it's not normal but some men enjoy it and she must be prepared for such incidents to come her way as she goes through life. I warned them they were not to get a taxi cab after that; just the normal bus, and if it was too full just wait for the next one.

Art College

Summar, Sahar and Yasmina had artistic talents. Summar spent time at home drawing and had painted a mural of a Japanese mountain scene on her bedroom wall. She desperately wanted to go to art college.

We decided to put in a request to her father. "Dad, some of my friends from school are applying to the art college, would it be okay for me to apply as well?" she said.

"What! ART COLLEGE! No daughters of mine are going to art college, it's full of prostitutes and pimps!" was his outburst.

He said this about hairdressers, too. They were all seedy places for meeting lovers clandestinely, which made it very difficult for us to go and get our hair done!

Although she tried again and again, his answer was always the same. She became depressed, tore up all her lovely paintings and drawings, cried a lot and one day I discovered she had been self-harming. I was at my wit's end on that day. Hugging her close I begged her to never do such a thing again. She promised me she would stop and thankfully she did. But she never painted or drew anything else while she was in Iraq.

Faris in UK

Another incident that we found out about long after the fact, involved Ahmed giving Faris money in the UK. I had no idea, what a dark horse he was, to have saved up quite a substantial sum and then handed it over to Faris to invest it in a property.

In those years, properties, especially in Hull where Faris was staying, were available for the amount that his father had given him.

Instead of carrying out his father's wishes, Faris decided it would be a better idea to rent an empty shop, stock it with various car parts and open it. This did not succeed. The shop went bust and Faris sold what he could of the stock.

I only discovered this when Ahmed had come in one day ranting about how MY son had taken HIS money and wasted it. When my father had died, no matter how many times I had asked my husband to pay for his burial, he had never agreed stating he did not have the money. Another nail in the coffin of our marriage.

Leaving Iraq (August 8th, 1997)

I was leaving Iraq. After much discussion Ahmed and I decided that the only way for us forward was for me to leave and once I had established myself in England I could start the procedure to get the rest of the family out. We both felt that the coming months and years would be difficult for everyone. We at least had a chance to move to a safer environment, most of the population of Iraq did not.

My exit visa and that of Samer, who was 12 years old, had already been obtained. Mohammed had tried to get an exit visa for Yasmin, she was still under 18 years old so she could accompany us, but unfortunately, there were complications in getting her passport ready on time.

It was heart-breaking to leave the children behind. I knew that there was no choice. I comforted them and myself with the thought that soon they would be joining me. I would apply for a settlement visa for each of them in Jordan before I travelled on to England. I did not know at the time, that I would not see most of my beloved children again for the next five years. The settlement visa for them was rejected by the British Embassy, the reason given that my daughters had a brother in Iraq who could look after them. Of course, the large amount of money that I had paid the Embassy to process their visa applications was not refunded.

Chapter 48

Trebil

Samer and I travelled to the border of Iraq and Jordan on a bus. It was a long and arduous journey through miles and miles of bland landscape. There were supposed to be two drivers, one to take over while the other slept on the long journey of 548 kilometres.

It normally takes about 5 hours, but the old and rickety bus, which had done this journey along these pot-holed roads for many years was not up to going very fast. The second driver had called in sick, so we only had one.

After a few hours I noticed the driver was continuously rubbing his face and moving his head. This made me anxious and I kept my eyes on him thinking that he was becoming sleepy and I was right. After a while, the bus moved erratically from side to side and he began nodding off. Terrified we would crash or go over onto the other side of the busy highway and get hit by a vehicle, I asked one of the male passengers in front of me, who was travelling with his family, to tap the driver on the arm and keep him talking until we got to the halfway stop which was coming up soon. I was relieved when we finally made it to the stop, then it was decided amongst us passengers that the driver should go and lie down for a nap. He told us that he had done two straight shifts to Jordan without a break and was very fatigued.

While he had his nap, I purchased something to eat and drink at the truck stop for Samer and myself. We waited for an hour before the driver woke up, had something to eat and some tea, then was refreshed enough to continue.

The rest of the journey was without incident, arriving at the border of Iraq and Jordan at 6 pm as the sun was setting.

We were all asked to leave the bus and give our documents to the driver who could then take them into the office for the various stamps. The bus was also searched for any possible contraband.

I sat on a spare stone bench with Samer. One of the ladies we were travelling with came over quickly to tell me that I had a cockroach crawling up my back. Jumping up, screeching I begged Samer to brush it off for me, it didn't have a visa for Jordan.

The ladies were all body searched by women guards, I had hidden a few bits of gold and some dollars in my bra, along the line of the wired part, so it could not be felt by anyone patting me down (but quite chaffing for me). Despite my thumping heart and sweating brow, it was not discovered in the body search.

Soon we clambered back on the bus for the short journey to the Jordanian side of the border. There was a marked difference in the attitude of the Jordanian border officers. They were much more, polite and respectful, smiling and joking with the passengers - a sharp contrast to the dour faces of the Iraqi border guards - although we were delayed by four hours there.

The rest of the journey to Amman took but a short time. I was able to get a cab to the apartment's hotel complex address for Saada Apartments only to find it was full! The taxi driver took us to three more places, all were either full or beyond our budget.

Panic stations ensued. I envisioned Samer and myself having to sleep in the street, then I remembered my friend, Moira. I went into a shop, asked to use the telephone and called the number of her home in Amman. A short while later her husband came in his car and collected us. He paid the eight JD we owed our taxi driver (I only had US dollars) and took us to their home.

Moira contacted my other friend, C, who graciously allowed us to stay with her in her apartment along with her daughter, Aseel, and her grandson, Mohammed. They had been waiting for six weeks in Amman for their settlement visa to come to the UK.

We were able to rent two mattresses from the manager of the apartment block for 5JD per night, at least we had somewhere to lay our heads. Moira kindly brought us some supper.

The next morning, I called Faris (5 JD) and left him a message on the answering machine telling him the number of the apartment and asking him what was happening about our tickets.

The next week was an absolute nightmare for us. We were in a strange country, with little funds and no tickets for our onward journey to the UK. Here are some excerpts from my diary at that time.

August 10th 1997

Faris called at 1.30 am, he promised to try and book us a flight at the earliest opportunity.

Sam and I walked to the British Embassy (took us 45 minutes in the hot sun and we got sunburnt).

I was able to get Sam a British passport for 23 JD and lodged Yasmina's papers. We took a taxi back to the apartment.

I am sharing the price of food with C with what little money I have, I must be very frugal. C has been here for a while so she knows a lot of the cheapest places for food and groceries.

A hamburger van comes in the evenings and parks outside the complex. One hamburger and chips are 500 fils, plus 150 fils for a Pepsi.

I have the number of one of Ahmed's friends, Rauf and his wife, Um Salah. When I called she arranged for us to go to their home tomorrow morning.

August 11th 1997

Got up at 9 am, Aseel's visa has finally come through. We decided to go into town for her to get some shopping before her flight. I had only 3 JD left in my purse though, no spending for me. I hope to get some good news from Faris today.

I waited all evening for Faris to call but he did not, now I am beginning to panic.

August 12th 1997

After a very bad night, I got up at 7 am. Suddenly it seems so hopeless, I stood by the window and burst into tears which lasted all morning. Aseel went and spoke to the owner of the apartment, Abu Mustafa. She persuaded him to let me stay on till I get some money, but what do we eat?

I phoned a number that Ahmed had given me for one of his friends in Amman, Captain Amer Selby. I explained the situation, he told me that he would call Ahmed and check with him if he agrees, Capt. Selby would give me some money to tide me over.

Faris called me in the evening, he said he has booked us on a flight for Friday. He also gave me yet another number to call, Ragheed, a friend of Ahmed's. I called him and we will meet up tomorrow in the morning. Faris promised to transfer some money tomorrow.

Samer looks a bit better (when he heard this news, he had been very upset), he wanted us to go back to Baghdad.

August 13th 1997

C and her family left this morning, they will fly to Cyprus and then on to LHR.

Ragheed came and took us to the Egypt Air Office in Baled where I collected the air tickets. He then changed some money and gave me 50 JD to pay the rent and get some food, what an angel!

When we got back to the apartment, I paid the owner what I owed and got lunch for Sam and myself.

We are due to leave tomorrow at 1 am.

In the evening we were invited to Dr Aliyah and her husband's house. She has a son of 10 and two daughters, one 6 years old and one younger. Her husband works in a bank in Shmeisani, Amman.

August 14th 1997

Up early, went to get some eggs and milk for breakfast, Sam said he was hungry.

Moira came to see us and say goodbye, I gave her some towels, a magazine and a book that C had left, 'The Summer of the Barshinskies'. There was also some whisky and gin left from C, which I passed on to her.

She asked me for the 8 dinars that her husband had paid for my taxi. As my cash was little, I told her I would send it to her with one of the ladies at a later stage, which I did.

We spent the rest of the day getting our things ready, Sam had a shower and I put his clothes out for the trip. We have to get to the airport by 11 pm tonight for the flight which leaves at 1 am.

We got a taxi to the Express bus station for the connecting airport shuttle bus.

Our taxi driver was a fundamentalist nutter who kept ranting on about me and my trousers! I wanted to tell him to mind his own business but kept quiet. It would not do to get attacked before I had a chance to leave Amman.

The flight was delayed, we finally took off at 2 am for the flight to Cairo.

August 15th 1997

Landing at 3 am, we disembarked and waited for ¾ hour for our room to be prepared at the airport hotel (we were in transit for London).

Sam and I slept straight through until 10 am. We went for breakfast at 10.30 am. Two boiled eggs, croissant, jam, cake, coffee and some weird fruit called guava.

Checked into our flight on Boeing 777. Sam was excited, he watched the in-flight movie '101 Dalmatians'.

I got violent cramps just after take-off, had to spend 10 minutes in the loo. I remembered that Ahmed had given me some medicine before I left (Baghdad), just in case. I took two Enthrostop and two Vitasporin capsules, felt fine after ½ hour, did not want to land in London in a mess!

We landed at 6 pm at London Heathrow Airport. Faris and Reem (his wife) met us in the arrivals' hall, we all went to their flat in Brondesbury Park-we had made it!!

Slept on their sofa bed-we were exhausted.

August 16th 1997

Cornflakes for breakfast! What a delight (it had been some time since we had cornflakes so we were enthralled).

Faris took us to the shops, then to a car boot sale nearby. He bought a Sega Mega Drive for Sam who was delighted. I got some t-shirts for the girls (back in Baghdad), and Reem bought me some perfume for £1.99.

Ahmed called us from Baghdad to see how we were (reverse charge call).

Met Reem's sister, Abeer, and her husband Sinan.

So, we had finally made it back to the UK. It had been a scary few days not knowing what was going to happen to us. Not something I would ever want us to experience again.

That was 1997, the 2nd part of my story will be the next 20 years or so. I hope you will continue to read it when I have finished writing it.

Sandra D. Ekelund

2022

Lightning Source UK Ltd.
Milton Keynes UK
UKHW020000111022
410244UK00012B/435

9 781915 492272